Mallarmé on Fashion

Mallarmé on Fashion

A Translation of the Fashion Magazine *La Dernière mode*, with Commentary

P. N. Furbank and Alex Cain

Seagull Books

CALCUTTA 2006

First published in 2004 by Berg

Reprinted with permission from the original publisher

For publication and sale in South Asia
(Bangladesh, Burma, Bhutan, Sri Lanka, Nepal and Pakistan) only.

ISBN 81 7046 284 3

Cover design by Sunandini Banerjee

Published by Naveen Kishore, Seagull Books Pvt Ltd
26 Circus Avenue, Calcutta 700 017, India

Printed and bound by Gopsons, Noida

Exclusively distributed in South Asia by Foundation Books Pvt Ltd
Cambridge House, 4381/4 Ansari Road, Daryanganj, New Delhi 110 002

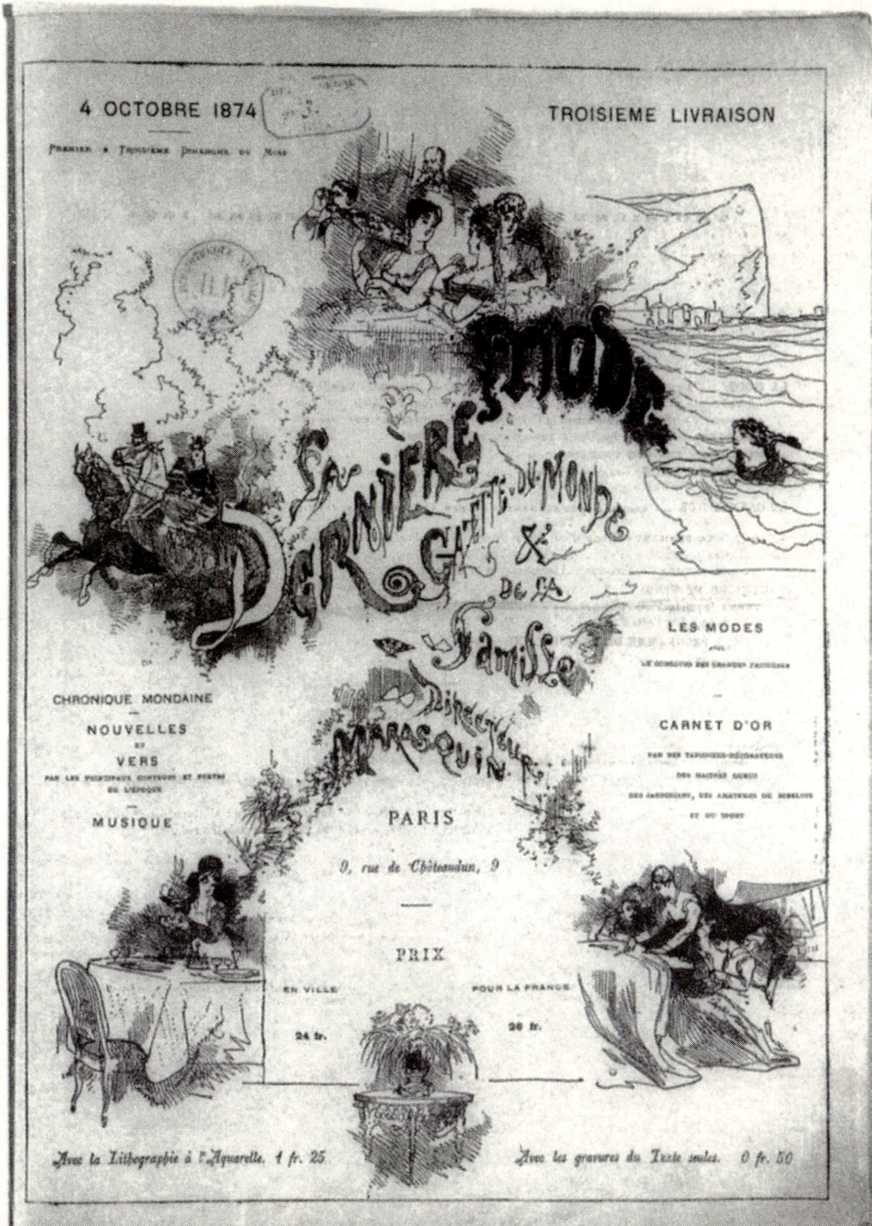
4 OCTOBRE 1874
TROISIEME LIVRAISON
La Dernière Mode
Gazette du Monde & de la Famille
Directeur Marasquin
CHRONIQUE MONDAINE
NOUVELLES
VERS
MUSIQUE
LES MODES
CARNET D'OR
PARIS
9, rue de Châteaudun, 9
PRIX
EN VILLE
24 fr.
POUR LA FRANCE
26 fr.
Avec la Lithographie à l'Aquarelle. 1 fr. 25
Avec les gravures du Texte seules. 0 fr. 50

Contents

Part I
La Dernière Mode, and its Pre-history

People today say: Napoleon AND Stendhal.

Who could have told Napoleon that people would say Napoleon AND Stendhal?

Who would have said to Zola, to Daudet, that this little, so amiable, so articulate, man Stéphane Mallarmé, would, with his few little bizarre and obscure poems, have a more profound and lasting influence than their books, their observations of life, the 'lived' and the 'rendered' of their novels?

So wrote Paul Valéry,[1] the disciple of Mallarmé, and it will do to introduce the subject of Mallarmé, that very great and deeply puzzling poet. By 'puzzling' one is not meaning 'baffling' (though no doubt some of his writing – *Igitur,* for instance – is baffling enough), but rather, intriguing, overwhelmingly original, and *appealingly* enigmatic.

It is not that we have no insight into his development, or the way in which he created himself as a poet; for his letters of the 1860s, written when he was in his early twenties, give an astonishing, and indeed harrowing, account of his aesthetic adventure, which took the form of a kind of suicide in the cause of the Dream. 'Having reached the horrible vision of a pure work (an *œuvre pure*),' he wrote to François Coppée on 28 April 1868, 'I have almost gone out of my mind and forgotten the meaning of the most familiar words'. 'The *œuvre pure,*' he writes, 'implies the elocutionary disappearance of the poet, who cedes the initiative to words.' The pursuit of the *œuvre pure* goes with the discovery of *le Néant* (Nothingness): 'having found Nothingness,' he announces, while at work on an early version of his *Hérodiade*, 'I have found the Beautiful.' A little later, on the road to recovery, he tells his friend Cazalis how the new man is being born, and how he or it will have to 'relive the infancy of Man'.[2]

This epic of discovery takes place whilst, with his wife Marie and their daughter, he is living an impoverished life in Besançon or Avignon, earning his living as a (rather incompetent) lycée teacher. By the time that he returned to Paris in 1872, the travail was, in a sense, over. Baudelaire by now being dead, Mallarmé was regarded by his fellow-poets as the 'master'. Indeed, in literary circles, he seemed sure of himself: elegant, poised and amiable, ready to pontificate on literary matters, and – outwardly at least – by no means hagridden. He was, nonetheless, inclined to say very puzzling things, and there were those – the Goncourt brothers especially – for whom the Mallarmé cult was extremely irritating. The Goncourts put it about that Mallarmé was clinically mad – either that, or

1. Paul Valéry, *Mauvaises pensées et autres* in *Oeuvres* (Pléiade edition, 1957) vol. 2, p. 802.
2. To Cazalis, 18 February 1869.

a charlatan. (It is a real-life example of what Valéry imagines about Zola and Daudet.) Edmond de Goncourt notes in his Journal for 3 March 1875:

> There is, among these exquisites, these Byzantines of the Word and of Syntax, a madman madder than all the rest: this is the nebulous Mallarmé, who professes that one must not begin a sentence with a monosyllable, saying: 'Cannot you see that this *nothing*, these two poor little letters, cannot reasonably serve as the basis of a great sentence, a sentence truly immense?'
>
> This search after the little animal stupefies the best endowed; it distracts them, preoccupied as they are with the microscopic study of a sentence, from all the strong, the great, the warm things which give a book life.

Others said that he was a *roublaud*, a 'fox'. There was certainly some truth in that, and perhaps even in the idea that he was in certain respects just a shade crazy,[3] though certainly none in his being a charlatan.

But what the Goncourts seem to have missed in Mallarmé, and others perhaps sensed only dimly, was his immense fund of irony: a kind of irony, moreover, that was unique to him. One small part of it was his engaging penchant for the Absurd. According to him, the top hat should be thought of as the pot from which Man grew from the head upwards, bifurcating plantwise at the hips. Or again, François Coppée reports him as saying he attached great importance to the stars (their disorderly arrangement symbolising Chance), but he had no patience with the moon, that 'cheese'. He hoped that some day scientists might find the way to dissolve it with chemicals. The only problem was, he said, that this would interfere with the tides, which were so important a feature of the terrestrial *décor.* (Though the fantasy is of course the purest nonsense, the wide sense he is giving to the word *décor* is by no means nonsense – a point we shall come back to.)

We have stressed both the irony and the enigmatic aspect of Mallarmé, because another and different puzzle arises, one which forms the subject of the present book. For in 1874 Mallarmé emerges as the editor – or rather the editor, the designer and the author – of a women's fashion magazine entitled *La Dernière mode.* This was the speculative venture of a friend of Mallarmé's, an impecunious publisher named Charles Wendelen, who lived a few doors further up the rue de Moscou. But, apart from a poem and short story in each number, commissioned

3. Everything concerned with his theatrical theories and endeavours seems to show a trace of an almost mad irrationality. He imagined producing a 'vast popular melodrama', capable of speaking to and for the 'crowd' more effectively than Wagner's *Ring*. But in fact he was unable to conceive of any theatrical enterprise other than a one-man drama. This, he said explicitly in his essay on *Hamlet*, was where the future of the theatre lay. The notes towards the work which Jacques Scherer attempts to reconstruct in his *Le 'Livre' de Mallarmé* (Paris, 1957) envisage a solo dramatic reading by Mallarmé, in which, taking the pages of a work from a set of pigeon-holes, he would read them over in different orders, according to an elaborately calculated series of permutations, over a period of two years.

from friends, every word of the text was written by Mallarmé himself, under a variety of pseudonyms. These included 'Marguerite de Ponty' (for fashion, and the theory of fashion); 'Miss Satin' (giving news of the fashion houses of Paris); 'Ix', a male critic (for theatre and books); 'Le Chef de bouche chez Brébant[4] (for food), etc. Each number would normally contain black-and-white engravings of at least two complete new costumes, designed by 'Mme de Ponty' (i.e. Mallarmé himself), together with a prose explanation. As 'Mme de Ponty' he would promise to supply dress patterns and undertake commissions at dress-shops and emporia on behalf of readers; and he conducted a correspondence column, in which he (or she) answered their queries. The letters frequently came, or purported to come, from countesses, duchesses and the titled generally; and it was a tacit assumption throughout the magazine that readers were mainly interested in, if they did not actually move in, 'high-life'.[5]

To distinguish fact from fantasy in these practical features of the magazine is difficult, maybe ultimately impossible; but some of it must have been genuine. For it should be remembered that this was a real journal, with real subscribers, which lasted under Mallarmé's control for eight fortnightly issues and could be said to have been moderately successful.

The journal meant a lot to Mallarmé, and he was deeply chagrined when it was taken out of his hands, furiously imploring his friends and contributors, in a circular letter, not to have anything to do with it under the new management.[6] Years later, in a letter to Verlaine, he wrote nostalgically of how, after sending out articles here and there, he had been 'tempted to compile, unaided, *toilettes,* jewels, furniture and even theatres and dinner-menus, to form a journal, *La Dernière mode,* of which the eight or ten numbers published serve, when I remove the dust from them, to make me dream for many an hour.'

One puzzle, then, is why he decided to carry out this enterprise. But a larger one is why this strange work, undertaken by him when he was at the height of his powers[7] and (one cannot help thinking) a work of genius, has received very little attention. The editors of the old Pléiade edition (though they included his

4. Brébant was celebrated for his dinners, frequented by authors, and especially during the Franco-Prussian War and the Siege of Paris when Paris was starving. After the Siege, the authors presented Brébant with a testimonial, praising him for his culinary skills during the hard times. Chez Brébant was located on the boulevard Poissonnière.

5. The first recorded use of the Anglicism 'high-life' is by Stendhal in 1823.

6. Wendelen placed it in the hands of a certain 'Baronne Lomaria', and it survived until May 1875. Under her editorship it lowered its sights socially, aiming more at ordinary housewives. It admitted news of sport and the stock exchange; clergymen contributed to the Correspondence columns; and the disquisitions on the theory of fashion were much diminished.

7. 'Brise marine', 'Tristesse d'été' and 'L'Azur' were first published (in *Parnasse contemporain)* in 1866, 'L'Après-midi d'un faune' in 1876.

biographer Henri Mondor) seem to have regarded it as no more than a piece of hackwork, like his handbooks of mythology and English grammar.[8] Accordingly they printed it in a smaller type size, gave it very meagre annotation, and even left out chunks of the text. Rémy de Gourmont wrote a rather flimsy essay about it; an incomplete translation of it was published in America in the 1930s;[9] a facsimile edition by Editions Ramsay appeared in 1978; but nobody seems really to have grasped the extreme interest and value of the work until Jean-Pierre Lecercle, in his valuable *Mallarmé et la mode,* published in 1989. Lecercle managed to elucidate a certain intricate 'mystification,' – or in his words, immense *coup de bluff* – indulged in by Mallarmé over the origins of the magazine, and we shall draw freely on his account of this. He also puts forward a powerful thesis about the meaning of the work, which seems to us half, but only half, right. We shall come on to this in a moment.

* * *

Mallarmé seems to have had a long-term interest in decorative art. In 1871 he was appointed to a lycée in Paris, and soon afterwards (in August 1871), he received a commission to review the French stand at the International Exhibition in London. The attitude that emerges from his articles, written under the pseudonym 'L.-S. Price', is clear-cut and intransigent: it is that, in the sphere of furnishing, there has been no new style created since the 'Empire' one – which was a real style though a depressing one. Returning next year for the second season, his report expands this sentiment into an 'axiom'. 'All invention having ceased, in the decorative arts, at the end of the last century, the critical task of our century is to collect and compare the usual and the out-of-the-way forms engendered by the fantasy of each people and each epoch.'

Despite this, he was evidently fascinated by the decorative arts, and on 7 April 1872 we find him writing to the 'Parnassian' poet Hérédia, saying he has been very busy.

> I am now collecting in the various corners of Paris the subscription required to begin a beautiful and luxurious review, which obsesses my mind: *L'Art décoratif, Gazette mensuelle* [Decorative Art: a Monthly Journal], Paris, 1872.
> Now you will see the thin pretext for this letter. There is only one man who could do the frontispiece, Claudius Popelin. He has been exquisite towards me and has agreed. It is all arranged: there is no need to question him. Only, as he is very fond of you, chat with him a little about it all in your next letter. Soon.

---

8. The wrongness of this is confirmed, if any confirmation were needed, by the letter from Mallarmé to Verlaine from which we quote.

9. Edited by S.A. Rhodes, for the Institute of French Studies, New York, 1933.

Mallarmé's friends told him that to plan such a magazine only a year after the *année terrible* of the Franco-Prussian War and the civil war with the Commune was madness, as indeed one would suppose oneself. However, the revival of Paris and of France took place remarkably quickly (the massive German reparations had been paid off by September 1873 and the last German soldier left French soil in the same month), and sometime (most probably in May 1874), Mallarmé reshaped his conception, giving it the form of a fashion magazine – in a way a more ambitious, and more complex, project. Invitations to subscribe, and a month or two later a 'specimen number', were sent out to his friends. He also invited several writer friends to contribute a poem or a short story.

The magazine was beautifully designed, avoiding the awkward 'continued on page so-and-so', usually found in such journals. The cover was an attractive blue, and the admirable cover design, with its vignettes of women at the Opéra, a woman on the hunting-field, swimming in the sea, decorating a dinner-table and cutting out a dress, was by Edmond Morin (1824-82), a landscape-painter and illustrator who worked for some years in England but returned to Paris in 1849 and drew for *L'Illustration, La Vie parisienne*, etc.

We come now to the immense *coup de bluff* of which Lecercle speaks. *La Dernière mode* repeatedly refers to itself as the 'second year', of a magazine which, during its first year, had consisted purely of engravings and lithographs. Thus Mme de Ponty writes in the Sample Issue 'The coloured lithograph . . . cannot, given its date, illustrate the September fashions: it has thus been chosen at random from the rich collection already published during the summer (in the edition without text)'. Similarly, in the 'Correspondence with Subscribers' in the Sample Issue, she writes that, since the Letters addressed to the Journal up to now have mainly been to ask for a verbal description of engravings previously published without text, the best thing she can do, in this issue, is to give explanations or descriptions of some of these engravings. This she proceeds to do for seven of them, the first, a 'Formal Visiting Costume', being dated 1 May 1874, and the last, a 'Costume for a grand ceremonial occasion', dated 1 August 184.

Now, what Lecercle seems to have established is that no such earlier magazine ever existed. There is a kernel of truth within the deceit, in that Charles Wendelen, under the pseudonym 'Marasquin', had published six fashion lithographs at irregular intervals between 11 August and 31 December 1873. But the 'rich collection published during the summer' (i.e. the summer of 1874), referred to by Mme de Ponty, was a fiction; and *a fortiori,* her seven descriptions of costumes, just mentioned, relate to engravings that never existed.

If what Lecercle says is correct (and his argument is intricate but on the whole convincing), one is left puzzled as to what Mallarmé was up to. However, it would be only one mystification among many in *La Dernière mode,* and somehow the theory sounds right.

The finances of the journal were evidently rather shaky. Mallarmé made a modest subvention of 100 francs himself, and on 26 September Wendelen's wife Constance writes to him to apologise for this sum, which he 'so obligingly put at our disposal', not having yet been repaid to him.

The journal began with a print-run of 3,000, but in November there was a change of printer, and the print-run was reduced to 1,000.

It is strange, and frustrating, that there is very little evidence (at least, we have so far not found much) as to what friends and others thought of *La Dernière mode* at the time. Luigi Gualdo writes to François Coppée on 27 August 1874 saying that he recognised Mallarmé under the pseudonym 'Ix', but by November, writing again to Coppée, his guesswork has still got no further. Is the magazine all by the 'Master', he writes, 'or has Mallarméism made such strides that all the contributors write like him? It is quite simply delicious'. Philippe Burty writes to Mallarmé, on receipt of Issue 2, that 'It is perfect'.[10]

* * *

Mallarmé was by no means the only writer in his period to theorise about Fashion. Théophile Gautier for instance, in his essay 'De la mode' (1858), made an ingenious defence of modern dress. He put it down to a false classical education, an outmoded prejudice in favour of the nude, that painters should look down on modern clothes. It was absurd even in regard to men's clothes, and doubly so in regard to women's, or to women's coiffures. ('The Parisian comb is the equal of the Greek chisel, and hair obeys more docilely than the marble of Paros or Pentelicus.') It was, he argued, even possible to construct an aesthetic defence of the crinoline, conventionally stigmatised as hideous, savage and abominable. 'From that abundance of folds, which spread out like the fustanella of a whirling dervish, the waist emerges elegant and slender. . . That mass of rich fabrics serves as a pedestal to the bust and the head, the only important parts, now that nudity is no longer permitted.' The theme of Gautier's last paragraph, which evokes the beauty-and-fashion parade in the vestibule of theatres, is one that Ix is fond of, with the tacit (or sometimes not even tacit) implication that this is really what theatres exist for.

> Let a great painter like Veronese paint the staircase at the Opéra or the vestibule at the Italiens, when the duchesses of the *beau monde* or the *demi-monde* are waiting for their carriages, draped in white burnooses or striped cloaks, ermine hoods, opera-cloaks stuffed or edged with swansdown, and marvellous fabrics from every country; their head starred with flowers and diamonds, their gloved fingertips lain on their cavalier's sleeve, in all the insolence of their beauty, youth and luxury; you will see then if, in front of his picture, any word is said about the poverty of our costume!

10. This and the Gualdo letter are quoted by Lecercle, p. 25.

Baudelaire wrote equally brilliantly about fashion. In the essay on 'Modernity', in his *Le Peintre de la vie moderne*, he castigates the painters of his day for dressing up their subjects in medieval or Renaissance or oriental costumes, on the pretext that modern costume is hopelessly ugly. This, he argues, is pure laziness on their part; for the proper aim of the artist is to extract the mysterious beauty of the modern, of the fugitive, the contingent and the transitory. It, moreover, ignores an essential point: that the language of fashion of any epoch is a matter, not merely of dress-design but of gesture and facial expression and manners. Any fashion constitutes a system and can only be understood as such. It is foolish, as he argues in 'Beauty, Fashion and Happiness', to laugh at past fashions. The transition from one fashion to another follows a clear logic, like that governing the changing shapes of animals.

Most characteristic of all is his 'Eulogy of Make-up'. In this he attacks what he calls the false eighteenth-century conception of Nature, as the 'base, source and type', of all that is good and beautiful. Here, he says, one sees the fatal consequence of ignoring original sin. For Nature is in fact an evil tyrant. She does not teach, she merely constrains: she forces us to sleep, drink, eat and protect ourselves from the weather, and likewise to torture and kill. Evil is natural. Virtue, by contrast, is always artificial; and it is possible to consider costume and fashion as one of the signs of spirituality and of longing for the ideal. Women, in particular, have a duty to use all arts to elevate themselves above Nature, and among them make-up, which is so frowned upon by philosophers. But they should employ it for the right motive, which is not to imitate the beauty of Nature or to try to rival youth (in which, anyway, it will not succeed). Make-up needs to be frankly and visibly what it is, a challenge and rebuke to Nature.

It is to be seen that, at least for the purposes of a fashion magazine, Mallarmé takes almost exactly an opposite attitude to Baudelaire's, and for him there is no difference between Nature and art. According to Ix (see p. 33), why holidaymakers hurl themselves in express trains to the seaside is to inspect the new *toilettes* woven by the waves. Again, one of the favourite tropes or principles of Madame de Ponty, as of Ix, is that the *monde* (world) in the 'high-life' sense (i.e. the scene of worldliness and fashion) is synonymous with the *monde* or world in the everyday sense (i.e. as meaning everything that there is); and this is closely related to a further trope, that 'Nature' is a false concept, 'Nature' and the man-made are not to be distinguished. There is an example of this latter in Madame de Ponty's remark in Issue 4 (see p. 96) that the glamour of the theatre and its costumes does not befit the Town, which calls for more sobriety, 'even when the Town is the Forest!' When we come to Ix's column in Issue 1 (see pp. 29–33), we shall see these notions at work on a wider scale.

But then, it should be remembered, what Mallarmé did was unique. He made himself, in all seriousness, a fashion designer, and at the same time a parody of a fashion journalist, or rather of several different kinds of fashion journalist, and this opened up to him possibilities not available to a mere critic or theorist, like Gautier or Baudelaire. It was a way of exploring Fashion – its rules, philosophy and rhetoric of persuasion – from the inside; and at the same time it allowed him to have a vision of Fashion which extended far beyond women's clothes.

But that said, there are some striking convergences between Madame de Ponty's theories and those of Roland Barthes, in his *Système de la mode*.[11] For one thing, they seize on the obvious but fundamental point that, as regards women's clothes, Fashion is the fashion of a calendar year. One of the reasons why Barthes decides to analyse, not women's clothes themselves but women's fashion magazines, is that 'printed' dress gives the analyst what human languages refuse to the linguist: a *pure* synchrony. 'The synchrony of Fashion changes suddenly each year, but during the year it is completely stable'.[12] The same point is made much of by Madame de Ponty in Issue 1, where she pictures herself as writing in a temporal void, neither last year nor (in the fashion sense) this year. It reminds one of her again when Barthes writes that 'Fashion "tames" the new even before producing it and accomplishes the paradox of a "new" that is unpredictable and yet law-bound (*legifère*).'

Barthes also nicely catches a feature of Madame de Ponty's tone.

> A fashionable woman does not suffer financial pressures, because Fashion has, precisely, full power to defeat them: the expensiveness of a garment is not mentioned except to justify calling it a 'folly'. Financial difficulties are never evoked except in so far as Fashion resolves them. Thus Fashion plunges the Woman of whom, and to whom, it speaks into a state of innocence, where everything is for the best in the best of worlds. The *'bon ton'* of Fashion, which forbids it to propose anything aesthetically or morally disgraceful, merges here with maternal language. It is the language of a mother who preserves her daughter from any contact with evil.[13]

As any reader of *La Dernière mode* will perceive, Madame de Ponty loves to adopt, and indeed to exaggerate, this 'maternal' tone – which, as Barthes rightly adds, used to be found in all literature for young women but is by now only to be found in fashion-writing.

* * *

---

11. It is a little surprising that, so far as we know, Barthes never mentions *La Dernière mode* and perhaps was not even aware of its existence.

12. Roland Barthes, *Système de la mode* (Seuil, 1967), p. 18; our translation.

13. Ibid., p. 264.

The argument of Lecercle's *Mallarmé et la mode* is that it is a mistake to find 'poetry' in *La Dernière mode*, to see the articles as 'prose-poems' etc., as some critics have done: on the contrary, its aim is to create a desperate hunger for poetry. '*Toilettes*? let us consider them as an epitaph: "Here lies poetry"; or, more properly, as the winding-sheet of a poetry buried alive'.[14] It is, he argues, a fundamentally ironic work. 'A poet, a veritable maniac for poetry – later he will even rhyme, for his friends, on fans, pebbles and envelopes – makes himself heard in a fashion magazine. And lo and behold, he installs poetry and reflection in a postponement. They shimmer in the far distance, like forbidden fruits, of which we – the embodiments of that high-life which he takes such care to target – will never know the flavour.'[15]

There is an important half-truth in this, but – we would argue – only a half-truth. That Mallarmé is conceiving of poetry and fashion as polar opposites is true, and represents a great originality in his vision. But in face of the brilliant insights and paradoxes about the nature of Fashion that he offers, in the guise of Madame de Ponty and of Ix, it seems absurd to suggest that he is denying us 'reflection'; and, as we shall argue in a moment, his response to dress and decoration can hardly not have involved love.

It is worth adding a remark or two about a book by Roger Dragonetti, *Un Fantôme dans le kiosque* [A Phantom in the Kiosk] (Paris, 1992) – the word 'kiosk' referring to the newspaper kiosks at which a fashion magazine might be bought. Dragonetti supposes that *La Dernière mode* never actually existed in the full sense: it was a piece of private publication for the eyes of a group of friends, who were bound by a vow of secrecy about it. It was not merely, under one aspect, a fantasy about and take-off of a real fashion-journal (which indeed it was); it was wholly a fantasy or 'phantom'.

Moreover, according to Dragonetti, it was, under heavy disguise, a portion of that 'Book' of which Mallarmé spoke in a famous letter to Verlaine in 1885. He wrote there of a book which he had already dreamed of writing, 'architectural and premeditated, and not a mere collection of random inspirations, even marvellous ones'; an 'orphic explanation of the Earth'; a book which needed to be called '*the* Book' – for he believed that there was only ever one, which is 'attempted unconsciously by anyone who writes'.

It is hard not to feel that Dragonetti's own ingenious book is, from beginning to end, on a totally false track. One easily sees what prompted his initial suspicion about the irreality of *La Dernière mode*. For, as has already been mentioned, it embodied quite an array of mystifications – for instance, inventing for itself an imaginary earlier existence – and it would be an ingenuous reader who believed in

14. Lecercle, p. 122.
15. Lecercle, p. 143.

the flesh-and-blood existence of all the titled ladies contributing to its Correspondence columns. But there is an overwhelming common-sense objection to Dragonetti's thesis. For it is quite conceivable that an author with a fondness for mystification might, to entertain his friends, forge a single number of a fashion journal – even given the enormous labour of assembling so much detailed information, about dress and dress shops, theatres, menus, railway services and holiday resorts, and leaving aside the commissioning or buying-in of illustrations and soliciting of advertisements. But that he should contemplate doing it eight times over is beyond belief.

Anyway there is evidence, including a police dossier on *La Dernière mode* and on its final cession to another proprietor, that the journal was a real one.[16] But it is hardly worth attacking Dragonetti from that angle, for what is more to the point is his interpretation of Mallarmé's text. He assumes that, fundamentally, it is not about Fashion at all, but about literature and writing. (One senses a bizarre but rooted prejudice on Dragonetti's part, that Mallarmé simply could not have been interested in Fashion.) Dragonetti's proof depends a good deal on the detection of puns. Thus, behind the title, the 'Anchor Line', of an English steamship company advertising in the journal, he detects, by way of *lignes d'ancre,* a pun on *lignes d'encre* ('lines in ink'), this decoding being reinforced by the fact that the company's office in Paris is in the rue *Scribe.* Madame de Ponty's instructions about a baby's *layette*, so he would have us believe, are meant to send the mind running on the Breton *lai* (song) and the *lais* (legacy) of Villon.

What this really adds up to is that Dragonetti wants to deny that Mallarmé ever could have been interested in Fashion; and to this rooted prejudice he is ready to sacrifice all the wonderful cleverness, and philosophical acuteness, and barbed ironies and inspired inventiveness of décors, of Mallarmé's text. No new and different work of art emerges from his exegesis, and it is hard to see how such a work could take its life from furtive and savourless puns.

But, indeed, here one comes up against a recent problem for Mallarmé criticism. It tends to be the fruit of too much interest, or the wrong kind of interest, in Mallarmé's *Livre*, which was largely a private fantasy and diverts attention from the magnificent poems of his early prime 'Tristesse d'été', 'L'Azur', 'Brise marine', 'Soupir', etc. and the great 'Hérodiade' and 'L'Après-Midi d'un Faune' – works of intense human force which have become so much part of one's own being.[17]

16. See Lecercle, pp. 153–161.

17. Some critics have even suggested that Mallarmé's *Un Coup de dés* is a realisation of Mallarmé's 'Book', and others identify it with the strange numerological project of Mallarmé's reconstructed by Jacques Scherer in *Le 'Livre' de Mallarmé* (1957).

As regards the text that we offer in the present volume: we have in fact translated every word of Mallarmé's magazine, but it became plain to us that, to give a full account of the original, one would need to offer something like a facsimile. For the layout and the interrelation of the various items (discourses, reviews, menus, timetables, etc., not to mention the illustrations) form an essential part of the journal's 'decorative' function. But a facsimile in translation presents its own special problems, which may indeed be insuperable. Accordingly we have opted for a different plan. We reprint in full the main articles of 'opinion' in each number, commenting, sometimes at length, on each as we go along, and we reproduce the columns of more practical information (about theatres and travel and books), but we have done a little discreet pruning of these latter where there is too much repetition. More importantly, we omit the story and the poem by another writer which appeared in each issue.

Each issue of *La Dernière mode* opens with a contents list, a black-and-white engraving of two newly designed *toilettes*,[18] and a leading article on Fashion and its nature and principles, by Marguerite de Ponty. There follow a Chronicle by Ix; some 'leaves' from a 'Golden Notebok', about food or interior decoration, etc.; a poem and a short story; a *Gazette for the Fortnight*, dealing with Books, Theatres and Travel; a column of 'Correspondence with subscribers'; and the 'visiting-cards' of various recommended shops and agencies.

The poems and short stories, which we are omitting, are as follows:

Issue 1. Poem, 'La Dernière pensée de Weber', by Théodore de Banville. Story, 'L'Aveu', by François Coppée.
Issue 2. Poem, 'Conseil', by Sully Prudhomme. Conclusion of 'L'Aveu'.
Issue 3. Poem, 'Inquiétude', by Léon Valade. Story, 'Les Voies de fait', by Alphonse Daudet.
Issue 4. Poem, 'At Home', by Ernest d'Hervilly. Conclusion of 'Les Voies de fait'.
Issue 5. Poem, 'Le Veilleur de nuit', by Emmanuel des Essarts. Story, 'La Petite servante', by Catulle Mendès.
Issue 6. Poem, 'Marguerite d'Ecosse', by Théodore de Banville. Story, 'L'Hercule', by Léon Cladel.
Issue 7. Poem, 'Menuet', by François Coppée. Conclusion of 'L'Hercule'.
Issue 8. Poem, 'La Vierge à la crèche', by Alphonse Daudet. Story, 'Eudore Cleaz', by Théodore de Banville (first instalment only).

In the next part of our book we follow the journal through fortnight by fortnight.

18. Except in the case of Issue 1, where one *toilette* is illustrated.

Part II
The Journal, Fortnight by Fortnight, with Commentary

Issue 1

PREMIÈRE LIVRAISON — DIMANCHE 6 SEPTEMBRE 1874

LA DERNIÈRE MODE

GAZETTE DU MONDE ET DE LA FAMILLE

MARASQUIN

PARAIT

LE 1er ET LE 3e DIMANCHE DU MOIS

AVEC LE CONCOURS

DES GRANDES FAISEUSES, DE TAPISSIERS-DÉCORATEURS

DE MAITRES QUEUX, DE JARDINIERS

D'AMATEURS DE BIBELOTS ET DU SPORT

NOUVELLES & VERS

LÉON CLADEL

FRANÇOIS COPPÉE

ALPHONSE DAUDET, LÉON DIERX, ERNEST D'HERVILLY

STÉPHANE MALLARMÉ, CATULLE MENDÈS

SULLY PRUDHOMME

AUGUSTE VILLIERS DE L'ISLE ADAM, ÉMILE ZOLA, ETC.

TOILETTE DES PREMIERS JOURS D'AUTOMNE

FASHION

On the argument that, in this late-summer hiatus between years, it is not plain what the new or 'latest' fashion is going to be, Madame de Ponty chooses for her first article a permanent and unchanging topic, jewellery.

JEWELLERY

Paris, 1 August 1874

Too late to speak of summer fashions and too soon to speak of winter ones (or even autumn ones). Though several great Paris Houses, as we happen to know, are already busy over their end-of-season selection. Today, in fact, not having to hand the elements needed even to begin designing a new toilette, we would like to chat with our readers about the objects which serve to complete a toilette, i.e. jewels. A paradox? No: is there not, in jewels, something permanent, fitting to speak of in a fashion journal still in suspense as to what was fashion in July or will be in September?

Let us study the Jewel, in isolation, and in its own right. Where? Everywhere: that is to say, a little all over the globe, and much in Paris, for Paris furnishes the world with jewels. What, you may say? Does not each region, as by nature it offers a flora, likewise offer, moulded by the hands of man, a complete jewel-casket? That instinct of beauty, and of relation to climate, which, under each different sky, governs the production of roses, of tulips and carnations: has it nothing to say as regards ear-drops, finger-rings and bracelets? Flowers and jewels: has not each of them, as one might say, its native soil? This sunshine befits that flower, this type of woman that jewel. A natural harmony of this kind used to reign, but it seems to be lost today, except among peoples generally thought of as barbarians, or peasants regarded as rebels to civilisation. Civilisation! Say rather the epoch when all creative force has disappeared – in Jewellery, as in Furnishings – so that, in the one as the other, we are thrown back upon exhumation or importation. Importing of what, then? Spun-glass bracelets from India and cut-paper earrings from China? No, but often enough the naive taste that encourages their manufacture. Exhuming of what? The heavy clusters of jewels of long-forgotten centuries, employed to set off, by contrast, the glare of stage-scene velvets and the brocades of the sacristy? No: but the boldness with which, by a master touch, they could be combined in a costume. Who knows, we may need to return to the earlier convergence of those two so different inspirations of the jeweller's art, the classic and the barbaric. Remember our Musée Campana;[19] *ask the great jewellers (whether named Froment-Meurice,*[20] *Rouvenat or Fontenay*[21]*) if their admirable (and supremely critical) science does not derive from there, as much as from the show-cases of the Musée de Cluny*[22] *or the Paris shopcounter of Japanese or Algerian traders.*

Thus Paris, unaided, likes to comprise the universe, itself as much a museum as a bazaar. Nothing so strange but it will accept it; nothing exquisite that it cannot offer for sale. London, certainly, has jewels, strange and massive ones, and I can see in them a certain intimate charm, preferable (if in this alone) to one of our defects – that is to say, of introducing wit into jewellery. Let us, in this sphere, remain severely sculptural. Decoration! Everything is in that word; and I would advise a lady, hesitating whom to apply to, to design a particular piece of jewellery, to ask the architect who built her town house, rather than the famous dress-designer who created her festal gown. Such, in a word, is the art of the Jewel; and, this said once and for all, let us pass on from the general to the particular.

It is simplicity itself: we now have proof that a stroll, on several afternoons, along the boulevards and the rue de la Paix, to the Palais Royal[23] *and to certain celebrated workshops, is enough to show us 'the best the world can provide', to give a trite phrase its true meaning.*

Let us mention, with your gracious permission dear ladies, what rare objects of precious stone and metal may form part of the chaste jewellery of your daughters – before enlarging on the needs of womanhood in its full splendour.

Here are some jewels for an elegant mother to choose from for a young person of eighteen or twenty years of age. For a walking dress: plain gold earrings, with a little matching buckle or a black velvet choker round the neck. Or again – let me ransack yesterday's memories – I call to mind a charming parure, *again designed to go round the neck, in pale (extremely pale) pink coral, with a necklace to match; another of turquoises, with the same little buckle (very 'young girl' this), or turquoises and pearls. I even conjure up in my mind's eye long earrings and a little brooch in the shape of arrows, with a fine pearl at the end: delicious. Everyone has a good-luck bracelet on their arm, made of simple gold or with pearls and turquoises; and on their finger a ring, just one, and always simple, without brilliants*

---

19. The great archaeological collection amassed by Campana di Cavelli (1807–80) was acquired by France in 1861 and exhibited in Paris in the Palais de l'Industrie as the 'Musée Napoléon III'. It was subsequently divided up and dispersed.

20. François Froment-Meurice (1802–55) was known as 'the Benvenuto Cellini of the day'.

21. Claude Fontenay (fl.1567) or Julien Fontenay (fl.1547).

22. Since 1842, the Musée de Cluny occupied the former hôtel of the Abbots of Cluny in the Latin Quarter; it is a treasure house of mediaeval art.

23. According to a Baedeker of the time, the most attractive shops in Paris were to be found on the boulevards, the Palais Royal and the rue de la Paix.

or emeralds, in enamel, or at most enclosing a little miniature. In the sphere of costume jewellery one has the choice of ear-drops and a cross of old silver encrusted with precious stones, in the antique style: it may come from Brittany or Provence, from Normandy, Germany or Holland. Jewels worn by day being quite different from those worn in the evening, we shall take great care – if, for instance, we have to design a corbeille de mariage – to *include both kinds.*

A corbeille de mariage![24] *We would begin by including a pair of ear-drops all in gold, of really artistic design: long ones (for so fashion decrees), with which we would match a pretty cross with a chain; a second* parure *in lapis lazuli, a stone very much in favour these days; and a third more elaborate one: cabochons of garnet in the shape of pears or apples, with a stem studded with diamonds. Sleeve buttons suited to each of these ornaments.*

Next, for dinner parties and soirées, *we would choose ear-studs and a locket, with, in its middle, a great black pearl surrounded by a triple circle of brilliants: an object just this moment arrived in the great jewellery-houses (those we named above, and others too).*

A very beautiful parure *would have its place beside this previous one: composed of sapphires cut* en tablettes *and surrounded with brilliants. The softer glow of this stone, in demand more than ever at the present moment, will somewhat dim the dazzle of the emeralds. Necklace to match. I would prefer these varied jewels to those eternal* solitaires, *with their brilliants, known to us for so long.*

Who is interested in bracelets? I saw a splendid one yesterday made of gold and rubies; then several rings of brilliants, or emeralds, or with cameos (these last are coming back into fashion). I leave it to you to choose the clasp for the shawl.

A little scent-flask in various hues of gold; or pink, or green, or yellow; or Louis XV or Louis XVI; or garlanded (or modern, in enamel, with Japanese foliage or birds). Being indispensable, like its companion the lace handkerchief, it will hardly get forgotten, any more than will a fan: a black silk fan with a pink, blue or grey edging for the Morning Toilette, a white silk one with a 'subject' for great occasions. The 'subject' must lie at one side now, not in the middle. Nevertheless nothing can ever rival a fan, with a setting as rich as you please or quite simple, but affirming, above all, ideality. What sort of ideality? That of a painting: an old-master one, of the school of Boucher or Watteau,[25] or even by them; or a modern one, by our collaborator Edmond Morin. Scenes of noble flights-of-steps or ancestral parks – or asphalt and gravel, scene of the contemporary monde *whose festival lasts the whole year round. These are what they reveal to us, those rare masterpieces placed in great ladies' hands.*

24. Wedding presents (specifically, presents from the bridegroom to the bride).

25. The Goncourt brothers had recently tried to revive an interest in these eighteenth-century painters: Boucher (1703–70) and Watteau (1684–1721).

All this that we have been glimpsing must for various reasons have its place in the corbeille *and an Indian cashmere shawl, of a certain price – indispensable, even if only very rarely worn. (Fashion having declared it not to be formal dress.) Let it (this shawl) slip from the shoulders, with its oriental folds, and envelop other marvels – all that jewel-box which, stone by stone or pearl by pearl, we have been recounting. As for lace, we wish it to be of the rarest quality, fairy-like in workmanship, knowing no mediocrity. For flounces, shawls, tunic, fan, parasol: Chantilly lace? For flounces, tunic, fan, parasol or handkerchief: Brussels-style needlework? There is really no choosing! We shall not be loading our* corbeille *with velvets and silks, such fabrics being the province of the dressmaker; and, apropos of the fashion designer, I have allowed myself to declare – but has one the right to prophesy? – that we should expect an absolute revolution in the Bustle. People claim that its day is over, the waist no longer needing its support. For it is almost an old story now that waistlines should be long, or even very long.*

May not Fashion, this time, come to us from the Salon Exhibition of Painting?[26] *We saw there with astonishment, then not without satisfaction, a portrait – indeed several – in which youthful and modern faces were poised above the long outlines of bygone centuries. It will be curious to decide, at the beginning of September, if that revival is to last through the coming Season! But then, our eyes dazzled by irisations, opalisations or scintillations,*[27] *how are we to focus so vague a scene as the Future?*

MARGUERITE DE PONTY

It is, one may begin by saying, very distinguished, and, syntactically speaking, enormously subtle prose (and no easy job to translate). Subtle, elusive and sometimes most brilliant also in its argument: for instance, here, the likening of jewellery to local flora, and the paradox about time (what can a fashion-journal talk about when fashion itself is 'in suspense'?)

It is also, for much of the time, serious and truly original aesthetic thought. When Mme de Ponty says that the 1870s are 'an epoch from which all creative force has disappeared', she is echoing what Mallarmé wrote in his Exhibition review: that there had been no new style invented since the 'Empire' one, which was at least a real one. One therefore has to make do with eclecticism; and it is Mme de Ponty's pleasant duty to expound the ways in which fashion (so much at home with eclecticism) can supply the place, and emulate the creativity, of high art. We are aware of a swarm of little ironies here, as always with Mme de Ponty,

---

26. The Salon Exhibition, at this time held in the Palais de l'Industrie (now the Grand Palais), was an annual event of great importance to the artists of the day, as it was from it that the State selected works of art to adorn its offices and museums. It was notoriously conservative in taste.

27. i.e. by all this talk about jewellery.

though it is not altogether clear whom they will sting. Mallarmé has embodied in her the gushing but despotic manner of women fashion-editors; and the question of Authority, the problem of where the authorisation for new fashions derives from, is already adumbrated here and will be explored much further in later issues. Even Mme de Ponty, though always so authoritative and oracular, does not pretend to be an arbiter of fashion, only to be closer in touch with its (ultimately inexplicable) workings. This is the era of the bustle, and it will be her great triumph to have predicted that great revolution, the disappearance of the bustle.

We need to add a word or two about the bustle, which is important throughout the magazine, as indeed it was in the history of fashion. The French have two separate words for the bustle, *tournure* and *pouff* (as well as the sobriquet *le cul de Paris*). *Tournure* refers to the twisting and bunching up of the dress over the buttocks, *pouf* to the pad which supports this construction. Mme de Ponty was proved right, for the bustle did in fact disappear in 1875, driven out by the tightly fitting '*cuirass bodice*'. But what is curious is that in 1885 it would return, in fantastically exaggerated form. In the words of Charles Gibbs-Smith, 'The enormous bustle tends to arch up and away from the back, before plunging down to the ground, giving the impression that the woman is saddled with a shrouded bird cage which sticks monstrously out behind her'.[28]

Charles Blanc, in his *L'Art dans la parure et dans le vêtement* (Paris, 1875), pp. 373–5, gives a very striking analysis of this form of dress:

> Everything that could prevent a woman remaining seated was developed, and everything that could impede her walk was discarded. They dressed their hair and themselves as though they were always to be seen in profile; now, the profile is the outline of a person who is not looking at us, who passes and would avoid us. The toilette became an image of the rapid movement which bears the world onwards, and which threatens to carry along even the guardians of our homes. They are to be adorned with the braid like soldiers, walking in high heels which threw them forwards, hastening their steps, cleaving the air, and hurrying their life as though to swallow up space, which in turn swallows up them.

It was in the period of the bustle that Odette de Crécy became Swann's lover, and in Proust's description of her costume we have another vivid analysis of this extraordinary style:

> . . . as for her figure – and she was admirably built – it was impossible to make out its continuity (on account of the fashion then prevailing, and in spite of her being one of the best-dressed women in Paris) so much did the corsage, jutting out as though over an imaginary stomach and ending in a sharp point, beneath which bulged out the balloon

28. Charles Gibbs-Smith, *The Fashionable Lady in the Nineteenth Century* (1960), p. 7.

of her double skirts, give a woman the appearance of being composed of different sections badly fitted together; to such an extent did the frills, the flounces, the inner bodice follow quite independently, according to the whim of their designer or the consistency of their material, the line which led them to the bows, the festoons of lace, the fringes of dazzling jet beads, or carried them along the busk, but nowhere attached themselves to the living creature, who, according as the architecture of these fripperies drew them towards or away from her own, found herself either strait-laced to suffocation or else completely buried.[29]

Something else again about the bustle – its impracticality and messiness as a walking dress – is brought out by the hero of Dostoevsky's *A Raw Youth,* in his furious complaint to his patron the woman-fancying Prince:

I don't like women because they've no manners . . . Go to the theatre, go for a walk. Every man knows the right side of the road, when they meet they step aside, he keeps to the right, I keep to the right. A woman, that is a lady – it's ladies I'm talking about – dashes straight at you as though she didn't see you, as though you were absolutely bound to skip aside and make way for her . . .
They're not decently dressed . . . They openly hang bustles on behind to look as though they had fine figures, openly! . . . They walk along the parade with trains half a yard long behind them, sweeping the dust. It's a pleasant thing to walk behind them: you must run to get in front, or jump on one side, or they'll sweep pounds of dust into your mouth and nose.[30]

But to return to that first leading article, on jewellery: it would be a mistake to see in what Mallarmé writes here an arrogant literary irony at the expense of something so 'trivial' as fashion. One needs to bear in mind that each number of the journal contains the verbal description of several *toilettes* freshly invented by Mme de Ponty (which is in this case to say Mallarmé) – designed, one cannot help thinking, *con amore* (and, of course, often involving the actual employment of jewellery). How he contrived to become such an expert in dress-design is a mystery, but it could hardly have happened without love. Moreover, though, as we saw Lercerle rightly saying, fashion figures in this journal as, in some sense, the enemy of poetry and of high art in general, we must not think of this as the only, or even perhaps as the main, focus of its ironies. One senses too much affection for fashion on Mallarmé's part to read *La Dernière mode* simply as a rancorous attack on it.

It is, moreover, not for nothing that *La Dernière mode* begins with a discourse on jewellery. Jewels are an important theme in Mallarmé's verse. One recalls Hérodiade's soliloquy:

29. Marcel Proust, *Remembrance of Things Past*, (Penguin Books, 1983), vol. I, p. 215.
30. Dostoevsky, *A Raw Youth*, trans. Constance Garnett (Heinemann, 1916), pp. 25–6.

Oui, c'est pour moi pour moi que je fleuris, déserte!
Vous le savez, jardins d'améthyste, enfouis
Sans fin dans de savants abîmes éblouis,
Ors ignorés, gardant votre antique lumière
Sous le sombre sommeil d'une terre première,
Vous, pierres où mes yeux comme de purs bijoux
Empruntent leur clarté mélodieuse . . .[31]

But in addition, jewels figure prominently in Mallarmé's theorising about poetry. We will repeat and continue the passage, already quoted, about the *oeuvre pure*:

The *œuvre pure* implies the elocutionary disappearance of the poet, who concedes the initiative to words, mobilised by the shock of their own collision; they illuminate themselves by reciprocal reflections, like a virtual train of fire upon precious stones, replacing the afflatus of the old-style lyric or the personalising note in the conduct of sentences.[32]

This can be compared with a much later statement, in an interview with the journalist Jules Huet:

The childishness of literature up to now has been to believe, for example, that to select a certain number of precious stones and to write their names down, even with great skill, was to *make* precious stones. Well, no! Poetry consisting of creating, one needs to identify certain states of the soul, certain gleams of a purity so absolute that, well sung and well lit, they constitute, as it were, the jewellery of mankind: there you will have symbolism, there you will have creation, and the word 'poetry' here finds its proper meaning – it is, in sum, the only creation possible to humanity. And if, in reality, the jewels one adorns oneself with do not manifest a state of the soul, one has no right to them . . . woman, for instance, that eternal thief . . .[33]

Mallarmé, as Huet notes, is here making a mildly misogynistic joke, about thieving by women in shops and multiple stores.[34] But in essence this is the *Symboliste,* and also the 'Modernist', doctrine, of which he was so much the creator: its burden being that a work of art should not describe but *be.*

31. Yes it is for myself that I bloom, deserted! You know it, amethyst gardens, entirely buried in wise, dazzled abysses, yet unknown, keeping your ancient light under the dark sleep of a primal earth – you, gems where my eyes, like pure jewels, borrow their melodious clarity.

32. Letter to Cazalis (*Correspondence,* ed. H. Mondor, vol. I, p. 358.)

33. The interview took place in 1891: see Mallarmé, *Oeuvres complètes,* ed. H. Mondor (Pléiade edition), pp. 870–1.

34. Theft in department stores was a matter of great concern, and psychiatrists had even created a clinical entity, 'la névrose des grands bazaars'.

In Mme de Ponty's essay much is made, and more will be made later, of fashion's relation to Time. In a literal or historical sense, the magazine is firmly planted in a 'moment'. It is that of the rebirth of Paris after the agony and destruction of the Franco-Prussian War and the Commune, and of the need to come to terms with the loss of Alsace-Lorraine. This theme is dealt with or hinted at in a dozen ways: bitterly, in the hordes of foreign sightseers, come to view the 'ruins' of the city (many of them already repaired), and sanguinely in the preparations for the opening of Garnier's great new Opéra. That Paris, still or all the more the leader of fashion, should require a new and luxurious fashion-magazine is of course another assertion of recovery, of which its columnists make great capital.

But what the magazine also explores, in all sorts of brilliant and paradoxical ways, is its 'moment' in a more abstract sense. Fashion, it is suggested, being a thing so supremely of the moment, may arrive at having no moment, no temporal space, at all, existing purely yesterday or tomorrow.

Madame de Ponty's leading article on Fashion is followed by some 'explanations' of the *toilettes* illustrated in the separate coloured lithograph and the cut-out patterns, which came with each number, and of the black-and-white engravings forming part of the text. We give the version in the 'Sample Issue', which is not altogether the same in its wording as the actual Issue 1.

EXPLANATION OF THE COLOURED LITHOGRAPH OF THE DAY (NOT PART OF THE TEXT) AND OF THE BLACK-AND-WHITE ENGRAVINGS FORMING PART OF THE TEXT.

COLOURED ENGRAVING

[Not reproduced in this translation]

BLACK-AND-WHITE ENGRAVINGS

First page

1. Skirt in navy-blue silk. Tunic in cashmere of the same shade, with puffed folds and lining of turquoise silk. Little diagonal pieces of navy-blue silk on the folds and round them. The bodice has two points and is in cashmere with silk trimming in two tones. All this ornamented with black pearled lace.

Middle pages

2. Boy's costume (8 to 10 years old). Jacket, trousers and waistcoat of dark-blue cloth, edged with lacing, with a little black silk facing on the trousers, the sleeves and the pockets. 3. Serge costume for a little girl of 8 to 10. Pleated skirt with chestnut velvet decoration. Little jacket fitting closely behind but not in front. The basque receding in front, with very long side pieces towards the back; the back itself very short. Pockets at the side with chestnut-wood buttons.

III. – CUT-OUT PATTERN (ACTUAL SIZE)

* * *

The Sample Issue cannot contain a cut-out pattern, since the summer toilettes illustrated in our lithographic watercolours vary with each copy. Nevertheless, the special lithographic watercolour, supplied to subscribers on Sunday 6 September, will come with a cut-out pattern, both being explained on the Cover for that day.

We come next to a further and elaborate meditation on the moment – this time in the social sphere – by the feline, elusive and often malicious Ix.

PARIS CHRONICLE

Theatres, Books, the Arts; Echoes from the salon and the seaside

A 'Chronicle' – but without a past? For we arrive on the scene unknown, with only a future. The opening number of La Dernière mode *has to remain before the public almost from July to September;*[35] *and in the case of Paris, is not a whole month a period vaguer and more undefined than eternity itself? But let us take advantage of this phase of existence we are going through, with its lack of a present, to indulge a little in generalisation; it will be a suitable beginning for our causeries.*

The purpose of these brief chats is made plain by their position in the journal, between Fashion news and the Department of Literature.[36] *We shall speak of products of the intellect, but always in the light of the fashion of the moment. Here – shall we say – is a new volume of poetry, in which you will find the poem we publish in the present issue; or a collection of short stories, of which the present issue*

35. See also p. 21.

36. In point of fact, it *is* the 'Department of Literature', but, as Ix explains, viewed strictly from the 'fashion' point of view.

will give you a first taste. These products of the latest hour (or of other hours): are they in vogue? And ought they to be? You may call this a frivolous mode of criticism, but not so. For it proceeds from an axiom: that all women love verse, as they do perfumes or jewels or the characters in novels; it is as dear to them as their own selves. To please them, or at least deserve to do so: I know of no ambition, becoming a triumph if one succeeds, that is more fitting for a work in prose or in verse. They say there are no real readers any longer, and perhaps this is true; but there are women readers. Only a woman, in her freedom from politics and gloomy cares, has leisure, once her dressing is done, to feel the need to dress her soul as well. That a certain volume should linger a whole week, half-opened like a scent-bottle, on the silks of sofa cushions embroidered with dreams; and another be banished from this trial-ground to the shelves of a lacquered cupboard, joining jewel-boxes locked up till the next ball or gala: there you have our very simple manner of passing judgement. Add a word as to 'why?' if you like, but only a word: that elusive word which, like a book's title, will inscribe itself for ever in our memory, brief but complete. Sometimes a friend's smile, when she offers us a volume, will serve in lieu of all comment: the great, unforgettable friendships of our life often begin in this way. I shall be the friend who, all unknown, lends you books.

When the number of books so increases that the few lines devoted to them reads like no more than a library catalogue, so much the worse – or so much the better! It will often be the case: for the surprise I have in store, a magnificent and charming one for those who listen to me even with half an ear, is the proof that no other epoch produces so many works meant for the silent hours: disinterested works which, to the chosen few, means interesting ones.

This, for me, is a grateful task; but when, for example, it comes to the Theatre, things grow more disturbing. A book, if it is tiresome, is easily closed, and one's gaze can find refreshment in the cloud of impressions that the reader of today, like the ancient gods, can at will put between herself and trite adventures. But by contrast, what a catastrophe is a whole evening of our existence lost in that cave of cardboard and painted canvas – or of genius – a Theatre, if nothing there is worth our attention! No clouds to conceal us, under the all-too-real gaslight, save the cloudy tissue of our own gown, wrenched by our impatience. Vain, splendid and incomprehensible, the living marionettes declaim their loud nonsense before us, like figures in some rare nightmare, against a background of intense and exasperated boredom. Admittedly, for all its nothingness, the décor – a northern landscape or a southern, or a grand palace interior – will win our attention just a little, simply by evoking their sites, and we will find entertainment in bygone costumes, or in foreign ones, resembling our own but transfigured! Still, given that a dramatic art for our own time – vast, sublime and almost religious – has yet to come into being, and that these half-hour-long causeries of mine are no place to expound its theory,[37] *it will be better merely to offer guidance on theatre managers, before whose doors so many carriages stand in line. There will be occasion for this every day of the year. For, since curiosity never sleeps, Paris, whose stage is copied throughout the world, always has something to stir its attention. But, to avoid competition, let us leave it to the* feuilletons *– those familiar Sunday-paper supplements, or reports of dress-rehearsals, which arrive in households, under cover of their parent newspaper, many hours before we ourselves are admitted – to classify or analyse the new productions and pass professional judgement on them. Our own aesthetic principle may be stated in these words: 'Is there, at such-and-such a theatre, anything which will entertain us?', or 'This place is for laughter, this other one for tears'; or perhaps, 'On this festive evening, the real drama is the one lit, not by the footlights, but by the chandelier'*[38] *(or, as it may be, the other way round). Once or twice a year, nonetheless, we may, like the rest of the world, find the printed text stimulating, and then we shall actually discuss it.*

Intimate ceremonies. To insert an ivory paper-knife into the shadow between two uncut pages: that is one. Another luxurious – proud and peculiarly Parisian – is a première, *wherever it happens to take place. But are there no other notable dates? The opening of the 'Exhibition of Contemporary Artists' forms, in the eyes of the intelligent, a ceremony no less important; and, just as much as the* Salon, *those sales of* Objets d'art *and exhibitions of a single master – all dates to be marked with a red letter (if not just with the finger-nail) on the calendar of fashion. We shall do our duty by them, knowing how much pleasure a person of today can gain from these new customs. To give an example or two: 'This style of painting', we are liable to say, 'seems just made for the panelling and ceiling of our apartments; from this artist, the only one to bring out the truly modern character in a face, let us commission our portraits'.*

Who longs to dream, but cannot? These leafy or twilit images are dream-machines,[39] *groves of solitude rarer than the trim coverts of real gardens; here might stand the statue we admired this summer in the 'sculpture park' of the*

37. For some years Mallarmé himself had grandiose schemes for a new Drama, though they came to nothing.

38. i.e. what goes on among the audience.

39. *rêvoirs.*

Champs-Elysées. To teach the beauty in everyday things is our concern, or a part of it, but even more a putting-to-use in the cause of delicate enjoyment, of artists' visions.

'Books, the theatre, and simulacra in colour or marble: art, nothing but art!' I hear you complain. 'Will you tell us nothing about life, which is so vivid, so dear to us and so multifarious? Nothing even about our own life, and its tremendous trifles?' Yes, we shall. For, indeed, what does it signify, Madame, that in your salon, the scene of your triumphs, the pier-glass is carved with a tragic or a comic mask, a flute and paint-brushes, and a text half-unrolled,[40] *since all this bygone French style (still in fashion!) does no more than frame a mirror where you encounter yourself? When, this winter, the rhythm of the dance brings you and your sisters before this impartial glass, the look you cast towards it, seeking to find the queen of the ball, flies straight to your own reflection. For in truth, what woman, being always so much a queen for somebody, is not one, just a little, even for herself?*

A thousand secrets, the fleeting history of an evening overheard amid the fashionable hubbub, will find a brief echo here, drowned the next moment by the band. Discarded dance-programmes and faded flowers, concert-programmes or dinner menus: they compose, there is no doubt, a literature all of their own, immortal with the immortality of a week or two. Nothing but has its value, in the existence of an epoch: everything in it belongs to everyone. A smile! See, it circulates already, still only half-formed, in the rooms with their heavy portières: expected, detested, blessed, received with gratitude or with jealousy, enrapturing, chafing or appeasing souls; and it is in vain for the fan, which thought at first to have hidden it, to hope to retrieve it, now that it has broken loose, or to dissipate its flight. Forgive me! I mean to catch its grace, that unfolding of your two lips, which other lips, reading this, will be essaying in sympathy. It is in the nature of things, this diffusion, and properly so. Has not the world the right to borrow from this smile, which is the deepest expression of our instincts? It provokes it, and it refines on it. Everything, even beauty,

40. Symbols of the arts.

is learned 'from the life'; and the way we hold our head, just as much as the way we wear our gown, we borrow from one another.

'Flee this world?' Impossible, one is a part of it. 'Seek out Nature?' Only by hurling ourselves, at furious speed, through its outward scenes, its landscapes and its distances, to arrive somewhere quite else – a modern image of its insufficiency for us! Yes if – the pleasures of the salon giving way, in due season, to the sports of the open air, the river regatta and the woodland chase – you then turn your back even on the woodland and the river, seeking rest for your eyes in the oblivion of a vast and naked horizon, is it not, surely, to feast your eyes on a new fashion: the paradox of the toilettes, *simple yet sophisticated, embroidered by the ocean with its waves? This Journal, choosing, without apology, to appear in the holiday season, as the right and proper moment, can slip between your day-dreams and the double azure of the sea and sky – long enough for you to turn one or two pages, though not, perhaps, to read these words of your Humble Servant,*

Ix

This is our first introduction to Ix, a male columnist, and his attitudes call for a lot of unravelling. We may begin with the obvious distinction that he considers the present day a notable age for poetry but a terrible one for the theatre – a view with which we might well agree. How, on the other hand, he can find it in himself to praise the response of fashionable women to poetry: we have here a problem. Evidently he is, in part, satirising both the philistinism of high society, and women in particular; he is giving women a cruelly malicious compliment verging on calculated offence. But this is not the whole story. For if women readers prefer to *say* nothing about poetry, signifying their preferences by inarticulate means (such as the length of time they leave a new volume on their sofa, or the smile they give when lending it to friends), does not this at least have the advantage of avoiding literary chatter? This in a way takes us to the heart of the Ix problem: that he is a paid critic who will use any excuse not to write criticism.

But among his excuses there is a very powerful one: that this is a fashion magazine, and, logically speaking, this ought to mean that everything in it is written strictly from the point of view of Fashion. With this pretext, Ix finds the most ingenious and implausible explanations for 'high-life' behaviour. Why, these days, are seaside holidays as much a fixture in the social calendar as *château* entertainments and the pleasures of the hunting-field and river? Do not say that those who go on them are seeking 'escape' (for they cannot escape from themselves); do not say they are in quest of 'Nature', for they hurtle through Nature blindly on express trains. What impels them to spend long hours on the beach, apparently totally idle, is *fashion;* it is interest in the new *toilettes* woven by the waves!

There is a free-floating irony in Ix's standpoint, of a kind one has not quite come across anywhere else in literature; and what happens in this first essay of his happens again in others. The satire and *Schadenfreude* give way, leading to a fantastic and enchanting, and utterly original, reflection on the nature of Fashion – here typified in the Smile. According to it, people learn 'from the life' (that is to say from one another) not just how to dress, but how they shall smile, and hold their head, and walk. The principle of fashion is instant and universal exchange. This passage in Ix's article, in which the smile is depicted as escaping from behind a fan, belongs with Mallarmé's many lovely fan-poems. All this mode of thought in Mallarmé belongs to his concept of the human décor. ('La Décoration! tout est dans ce mot.')[41]

Appropriately in view of Ix's 'Chronicle', the menu (or first page of the 'Golden Notebook') in this issue is for a meal at the seaside.

First leaf

Menu for a luncheon by the seaside

No large pieces of fish: they come from Paris. No precise instructions as to vegetables, for this menu has to serve from Boulogne to Arcachon

Oysters, Canapés of anchovies

Fillet of sole à la Saint-Malo
Mutton cutlets Maintenon
Lobster Supreme, with Montpellier butter
Chicken à la Duroc

Port wine sorbet

Baby turkeys
Terns

Salads

Shellfish en buisson
Local vegetables

41. See Mme de Ponty on Jewellery, p. 22.

Praline ice with fresh almonds

Dessert

Wines
Vin de Saint-Bris
Vins de Nuits
Léoville
Haut-Brion

THE CHEF DE BOUCHE CHEZ BRÉBANT

Mallarmé appears to have been both a gourmet and a gourmand. His friend Lefébure, after a stay with the Mallarmés, commented on the poet's ferocious appetite and the huge meals customary in their household; and he pretended that, cannibalistically, they were fattening him up for the table. On the other hand, at least during his earlier years, Mallarmé would have been far too hard up to eat at expensive restaurants or to lay in vintage wines. There must therefore have been some wish-fulfilment in the sumptuous menus in his journal.

Next, in this first issue, we get 'A *corbeille du jardin* for the month of August', which is a play upon the *'moment'*, in another sense again. It is plain from this evocative little floral invention that, for Mallarmé, *décor* and 'decoration' are more or less the same concept.

Second leaf

Flower-display for the Month of August

A flower-display for August! No easy task, you will agree. The sun, which caused the garden to flourish, has faded it. So what to do? This: simply turn the very colour and defects of the season to advantage in your flower-beds: a very just, very precise, inspiration, which no-one had had till put into practice by the Municipal Gardener in Paris. A true summer corbeille *this, which goes to Nature herself for the pale, dusty and defeated look which all things must wear at this time.*

It is what those who enter the Park by the avenue de la Reine-Hortense[42] *see in the first bed to the right. The entire lassitude of the hour is expressed in* Centaurea Candidissima, *with its pale and lustreless foliage, bleached white by dust and lightly also on its two sad surfaces. All the effect of the* corbeille *lies in the nearness*

42. Now called boulevard de Courcelles.

of this plant to another, Obelia Erineus,[43] *which, brittle and delicate, with its sharp blue florets, creeps through the oval border of the bed to lose itself above. The leading tone of things is dun: now we must enliven it. A few brusque and simple spots of scarlet are needed: namely* Pelargonium Diogène *(red), its five petals, somewhat worn and shabby, giving way in turn to the decorative foliage of* Coleus Beauté de Vilemore, *wine-coloured and green and as if already touched by autumn.*

All this, in its unstudied way, creates a brave and subtle harmony, borrowing its tints from the noons and afternoons of August itself. The strong sun of Touraine or Provence will suit it, or any of France's skies that you may choose: plant it near a stone balustrade or flight of steps, or in the middle of an English lawn, if you want a contrast with freshness.

Four more or less ordinary plants (for the bed will cost no more than a louis, or at most two, according to its size), yet an effect quite new and out-of-the-way in our gardens – glimpsed already by the English, but never till this moment, I think, given rational explanation.

(PARC MONCEAU[44])

The 'Gazette and Programme for the Fortnight', another regular feature in the magazine, is normally unsigned; but from internal evidence, and occasional correspondence in phrasing to the 'Paris Chronicle', there are hints that it is also the work of Ix. As will be observed, the travel notes pay much attention to seaside resorts. (The reader will also note the appearance of Mallarmé's own name, right at the end.)

GAZETTE AND PROGRAMME FOR THE FORTNIGHT

Amusements or solemnities in 'Society'

August 1874

Just a quick word or two: a whole month, or even more, has to be covered in the space normally allotted to a few days. We ought to call it 'Gazette and Programme for the Season'! Paris opens her gates towards all horizons and departs: foreigners and provincials profit from this opening of her gates to come, in flocks, to admire the vestiges of Parisian splendour, contending meanwhile with the August sun. Such is the moment, and our task is simple.

43. This is perhaps in error for 'lobelia'.

44. The Parc Monceau was laid out as a garden in the English style and was situated in one of the most aristocratic quarters of Paris.

No 'society' news; so we turn our attention towards Theatres and Railway-stations; Drama, Fairy plays and Farces; and then, simply, Seaside Resorts. (For even the irresolute water-drinker finds it easy to choose a Spa, whereas the sea is always . . . just the sea.)

But two words first.

BOOKSELLERS AND AUCTIONS

More than ever, this is a time for reading: on trains, in the garden hammock, or on beach chairs. New books are comparatively few; but a winter book can be re-read in summer. Two firms, nevertheless, who follow or lead the literary movement of the day, have published or are about to publish the following volumes.

Bibliothèque **Alphonse Lemerre**[45] *(already published): three novels: Les Femmes d'artistes (1 vol.), by Alphonse Daudet; Une Ressemblance (1 vol.), by Louis Gualdo; Une Vieille maîtresse (1 vol.), by Barbey d'Aurevilly. Travel: Un Eté dans le Sahara (1 vol.) and Une Année dans le Sahel (1 vol.), by the painter Fromentin. – Poetry (the 'speciality of the House'): Livre de Sonnets (1 vol.), La Révolte des fleurs (1 vol.) and La France (1 vol.), by Sully Prudhomme; À Mi-côte (1 vol.), by Léon Valade, and Le Harem (1 vol.), by Ernest d'Hervilly; finally, Le Sang de la coupe (1 vol.), by Théodore de Banville.*

Forthcoming: Le Cahier rouge, verse, Une Idylle pendant le Siège, fiction, by François Coppée; Quatre octaves de sonnets, by Claudius Popelin.

Bibliothèque **Charpentier** *(already published): La Conquête de Plassans (1 vol.), Contes pour les grandes personnes (1 vol.), by our two contributors, Messrs. Zola and d'Hervilly.*

Let us await, before speaking of Hachette's publications, the return of the studious to Paris: the Guides Joanne[46] *are still in everyone's hands.*

At the **Auction House**[47] *no activity, or practically none: and in the present weather, nearly unbearable despite the watering of the streets, the dust on the curios would not be the 'dust of the centuries'. All interest in ancient things is now focused on the* **Exhibition** *of Paintings and Objets d'Art for the benefit of the Society for the Protection of our Friends in Alsace-Lorraine. This has been extended for two months.*

---

45. Alphonse Lemerre (1838–1912) had published Mallarmé in the *Parnasse contemporain*, and his bookshop in the Passage Choiseul was a meeting-place for avant-garde poets.

46. The *Guides Joanne* were a vast and excellent series of guidebooks directed by Alphonse Joanne (1813–81) and, from 1855, published by Hachette. They were the ancestors of the Blue Guides.

47. The Hôtel Drouot, or Hôtel des ventes mobilières, situated in the rue Drouot.

THEATRES AND RAILWAY STATIONS

I

In Paris

Leaving aside the theatres which, by tradition, never close and continue with their repertoire through the whole holiday season – the ***Théâtre-Français*** *(*Polyeucte*:* ***Mlle Favart and M. Dupont-Vernon****, then* Zaire*, with* ***Sarah-Bernard*** [*sic*]*; the* ***Opéra*** *(first performance of* L'Esclave*, by MEMBRÉE);*[48] *and the* ***Opéra-Comique*** (Le Pardon de Ploermel[49] *alternating, shortly, with* Mireille: **Mme *Carvalho, Ismaël)*** *– we would draw the attention of visitors to certain sumptuous or moving spectacles which are to be continued in their honour throughout July and August.*

At the ***Gaîté*** *the Opéra-bouffe-féerie,* Orpheus aux enfers, for *which the maestro has created, for those new to it, a 'marine Act', which will be marvellous both musically and scenically: no more dancing flies and midges but a ballet . . . of fish!*

At the ***Porte-Saint-Martin,*** *the fairy-ballet* Le Pied de Mouton *has sprouted new muslins, new silks and new skins designed by Grévin, in the style of 1874.*

At the **Châtelet,** Les Deux Orphelines[50] *will see many more tears – Russian tears. English, Italian, Asian or American ones – pour down cheeks for them.*

At the **Gymnase,** La Chute, *with a delightful costume-duel between Mmes Fromentin and Angelo.*[51]

At the ***Palais-Royal,*** *the home of laughter, a thousand admirable attempts to provoke it.* La Sensitive, *mainly.*

At the **Cluny,** L'Enfant, *a first success for the new management.*

Finally, at the ***Belleville*** *(it is one of the leading theatres in Paris nowadays) Frederic Lemaître will appear in* Le Crime de Faverne *and* Le Portier du no. 15.[52]

The **Odéon,** the **Vaudeville,** the **Variétés, the Bouffes, the Renaissance,** the **Château d'Eau** and the **Folies Marigny** have, at various dates, given notice of their annual closure; and, for the benefit of those on holiday, we can announce the date of their re-opening:

The ***Odéon,*** *1 September, continuing the success of their* La jeunesse de Louis XIV.[53]

---

48. This was the first work performed by the *Opéra* at the Salle Ventadour, in January 1874.

49. *Dinorah*: *ou le pardon de Ploermel*, opera by Meyerbeer.

50. Sentimental drama in 5 acts by Dennery and Cormon.

51. *Figaro* for 7 July 1874 announces the première of *La Chute*, a four-act play by Louis Leroy; and in its issue for 9 July (its 'amiable lady readers' liking to read about toilette from time to time) it analyses the women's costumes act by act.

52. These were the last appearances of Lemaître on the stage.

53. By Alexandre Dumas, *père*.

The ***Vaudeville,*** *1 September.*

The ***Variétés,*** *1 August, with* La Vie parisienne.

The ***Bouffes,*** *1 September, with* La Famille Trouillat, *an operetta in three acts, by Messrs Hector Crémieux and Ernest Blum. Creating the principal roles,* ***Thérésa and Paulin Menier.***

The ***Folies-Dramatiques****, 5 August, with* La Belle Bourbonnaise *and* Le Nouvel Achille, *except for a revival of* La Fille de Madame Angot *for the Burmese and Moroccan embassies and an excursion party of two hundred Lapps. However, we are promised, almost immediately,* La Fiancée du roi de Garbe, *with music by Litolff (the cast including* ***Mlle de Bogdani,*** *returning from the* ***Italiens,*** *and two other performers making their* début).

* * *

Other resorts for amusement or pleasure, by day or by night, include the ***Jardin d'Acclimatation*** *(animals, in particular the two little orang-utans and the pair of giraffes; flowers, orchestra).*

The ***Concert des Champs-Elysées,*** *with Cressonnois, and distinguished performers under his baton.*

The ***Cirque d'Eté.*** *M. Franconi promises to stage the famous illusion, 'The Maharajah's Cabinet', out of which (a special attraction) will materialise one of the prettiest members of his troupe. Meanwhile we have the début of those extraordinary skaters, Goodrich and Curtis, one of the season's attractions.*

The ***Théâtre-Miniature*** *re-opens on 15 August, with performances for school-prize winners, a schoolboy who has won a first prize receiving a ticket for* Le Vainqueur de Jemmapes. *A display involving little boys and even little girls; a grand military spectacle, replacing great fairyland ones. The cast: the talented Messrs. A and B, made of wood and rag. Surprise of surprises! the arrival of Mr. Punch himself, dispensing sweets and good advice; and, as a holiday extra, a round-the-world exhibition, with, as always, 'The Maharajah's Cabinet'.*

The ***Salles des Familles:*** *another 'sweetshop', but less devoted to barley-sugar than the preceding one, whose spectators return here older and more sedate. It stages genuine* premières, *alternating with established masterpieces like* Les Fourberies de Périne *by Théodore de Banville and certain of Musset's* 'Proverbs'. *A brilliant, and moreover edifying, repertory.*

For ***Dance-halls*** *in and around Paris, and* ***Café-Concerts*** *lit by gas or by the stars, consult the multilingual Guides which cater for younger visitors.*

II. – Railways

The Gare de l'Ouest[54] *is the most strictly Parisian of all stations. Located in the heart of the metropolis and in a very up-to-date quarter, it dispatches its expresses along all the fashionable Normandy and Brittany coasts. Here, when summer comes, is the sea, as in spring the greenery of Ville-d'Avray, Bougival, Chatou and Saint-Germain and the groves or parks around Paris.*

The resorts in Normandy being, all of them, so famous, and its villages so thronged with the summer-houses of the rich, we need only give those of our readers who are still detained here, in these early day of August, a list of place names to help them fix their wavering mind.

***Bathing-resorts in Normandy** – Dieppe: Le Tréport, Criel. – Motteville: Saint-Valéry-en-Caux, Veules. – Yvetot: Veulettes. – Le Havre: Sainte-Addresse. – Les Ifs: Etretat. – Fécamp: Yport, Etretat, Les Petites Dalles. – Trouville Deauville: Villerville, Villers-sur-Mer, Houlgate, Beuzeval, Cabourg, le Home-Varaville, Honfleur. – Caen: Lion-sur-Mer, Luc, Langrune, Saint-Aubin, Bernières, Courseulles. – Bayeux: Arromanches, Port-en-Bessin, Asuelles. – Isigny: Grandcamp, Sainte-Marie-du-Mont. – Valognes: Port- Bail, Carteret, Quineville, Saint-Vast, Cherbourg, Granville: Saint-Pair. – Saint-Malo – Saint-Servan: Dinard, Saint-Enogat, Paramé.*

The times of outward-bound trains on Saturday and Sunday, and homeward-bound ones on Sunday and Monday are as advertised or available: the Company, during the Season, offers cheap weekend return tickets valid at all times of the day.

***Bathing-resorts in Brittany.** – We would like to draw up a similar list of bathing-resorts in Brittany, of which every year all its admirers, artists or lovers of landscape and solitude, speak with such enthusiasm.*

Luxury, already acclimatised on the cliffs of Normandy, promises, in the near future, to bring its blessings to the beaches and rocks of Brittany. La Dernière mode *wants to be the first to publicise this trend. From this year onwards, but only at the beginning of next season, since our journal has come out so late, one of our staff will go down the coast from Brest towards the Loire, as far as Vannes, or will return up to Morlaix and Saint-Brieuc, reporting on the beaches. Douarnenez (on the line from Brest to Redon) and Roscoff (on the main line) are the only picturesque spots with hotels well known to some Parisians.*

A round-trip by the Orléans line *and the previously mentioned* West line, *combined, gives a view of the principal* **seaside resorts north of the Loire:** *such as Audierne, Concarneau, Le Croisic, Pornichet, etc.*

As to **resorts south of the Loire,** *i.e. Pornic, les Sables d'Olonne, La Rochelle, Royan, Arcachon, Saint-Jean-de-Luc, Biarrritz, etc., they are to be reached by the main Orléans-Midi line.*

54. Now the Gare Saint-Lazare.

After the Ocean, the Channel; or (since part of it bathes the Normandy shore) at least the northern portion. **Seaside resorts** *include Tréport (branch line from Amiens), Boulogne, Saint-Valéry (with transport to Cayeux), Berck-sur-Mer, Calais, Dunkirk.*

All this vast corner of the sea belongs to the Ligne du Nord, *which, for each beach, offers first-class tickets valid for ten days.*

* * *

We shall name (without saying that it goes to Marseille, the gate to the East or to Africa) the Ligne de la Méditerranée; *and, since we are in the 'blue' regions, revealed in their true glory only in summer, we must remind readers of the marvellous beaches of Cettes; of Marseille, Toulon, Hyères, Cannes, Nice; and of Monaco. The warm and waveless Mediterranean offers its cure for our ills. Other enchanted and unvisited spots are les Lecques, Bandol (between Marseille and Toulon), and, along this same line of scattered oases, Saint-Raphael (between Toulon and Nice).*

We are compelled this year to leave till September (that is to say, alas, till too late) all information regarding cut-price Excursions, of which the railway Companies have obligingly given us particulars. Families should consult the advertisements, to be seen on every wall, and should set out accordingly.

The Ligne d'Est *offers us the whole of Switzerland and of our own Alsace as a tour or a pilgrimage.*

Address all Books, and all information regarding the Theatre, Travel, the Beau-Monde or the Beaux-Arts, to M. Stéphane Mallarmé, 29, rue de Moscou.

The Proprietor: ***DAVID***

CORRESPONDENCE WITH SUBSCRIBERS

August 1874

Since the letters so far addressed to us have mainly been to ask for a text to attach to an engraving previously published by us on its own, we can think of no better response to anyone who has shown interest in our Journal than to send them a copy of this Sample Issue. Thus on this occcasion, the 'Correspondence' will be replaced by the description of Lithographs and Watercolours published by us between April and July, which will serve in place of the as yet-unknown **toilette**

for September. As a review of this summer's fashions, and as a specimen of the **toilettes** ***we have devised ourselves, does this not answer any question our Readers might ask?***

Formal Visiting Costume: 1 May 1874. *– Skirt in chestnut-coloured* faille,[55] *with apron ornamented with puffs arranged lengthwise and edged in blue* Japonaise. *Behind, four flounces of different length one upon another: a band of blue* Japonaise *forming the head of each flounce. Tunic of blue* Japonaise*: the apron is heavily pleated at its sides: the right-hand flap goes over the left shoulder beneath a knot with two loops, one chestnut-brown and the other blue. A chestnut* biais[56] *runs along the side of the tunic rising towards the shoulder. Puffed sleeves with facing puffed crosswise. The whole tunic is trimmed with blond lace pearled with white jet.*[57]

Costume for the races: 15 May 1874. *– Costume for the races in blue* poult-de-soie.[58] *There are printed bouquets of roses among the trimmings of this costume, which has had a great success this summer. Five superimposed flounces of different sizes garnish the bottom of the train, whilst the upper part, raised in a pouf, is held in place by a scarf of the same shade. The front, forming an apron, has at its bottom a fairly large flounce surmounted by four false tucks, held at the middle by a bow of* poult-de-soie *similar to the one used for the pouff; a blue scallop lined with pink satin makes a gathered edging. Corsage coming to points in front; sleeves up to the elbow with flounces as required, surmounted by a blue and pink* coquille *like that of the gusset of the skirt. Frock-coat in blue* poult-de-soie *with pink lining and buttoning lapels. The garment is close-fitting behind but not in front – Our model*[59] *is without sleeves. – Blue umbrella with pink* biais *and white lace.* Chapeau Felix *or garlands of roses and cornflowers with a long train; blue aigrette.*

Walking Costume, 1 June 1874. *– Skirt of very pale blue* faille*; the apron is made of large blue puffs separated by a black* biais *bordered with blue; the edging is made from two pieces of black lace, their foot being hidden under a blue border; buttons covered with blue and white Paisley-pattern* poult-de-soie *placed between the two pieces of lace. Large pleats sheaf-wise and made of Paisley* faille *are fixed by a button to the bottom of the skirt here and there, a* biais *of black silk joining them. Tunic of black* faille *lined and bordered with blue and white Paisley* poult-de-soie, *with a lace covering to the tunic; the latter is attached by the gusset right*

---

55. *Faille* is a coarse-grained silk.

56. A *biais* is a crossband, a long strip of material cut on the cross, to give elasticity and strength.

57. 'White jet' (*jais blanc*) was in fact not jet but glass beads.

58. *Poult-de-soie* is a thick silk, without lustre. (The word is related to Paduasoy.)

59. See Introduction (p. 7), where we mention Lecercle's suggestion that this and later references to 'our model' (meaning an illustration) are a blind, there never having been any such illustrations.

at the back; it is round on one side in front and raised a little by pleats on the side hidden in our model; behind, on the contrary, it is square, so that, on folding the middle of the rear part, the four superimposed pleats give a glimpse of the Paisley lining. Plain corsage without belt and terminated simply by a blue border; it has two little points in front which remain slightly open; a straight collar, slightly widening and lined with blue faille. *A long waist for this costume and very long for corsages with basques. Very pretty blue sleeves puffed at the top with a* biais *of black* faille*; below the elbow, two pieces of lace, one ascending, one descending, are separated by Paisley buttons. The same motif as at the bottom of the skirt, but smaller, finishes the sleeve, which is full of charm.*

Costume for the country: 15 June 1874. *– Overskirt of slightly yellow* poult-de-soie; *three draperies of the same material form the apron; they terminate in a very beautiful check-pattern fringe, with tassels and buttons of* passementerie. *Three flounces, one above another, with their frills hidden under a* biais *of emerald velvet, form the train. The first flounce goes right up to the waist to separate the apron from the rest of the skirt. A puffed tunic in glossy batiste thread, with a puff separated by a* guipure *insert; it is edged with a* biais *of velvet and a pointed* guipure *festoon. This is a style much in fashion at the moment. The tunic is raised only on one side. Puffed corsage coming to points in front and bordered with green velvet. Waist rounded at the back and very long. A sash, of green velvet on one side and yellow satin on the other, fits close and falls with two large puffed bows over the tunic. Sleeves smooth on the interior and puffed on the outside. A ~~straight little~~ scarf in batiste to tie negligently over the corsage. A ravishing hat in unbleached rice-straw, designed by Mlle Baillet, 22, rue de la Chaussée-d'Antin.*

Costume for a promenade concert: 1 July 1874. *– Skirt and waist* décolletée, *in salmon-pink* poult-de-soie; *apron with two rows of flounces with flat pleats, the upper part hidden by a piece of fan-wise pleating also in* poult-de-soie, *bordered with satin of the same shade. The cross-piece and the puff which join these trimmings together are in satin bordered with* poult-de-soie, *blonde lace, pearled with white jet, emerging from beneath and falling back upon the silk flounce. The upper tunic with train forms a kind of Court mantle: same trimming as on the flounce, but much higher. Second tunic in tulle of white lace: the stars are embroidered in white chenille and the inside is pearled with white jet. This tunic, which is in the shape of a scarf, is knotted so as to form the pouff. Sash and bows on the sleeves in salmon-pink* faille. *Hat all white, with plume and white wing – which is the height of fashion this summer.*

***Visiting dress in pale blue* poult-de-soie: *15 July 1874.* –** *Overskirt with three rows of flat pleats arranged horizontally. It is slit in the middle to allow the pleats to turn back on either side. These trimmings, three times repeated up the dress, are separated by a very large* biais *of the same material. The gussets are made of three superimposed flounces, edged with curled feather. Behind, an immense pleat forms* *the train. In the shape of a tunic, in front, three scarves, edged with feather, are draped: they end beneath the rear part of the tunic, which is not raised at all. This last is ornamented with three flounces of different sizes with 'heads' of flat pleats and* biais *to match, edged with feather. From under each flounce appears a bow of one* coque *only and with two ends. The bows must be bigger than those of our model. Corsage with tightly-fitting basques. It laces up behind and must fit closely over the hips to give the effect of a corset, being also supported by whalebone stays.*

***Costume for a grand ceremonial occasion: 1 August 1874.** – Skirt of* poult-de-soie, *trimmed at the bottom with a pleated flounce surmounted by four puffs and a pleated head. Tunic in white Chambéry gauze. It takes the shape of an apron, the large bottom of this coming to a point, which connects with the other* pointe *across an expanse of clear blue* faille, *surrounded by a very beautiful fringe. The tunic is adorned with a diagonal in white* poult-de-soie *and lace pearled with white jet. On the middle of the apron, near the bottom, is a big bouquet of artificial convolvulus. This, something altogether novel, is in the highest taste. Corsage in white gauze, pointed in front and with basques behind: the middle of the back is in blue* faille. *The sides and the pockets are trimmed with a white* biais *and a border of blue* faille. *The ruff, and the edging of the* pointe *in front, blue. Sleeves with the same trimming as the apron, whilst the collar is surrounded with a train of artificial convolvulus. At the bottom of the sleeve, a bouquet of the same.* Chapeau Mousquetaire *in Italian straw: 'Amazonian' feather beneath, the brim being raised at one side by puffs of* faille *and a semi-circular garland of convolvulus.* Torsade *of* faille *around the 'skullcap', with a bow in front, near the middle.*

***Costume of 15 August.** – Many Specimen Numbers, sent during the present month, will contain this Costume, with an explanation on a loose page, subscribers to* La Dernière mode *being entitled to receive this on the very day of publication, under separate cover.*

MARGUERITE DE P.

The Correspondence Column is surrounded by the 'visiting-cards' of recommended shops and other establishments, under the heading 'Maisons de Confiance'. (See p. 45.) There will be much about the shops, and the treasures to be found in them, in Mme de Ponty's causeries.

LES MAISONS DE CONFIANCE

DONT LE NOM SUIT

PRÉSENTENT AUJOURD'HUI LEUR CARTE AUX LECTRICES DE **LA DERNIÈRE MODE**

Associées au luxe de la Couverture et participant à la rédaction même du Journal grace au voisinage de la *Correspondance avec les Abonnées*, nos Annonces s'offrent, sous un titre spécial, comme les Cartes de Visites des Grands Établissements de Paris. Sans publier un amas d'adresses assemblées par le hasard ou en vertu de combinaisons étrangères à l'intérêt du client, nous fournissons les renseignements nécessaires à une personne, même éloignée, pour suivre de tous points les habitudes parisiennes.

CORRESPONDANCE AVEC LES ABUNNÉES

4 Octobre 1874.

Mme LA COMTESSE S..., A MILAN. — *C'est un coussin qu'il vous faut, Madame : on ne les fait plus beaucoup en tapisserie, il est de mode aujourd'hui de les broder avec application de drap de couleur sur drap noir. L'ouvrage, eschantillonné, avec toutes les fournitures, vaut, à notre Magasin Spécial d'Ouvrages de Dames : Au Sphynx, de quinze à vingt francs.*

Mme L..., A TOULOUSE. — *Faites faire, Madame, une robe de cachemire noire garnie de crêpe anglais ou de crêpe impératrice : ce dernier, d'aussi bonne qualité que le crêpe anglais, est d'un prix moins élevé. Vous n'ignorez point que vous ne pouvez pas porter de Confection (pardessus, etc.), dès maintenant, le châle et le voile long étant de rigueur pendant trois mois ; mais on est moins généralement au fait de ceci que les boucles d'oreilles sont en bois durci au lieu d'être en jais. Je poursuis, n'est-ce pas ? puisque vous voulez bien m'interroger sur l'étiquette absolue du deuil : cachemire noir et crêpe pendant les six premiers mois, soie noire et crêpe lisse noir pendant les six autres ; enfin du gris, du violet ou du noir et blanc pendant les six dernières semaines. On porte le deuil pour un beau-père, oui, de la même façon que pour un père.*

Mme DE B..., A FONTAINEBLEAU. — *Vous avez raison, chère Lectrice, une machine à coudre est indispensable dans une maison montée sur le pied de la vôtre : si vous ne l'utilisez pas vous-même, vous y faites travailler votre femme de chambre. Plusieurs fabricants donnent gratuitement des leçons, après acquisition faite chez eux ; sinon, les font payer. Je vous assure qu'en sept ou huit leçons, voire même en moins que cela, votre femme de chambre peut être apte à tout faire de votre machine. Envoyez ici cette personne, qu'on se chargera de conduire dans une maison sérieuse, qui lui livrera une machine garantie pendant plusieurs années ; elle pourra elle-même confectionner parfaitement les Costumes d'Enfants, dont nous venons de vous expédier les patrons. A propos de ceux-ci, donnez-nous, je vous prie, les mesures bien exactement, car tous les enfants de cinq ans n'ont ni la même taille ni la même carrure.*

Mme LA COMTESSE S..., A SÉVILLE. — *Nous avons vu chez* Frainais et Gramagnac *les Cachemires de l'Inde dans les mille à douze cents francs : ils sont jolis sans être d'un prix élevé, chose, du reste, tout à fait inutile aujourd'hui. Faites-nous savoir, Madame, si vous désirez le vôtre long ou carré : notre manque d'information à cet égard nous a seul empêchée de le choisir ; mais nous vous le conseillons carré, le châle ne se portant plus en pointe. Aussitôt votre réponse reçue, ce vêtement, dans sa boîte, vous sera expédié contre remboursement.*

Mme LA DUCHESSE DE LA T..., A MADRID. — *Madame, si vous n'avez que deux filles, habillez-les de même ; si vous en aviez trois, vous ne le feriez point, ou elles ressembleraient à des pensionnaires. Non, le même chapeau ne conviendra peut-être pas à ces deux sœurs ; pour la coiffure, choisissez-la différente, tout à fait selon le visage.*

Mme B..., TAILLEUSE, A BRUXELLES. — *Le costume de Jeune Fille que nous avons donné dans le dernier Numéro peut parfaitement convenir à une Jeune Femme : seulement, vous garnirez de volants ou de bouillonnés la jupe en velours, voire même de l'un et de l'autre juxta-posés.*

Mme LA MARQUISE DE C. L..., A BEAUVAIS. — *C'est à des religieuses seules que vous voulez confier votre enfant, Madame, sans quoi nous vous dirions de jeter les yeux sur la carte de visite placée ci-contre d'une excellente Pension recommandée par nous ; ou nous consulterions un conseiller précieux pour tout ce qui est de l'Education. Il nous reste à prouver notre expérience maternelle et conforme à l'énoncé de votre vœu, relativement à l'emploi de quatre années de jeunesse. La chose est toute simple : entre tous les couvents, il en est un, le Sacré-Cœur ; votre ville de Beauvais possède une des maisons de l'Ordre ? Y mettre deux ans votre chère enfant, afin que la séparation ne soit qu'à moitié cruelle et vous prépare à l'éloignement nécessité par deux autres années passées dans la maison mère de Paris, parmi des plus grands noms de France. Une même méthode d'enseignement, employée dans tous les pensionnats dirigés par les Dames du Sacré-Cœur, autorise ce changement dont l'instruction n'a rien à souffrir. Faut-il dire que ces dames savent également donner à leurs élèves une éducation parfaite et remplir ces jeunes cœurs de sentiments distingués ? Personne ne l'ignore et je ne prétends vous rappeler que ce que vous connaissez mieux que moi ; mais on aime à s'entendre répéter par quelqu'un de confiance les choses qu'on a déjà un peu projetées à soi seule. Il ne nous conviendrait d'insister que sur un point, c'est que si, dans ces pieux asiles, l'enseignement est poussé au dernier point, cependant on n'y néglige ni les travaux à l'aiguille ni les arts d'agréments. Intéresser autant qu'édifier les jeunes personnes, telle est la devise adoptée.*

Mme BRENC..., A MANTES. — *Le Capulet se portera aussi chez les jeunes filles : ce vêtement, fort simple, achève tout à fait leur toilette de sortie ou de visite.*

Mme M. Y., LONDRES (OU DANS LE WILTS). — *Oui, les fleurs naturelles sont bien jolies dans les cheveux, mais elles ne résistent guère à l'atmosphère du bal ; et après une heure et deux au plus, elles sont fanées ; c'est pourquoi je leur préfère, pour vous coiffer à cette fête, toute hors de saison, officielle et administrative, des fleurs artificielles merveilleusement travaillées.*

Plus de lettres; et nous parlons maintenant à toutes nos lectrices : d'abord

LES OCCASIONS

de Bibelots, Fantaisies, voire même de Villas et de Châteaux pendant les saisons d'Eaux; Bons Marchés dans les Magasins ou à l'Hôtel des Ventes, ou Échanges entre Gens du Monde. Non, il faut attendre, pour donner à ce chapitre tout son intérêt, la rentrée des amateurs. Dames et Messieurs, à la Ville et l'éclat subit que prennent les étalages de luxe au premier mauvais temps, c'est-à-dire demain.

CONSEILS SUR L'ÉDUCATION

Les express de toute ligne et de toute heure ramènent à Paris, avec les parents, les enfants. A l'intention des parents qui, désireux de garder leurs enfants près d'eux, ne choisiraient pas pour ceux-ci l'une des maisons d'éducation recommandées par nous dans les cartes de visite ci-contre; et hésiteraient, cependant, à leur faire donner une éducation tout à fait isolée par des précepteurs ou des institutrices (deux de ces dernières se mettent, par notre intermédiaire, à la disposition des familles, une étrangère, parlant presque toutes les langues du Nord et le Français, l'autre Française et remarquablement musicienne, mais plutôt dame de compagnie), citons un Cours célèbre de Jeunes Filles. Véritablement, est-il besoin de rappeler, sinon pour dire qu'il s'apprête à inaugurer sa 24e rentrée, ce groupe de mères, de professeurs et de jeunes filles le plus parisien de tous et dont le nom vient à l'esprit de nos Lectrices : le Cours Lévy Alvarès, qu'il se fasse rue de la Chaussée-d'Antin ou simultanément Place Royale, au Marais. Toute l'instruction que peut et doit acquérir une femme, la fillette et la jeune personne l'y reçoivent, et la mêlent, revenues dans leur famille, à l'éducation du foyer. Une chose charmante, c'est que plus d'une mère intéressée à des questions oubliées par elles depuis l'enfance ou renouvelées par les programmes, devient, dans ces leçons, la condisciple de sa fille.

Il n'y a à entrer dans aucun détail du prospectus, qu'envoie, sur une demande faite par les parents, le Directeur, Officier d'Académie.

Les livres de rentrée? Nous sommes prêts à recommander tous les bons ouvrages adressés à ces initiales : Monsieur S. M., 29, rue de Moscou, par les auteurs ou les libraires, autant qu'indiqués par les familles elles-mêmes; mais en gardant, toutefois, une complète liberté de jugement. Nous ne faisons à cet exercice de notre indépendance qu'une exception en faveur des livres publiés par la maison Hachette, qui, en ce moment, augmente, pour la rentrée de l'année scolaire 1874-75, son vaste catalogue d'ouvrages presques officiels et recommandés par le Conseil de l'Instruction publique avant de l'être ici. Tout ce chapitre, dans chacune de nos Livraisons, pourrait être rempli par l'appréciation seule des vastes efforts que font ces Editeurs pour être toujours au courant des programmes et de l'esprit actuels.

Terminons aujourd'hui cet entretien spécial dont les proportions, un peu vastes en raison du peu de place donnée aux Occasions, Bons Marchés, etc., montrent très-fort le désir que nous avons de prendre, tout à fait, possession d'un sujet appartenant, avant tout, à une Gazette, qui est celle, non seulement du monde, mais de la Famille.

Madame DE P.

Paris. — Imprimerie du passage de l'Opéra. Richard-Berthier, galerie de l'Horloge, 18 et 19.

Issue 2

DEUXIÈME LIVRAISON — DIMANCHE 20 SEPTEMBRE 1874

LA DERNIÈRE MODE

GAZETTE DU MONDE ET DE LA FAMILLE

PARIS	Directeur :	FRANCE
Un an . . . . . 24 f.	MARASQUIN	Un an . . . . . 30 f.
Six mois 13	9, Rue de Châteaudun, 9	Six mois . . . 14

PARAIT

LE 1er ET LE 3e DIMANCHE DU MOIS

AVEC LE CONCOURS

DES GRANDES FAISEUSES, DE TAPISSIERS-DÉCORATEURS, DE MAÎTRES QUEUX
DE JARDINIERS, D'AMATEURS DE BIBELOTS ET DU SPORT

NOUVELLES & VERS

DE THÉODORE DE BANVILLE, LÉON CLADEL, FRANÇOIS COPPÉE, ALPHONSE DAUDET,
LÉON DIERX, ERNEST D'HERVILLY, ALBERT MÉRAT, STÉPHANE MALLARMÉ
CATULLE MENDÈS, SULLY PRUDHOMME, LÉON VALADE, AUGUSTE VILLIERS DE L'ISLE ADAM,
ÉMILE ZOLA, ETC.

MUSIQUE

PAR LES PRINCIPAUX COMPOSITEURS

TOILETTES DE PROMENADE

Madame de Ponty, no longer feeling in a timeless void, begins to examine the features and crazes of the moment (the *chapeau Valois*, the *chapeau Berger*[60]) and certain subtly changing trends. She is here in her analytical vein. It is the era of the 'cuirasse' or 'chain-mail' style of tunic (suggestive, also, of the scales of a mermaid), and she puts her finger on a new tension, between the steely or polished and the feathery.

FASHION

Paris, 20 September 1874

What pretty things to be glimpsed this fortnight! I say 'glimpsed' because preparations for autumn are not complete yet, and the great creators of Fashion will not let us see their preliminary sketches. As for me, it is, I confess, thanks to a flagrant indiscretion that, in a moment, I shall be able to give my readers some definite news.

What calls for most care in a woman's costume is, unquestionably, the footgear and gloves; and after that, the hat, the sole duty of which is to be charming. These are truths in no need of proof: a small foot, a delicate hand though that hand has sometime picked grapes and the foot has trampled them – are the sure indications of race. But, badly shod, a duchess's foot cannot arch itself in noble style, nor her hand, badly gloved, reveal its form. The bottine *is, of all footgear, the one which shows the foot to the best advantage; and the time has come for the cloth shoe, though endlessly varied as an item of seaside wear, to give way to leather. No more slippers, save on the ballroom floor: one dances in slippers, but one walks on leather.*

Why do I say all this, if not that (except in the case of lingerie, which obeys other laws of fashion than those of the season) we wish, at this moment of renewal, to reclothe our lady-reader from top to toe? I said that a hat has to observe one rule only, to be ravishing: a vague prescription but not hard to follow, since the fashions are now so pretty; and moreover, does not the whole science of a good designer lie in subtly combining flowers, feathers and lace – and more so this winter than ever, when everyone will be wearing them? My visits to several of the best fashion houses over the last fortnight (for in this amazing Paris, a number of houses can claim to be the best, indeed they all can) enable me to assure you that the chapeau Berger *and the* chapeau Valois *divide fashion between them. They are both very*

60. See the illustration on p. 102.

becoming, but my heart goes out to the chapeau Berger, *which sits right on top of the chignon, leaving the whole coiffure visible. The top is decorated with a torsade of velvet and some feathers, and the underside imitates a garland of flowers. The* chapeau Valois, *which has its peak behind instead of in front, is generally covered in velvet or in jet embroidery: a bouquet of flowers, enwreathed with lace, lies behind on the* calotte,[61] *whilst in front there is beautiful foliage, making a* bourrelet[62] *and falling over the hair.*

To generalise: hats should be richly decorated with jet and blued steel; I have seen cock feathers covered in jet or blued-steel spangles, and whole leaf-sprays of one or the other; also fantasy wings, part feather and part jet, and splendid embroidery on tulle – this last highly expensive. There are many pretty silks for trimmings, one of which, whose name I have yet to discover (perhaps one of my readers will christen it) is glossy on one side and rough silk on the other. To our two autumn hats, the Berger *and the* Valois, *I shall add a very attractive model with a round* calotte *and an immense brim, also round or with one side turned up. The hat is of felt; the underside of the brim, if round, is decorated with a garland of flowers, and if turned up at one side, with a twist of material pinned by a wing to a velvet bow.*

From the hat I move on to the rest of the costume. The great success of the season will be the tunic of steel or blued-steel jet. This garment, a veritable feminine coat of mail, is knitted, in black, grey or blue silk worked with pearls. Elastic, it perfectly models the bust, the outline of which the tunic prolongs: somewhat long in front and very short behind, made of one piece with the corsage, and ending in a fringe of silken bows, with matching pearls. No belt and no sleeves, for this 'cuirasse' is worn over a faille *or* poult-de-soie *gown. Nothing newer, nothing more delightful: though, to tell the truth, there are reasons why we should not be so free with those epithets, our older suscribers remembering, no doubt, that the cuirass was already launched a year ago, and precisely by one of the coloured engravings in* La Dernière mode.[63] *But it is not to announce this, any more than to display false modesty, that we now supply that engraving with words.*

Let us pass on, all the more so since to have anticipated fashion by several seasons may seem to some like forgetting our duty, which is to create fashion day by day. So, instead of riddling the future, let us turn to the present and study that: for instance the favourite trimming of today, feathers. Nothing so pretty and shimmering as feathers, surely, whether curled or glossy and smooth? We shall not, in this case, be reproached for over-hastiness, for it is only this summer that we have used this feature in our toilettes – only three months or two months or even

61. The literal meaning of calotte is 'skull-cap'.

62. Bourrelet here seems to mean something like 'roll'.

63. See p. 7.

one month before it became general (and even now it is so only among the rarest of our élégantes, *or in the workshops which decide the fashion of the season).*

Let me add (to strike a less personal note) that glittering pearl passementerie[64] *will have even more of a vogue this year than last; for, as I have implied already, our task today is to ornament the integument of a she-warrior or goddess of the sea.*

Nevertheless, fashion does not repeat itself: and if this clear-cut, hard and already familiar form of ornament[65] *is to alternate with a softness and featheriness quite new, let us insist on one point: that the costumes in vogue at present leave so little silk visible that this (by now) almost ancient style of decoration will need to be applied in a quite new manner.*

What else remains to say? This: that the unifying scarf remains very close-fitting, the pouff[66] *placed very low, and the waist very long: but those two last details are by now common property and may be observed in the street, by any passer-by.*

MARGUERITE DE PONTY

EXPLANATION OF THE COLOURED LITHOGRAPH OF THE DAY AND OF THE CUT-OUT PATTERN, AS OF THE BLACK-AND-WHITE ENGRAVINGS WHICH FORM PART OF THE TEXT.

I

COLOURED ENGRAVING

[Not reproduced in this translation][67]

II

BLACK-AND-WHITE ENGRAVINGS IN THE TEXT

First page

1. – Garnet-coloured costume. Overskirt, with four gathered flounces, at the bottom of which is a little plissé[68] *of a brighter tint, ten centimetres high. Under-*

64. *Passementerie* is the name for pearl or gold lace, used to embroider silk.

65. i.e. pearl *passementerie*.

66. See p. 25.

67. The fact that the coloured lithograph and the cut-out pattern are not reproduced in the present translation applies throughout.

68. A *plissé* is an ornamental series of regular folds.

skirt, cut in front as a square apron and, at the back, attached to a knotted scarf, with coques *and long lappets furnished with plissés. Louis XV-style blouse, without sleeves, garnished all round, on the shoulders and around the neck, with a plissé of a brighter tint.* Chapeau Valois.[69]

2. – Iron-grey costume. The front of the skirt is folded down its whole length; it is furnished behind with two large flounces with hollow pleats, edged with the same material: two great knots with flaps join the flounces in front. A lightweight pouff *is hidden in the turn-up of the skirt. Costume for autumn in black* sicilienne[70] *embroidered with steel pearls: arched behind with very short basques, whilst the flaps in front are very long, this confection has all round it, for decoration, a ruche of black silk. Sleeves with 'musketeer' revers.* Chapeau Berger.[71]

Middle pages

1. – Young girl of fifteen or sixteen: toilette. *Skirt of black velvet, tunic of sky-blue cashmere, trimmed all round with a wide* biais *of black velvet. The corsage, with basques, has a square opening on to a Swiss-style pleated shirt-front, trimmed with black velvet like the sleeves. It closes behind by means of a silk lace. A flood of velvet ribbon falls over the back. 2. – Young girl of fifteen or sixteen: a garment. A blue or grey waterproof, lined, on the front only, with a striped material of a matching hue. Two great pleats in the back, held by a fastening with two buttons. At the side, a pretty pocket; a double range of buttons in front; and a collar with lapels, lined with striped material. The bottom of the garment forms a turn-up, with a movable button and buttonhole, in case of rain. – The old model, with a cape only in front and a hood behind, is very popular today because of its roominess.*

III

CUT-OUT PATTERN, ACTUAL SIZE

[Not reproduced in this translation]

In this second issue, Ix applies his wit and fantasy to another fixture in the calendar, the great first-of-August exodus from Paris. (It is a tradition which persisted until quite recently.)

69. See the illustration on p. 49.

70. A kind of silk.

71. See the illustration on p. 49.

PARIS CHRONICLE

Theatres, Books, Fine Arts
Echoes from the Salons and the Seaside

Rome n'est plus dans Rome.[72] . . . Have *you lived through them, those days which changed the town into a desert – what am I saying? – into an ancient city of the desert, like Ecbatan, Tyre or Memphis without the ruins: for I can no longer call them 'ruins', those facades, with their statuettes still, after three years,*[73] *blackened by fire, and visited now by the moon and by young persons in white-veiled Tyrolean hats – coquetry of a metropolis audaciously new, rich and splendid. In vain do the Hôtel de Ville, in its devastation, and the forlorn Tuileries see themselves photographed and minutely described in foreign guide-books*[74]*. It is not their still-gaping windows that, of a sudden, from July to September, attract, in travel-stained dress, by railways or across the Atlantic, an invading mob. No, it is Paris alive and herself! Lamentable spectacle!*

I would prefer to see them, those strange couples with their patriarchal beards or uncurled hair, studying, through their binoculars, the disappearance of the great city, see it eclipsed, dead, abolished, a heap of cinders and weeds, rather than making themselves at home in it – an empty city, abandoned entirely to tourists, by the Parisians in their lust for ocean waves and green leaves. But the grandiose vision, foreseen in that poem in Les Rayons et les ombres *which children know by heart,*[75] *has not yet been fulfilled – that of the capital of the world lying*

72. *Rome n'est plus dans Rome, elle est toute où je suis:* the arrogant boast of Sertorius in Corneille's tragedy of that name, Act III, scene 1.

73. i.e. after the devastation in Paris during the Franco-Prussian War and the Commune.

74. Such as *Paris incendié*, by E. Dangin [et al.], (Paris, 1872).

75. This seems to be a reference to 'Le 7 Août 1829' in Victor Hugo's *Les Rayons et les ombres* (1840), a poem which, though depicting the Arc de Triomphe and the Louvre as enjoying a 'repos solennel', ends with a vision of the desolation of Holyrood Palace in Edinburgh, which had been the residence of the exiled King Charles X.

in ruins, bare and overlain with dust, haunted by the double ghost of its Arch and its Column. No, the Arc de Triomphe has long been restored, though the Column has not quite yet been re-erected;[76] *and the new Opéra*[77] *– completed, all unexpectedly, no later than tomorrow – raises, amid the tempests of late summer and the first mists of autumn, its golden Apollo, drawing light from all points of the compass to his godlike form.*[78] *Only the other day, however – indeed, on the very evening thereof – on the square before this monumental and proud building, a famous feature of tomorrow's Paris, there was a coming-together, as if in an occupied and conquered country, of families and tribes, faithful to the rendezvous agreed, before setting out, on the banks of the Mississippi or the Marne.* 'Boulevard des Italiens', 'Rue de la Paix' *or* 'Champs-Élysées': *such names, only three or four weeks ago, were being pronounced in various idioms and dialects or simple patois, as one might say 'Valhalla', 'Eden' or 'El Dorado'; and – strange happening! – those who had pronounced them met and recognised one another, the other day, on the boulevard des Italiens, the rue de la Paix and the Champs-Élysées. Confident, serene and triumphant, as if exclaiming, 'Well, then, we were right; it all exists', they pointed out, with the tip of their umbrella, some tiny emblem of our glory, an architectural ornament or the shop sign of some famous* couturière; *and then they turned back towards blank space and bare perspectives as if safe back home and in their dressing-gown.*

Horror! Or rather, joy? We cannot but be pleased at these invasions, though the free-and-easy manners tended at first to grate on us. For we were not there! So where were we? That is the miracle. Whilst from the four points of the compass, forgetting Alps and Saharas, and avid and determined to see the city, the traveller arrives, we – who from birth onwards realised the lie of the 'exotic' and the disillusionment of world tours (having seen it all already, by courtesy of certain masterpieces, through the eyes of our mind and even of our body) – go, merely, to the shores of the ocean, where all that subsists is a pale and indistinct line, to gaze at what lies beyond our daily existence, which is to say infinity and nothingness. Upon seats like those old ones at Tortoni's,[79] *ranged in their rows on a hundred western beaches, we smile at the sea, which sprawls useless and dying at our feet, disdaining to invade it.*

76. The Vendôme column was overthrown by the Communards in May 1871, at the instigation of the painter Courbet, but the fragments were preserved and eventually re-assembled in 1875.

77. The Opera House designed by Charles Garnier (1825–98) was begun in 1868 and completed in 1874. It is unrivalled in the sumptuousness of its ornamentation.

78. The statue of Apollo, holding aloft a gilded lyre, on the summit of Garnier's new opera house. It was the work of Aimé Millet (1819–91).

79. The café Tortoni, on the corner of the boulevard des Italiens and the rue Taitbout, was a famous haunt of writers and politicians, who sat at tables outside on the pavement.

Object of endless amusement, and one of the richer paradoxes of the universal comedy, what do they know, these nomads, male and female, even with their white veil rolled round their hat like a little tent, and their spyglass, souvenir of the stargazing shepherd of the Chaldees, returned lovingly to its leather sheath? Yes, what do they know of Paris, when we are not there? In despair, after a day's trudge over the deserted asphalt, wondering whether, in our vanishing at the very moment they arrived, there might lurk a trace of that Parisian esprit *which it is their fate never to share, they are to be seen, alas!, reunited in the evening, in one of the theatres which refuse to close, watching the lowered curtain in suspense. Surprise! The curtain rises, for the hundredth time, but before eyes instantly in tears or dazzled with amazement. It is* Les Deux orphelines *at the Châtelet, or* Le Pied de mouton *at the Porte Saint-Martin, happy to repeat their never-waning success. But the grace, so perfect, so typical, of the Maestro,*[80] *who, famous in Paris as at the ends of the earth, treats the children of all races as one, is here at its most incomparable: in the Kingdom of Neptune, a new third Act to his* Orphée aux enfers. *A* première, *dedicated to the cosmopolitan public, and of which we all, amazed next day by a review all the way from South America, but furious and envious too, wish to see the glory prolonged till the middle of the winter.*

Nor have they ever closed, those noble institutions: the Opéra, *with yesterday's* L'Esclave[81] *and its perennial masterpieces; the Comédie Française, which puts on* Polyeucte,[82] *to prove that, rivalling the efforts of today's drama, there are never-dying successes, and which, following on from Corneille, revives Voltaire,*[83] *to display Mademoiselle Sarah Bernhardt, who is Zaire herself, and Mounet-Sully.*[84] *Thanks to this custom, every year visitors take away with them, as a traditional local treasure, all the purity of French taste and our ancient 'sublime'; and with them the sole true laughter – loud and youthful and whole-hearted – of the only theatre not afraid to clown at Molière's own front door,*[85] *knowing that after his comedy all that remains is farce, whether it be called* La Sensitive, Bobinetti *or* Les Jocrisses de l'amour, *etc. (the holiday-time repertory of the Palais-Royal).*

Let them go home now, those strangers, being no longer foreigners and puzzling no further over that fraud, a Paris without esprit, *that is to say without Parisians; and let us return to our hearths without remorse for that strange sort of hospitality, that of relinquishing to our guests, for all purposes, our four or our thousand walls.*

---

80. Offenbach.

81. *L'Esclave,* opera by Membrée.

82. By Corneille.

83. i.e. his tragedy Zaire

84. Jean-Sully Mounet, known as Mounet-Sully (1841–1916), French tragic actor.

85. The Palais-Royal was Molière's own theatre, and his bust is over the chimney piece in the public foyer..

All honour to our Theatre, both the noble and the absurd, for initiating those who have never, or who have now, seen – what? – La Fille de Madame Angot,[86] *with a young tenor and a new house:*[87] *the former's voice, roving in the balcony and the boxes and up to the ceiling, and round the chandelier, in pursuit of that gold, so profusely lavished everywhere, for which the tenor voice is made.*

Meanwhile ordinary life is already stirring. Names that, in the 'Society' columns of newspapers at the seaside or at spas, were mixed with strange and unfamiliar ones, reappear, disencumbered of such associates, in their wonted place. The first theatre-reviews begin to be written.

And now is the moment, alas!, for us to stop, for it would take not merely the 'Chronicle' of this Journal, but the entire journal, to report on the doings of these last days, which have seen not just soirs *but* soirées. *There is a whole past month or more, with its vast nothingness, to report on; for without first doing this, without postponing to the next number the happenings, which promise to be so brilliant, of the present moment, how shall we link our new causerie to the echoes of the old and the yet-to-come – in a word, fix our place in time?*

So, for this once, the past; next time, it shall be the present, mingled with the future: the holiday-season Theatre (already described), and the new season announced in our 'Gazette and Programme'. Such is our plan, as is to be seen in the layout of this very page, with its ample margins and its cameos of young ladies. It is this alone, much more than the prolonging of the great villégiature, *which makes me wait for the return of women, not from Fashion's last brief and charming week-long emigration to the warmer waters of Biarritz, but from their* châteaux *and their task of gilding, illuminating and emblazoning the white vellum of the coming winter's writing-paper – this, and the aiming of dainty gun barrels down seigneurial forest-ways, where the stag will pass, being the great employment of aristocratic hands, thus foregoing their chance to applaud, with the tips of their gloved fingers or their fan, at the*

86. A celebrated operetta in three acts by Charles Lecocq, to a libretto by Clairville et al., first performed in Brussels in 1872 and in Paris in 1873.

87. Presumably the Folies-Dramatiques, which had recently been redecorated.

Comédie-Française, the Opéra-Comique, the Porte Saint-Martin, the Ambigu, the Château d'Eau, or (see below) the Cluny and the Hungarian Gypsies at the Folies-Bergère, i.e. all that is good and is not so good in our Theatre.

But no regrets for the delay of this Chronicle could come near (by a whole world!) our remorse if we failed to mention the (now long-past) opening of the Exhibition of Décors, *by the painter Baudry,*[88] *for the new* Opéra, *the theme with which our causerie ends as it began. For, for several months, it will practically be Paris itself. Its importance will be no secret to Nilsson*[89] *and the marquise de Caux,*[90] *who tried out their roulades there while still in their travelling clothes, nay tried out the walls themselves – no secret, either, to Faure.*[91] *First, nevertheless, a word about the paintings. Everything has been said about the long and inspired labours of this painter, the true hero of the day: the critics' appreciations are well known to all who wish to judge his work, as are its various titles, as set out in a catalogue. To the loud cries of admiration or rage I shall add no more than a low murmur, mingling with the rustle of the dresses and clicking of the jewels of astonished ladies as they pass to and fro. 'That head there, why, it is —'s!' 'My dear, aren't those your features? You must have posed for him.' 'What features? But look at that mouth, that chin! Surely they are yours?' – 'Whose are they, that noble forehead, that look? I'm sure I know them,' etc. etc. I hear such things as I jostle among the visitors, who, secretly, recognise themselves in 'Tragedy' or 'Comedy', in 'Melody' or 'Salome dancing'. It is no banal compliment but a just and new one, bestowed by women on a ceiling-painter, who, though a product of the Schools, has found how, in place of the generalised and almost abstract models of classical Beauty, to give us the Types we see at every moment: their special perfection, emerging from a* loge *or a carriage, or leaning on a shoulder in a ballroom, always with a faraway gaze, dreaming – of what? – of perpetuation in some higher and ideal heaven, a longing which Art, this time, has fulfilled, through the talent of an artist bold enough to apotheosise the contemporary face. For all women, it is the great event of the Season.*

Ix.

Ix's approach to his lady-readers, as we see, is highly insidious. He keeps encouraging them in a ferocious snobbery and chauvinism, until it dawns on us that his

88. Paul Baudry (1828–86), a successful *Salon* painter. When commissioned to decorate the *foyer* of the new Opéra, he took a long time (six years at least) to study and prepare. The whole thing took about twelve years. He drafted his compositions in words, first of all.

89. Christine Nilsson (1843–1921), Swedish soprano. She sang at Covent Garden, the Paris Opéra and the New York Metropolitan.

90. i.e. Adelina Patti, who was briefly married to the marquis de Caux.

91. Jean-Baptiste Faure (1830–1914), French baritone.

cruel mockery of the foreign tourists can be read, equally well or better, as mockery of the Parisians, vainly pluming themselves on their high culture and *esprit* and the supremacy of their city. (For after all, according to the logic of the argument, they have not actually *seen* these foreign invaders, they are merely imagining them.) It may be a mockery, too, of the fashion for seaside holidays, towards which Ix is evidently very ambivalent. The grandiose claim made for these Parisians as they lounge on their beach chairs – that they are enjoying the 'double azure' of the sea and sky and the spectacle of 'infinity and nothingness' – may suggest a quest of the 'Absolute', but it could equally be a way of saying that their minds are simply vacant. That the 'golden' tenor voice was made for women, and that a superabundance of gilding is what is to be demanded of an opera-house: for all the brilliance of Ix's style in pursuing such banal fancies, they are covertly insulting. Ix is not altogether a nice character.

We must turn next to the problem of Ix as a drama-critic. The awkward truth which gradually reveals itself is that he regards most of the current plays in Paris as, artistically or intellectually, absolutely frightful, a mere string of clichés, and he far prefers tightrope-walkers and conjurers. He has, however – once again – a legitimate escape from frankness over this, in the fact that he is writing in a fashion magazine. For if, as sometimes happens, he comments on a play as though its most important feature, or even its sole feature of any significance, were its costumes, this can, in theory at least, merely be put down to a strict interpretation of his duties. If readers wish to take it as a judgement on the play as a whole, that is their business, not Ix's.

His review in Issue 2 is fairly discreet, though the hint given about *La Jeunesse de Louis XIV* is clear enough.

Third leaf

Menu for a hunt luncheon

Salt herrings, Paris sausage (Duthé)
The local butter

Terrine of leveret in the ancient style
Grey partridges piqués, *cold in jelly*
Fillet of beef en Bellevue

Muslin brioche, Gooseberry jelly of Bar
Cheese from Sept-Moncel or locally, and Fruit

La Dernière Mode, 2

HAMPER OF WINES
Barsac
(Condillac water)
Thorins and Pontet-Canet 1864
Tisane de Saint-Marceau
(with ice)

Another menu

Tongue à l'écarlate[92]
Remoulade of celery
The local butter

Veal cutlets piquées[93] *and braised, cold in their ice*
Salmon trout with Montpellier butter
Pheasants cut into salmis with jelly

Russian salad
Rolls stuffed à la duchesse

WINES
Pouilly blanc
(Saint-Galmier water)
Médoc and Richebourg 1859
Crême de Bouzy rosée

THE CHEF DE BOUCHE CHEZ BRÉBANT

Fourth leaf

Adapting gas to Dutch-style Jewish Lamps

Gas must not penetrate further indoors than the stairs and landings: it should not cross the threshold of our apartments to light their anterooms unless softened and veiled by the transparent paper of a Chinese or Japanese lantern. Glaring through

92. Pickled beef tongue.

93. This is Carême's recipe for veal chops in jelly, in which the chops are 'studded with ham and bacon fat or pickled tongue'. He says (*L'Art de la cuisine française,* Paris, 1833–47, vol. 3, p. 295) that such things cannot be analysed: practice constitutes the whole talent of the *piqueur.*

glass, it gives, in the intimacy of our own house, a reminder of public places, a thing to be eschewed, despite all the benefits of this modern form of lighting. If the lamp, pouring forth the golden calm of oil, suggests study, as the candle, with its ardent flicker, evokes worldly enjoyment, gas, too, has very special characteristics: above all, that of being an ever-present though invisible slave.

Now, since all the devices for dispensing this illumination – bronze, zinc, etc. – are hideous and associate it with the shoddy and the banal, the plan is to adapt gas to some traditional and beautiful object: not so as to play tricks with it, but to display it in its very essence (I might say naked, if its nakedness were not what is impalpable!). In short, to allow it all its suggestiveness of magic.

Nothing could fulfil this intention better than the Dutch-style Jewish lamp, a clear and polished ring of six radiant bronze burners. Each a horizontal jet of light. Problems? There are none. The tube which sustains it, made of the same material, a rich fabric of flexible rubber, and sliding up and down to raise or lower it, to balance it, has simply been substituted for the original rod and cord, so as to provide continuous gas in the cavity which used to hold the evening's oil. As for ancient burners, one simply replaces them with silex ones, which are indestructible by gas.

Anywhere in a small room – the dining-table or work-table – where one wants a relatively brilliant light, this object, six tongues of flame in a metal frame, hangs up a gay Pentecost: no, a star, for truly all ritual and Judaic association has disappeared.

It would also suit a small dining-room, or a study in a seaside chalet, where the master of the house could work on through the early nightfalls of September.

Advice from MARLIANI,[94]
Upholsterer and interior decorator.

GAZETTE AND PROGRAMME FOR THE FORTNIGHT
Amusements or celebrations in 'Society'

From 20 September to 4 October 1874.

I

BOOKSHOPS AND EXHIBITIONS

For reading or re-reading by the first fires in the château *and in the railway-carriage returning to Paris.*

94. See his *'visiting-card'*, reproduced on p. 46.

Bibliothèque **Alphonse Lemerre** *(already published):* Montaigne (vol. II); Molière (vols. I–VI), *with thirty-five etchings after Boucher;* Racine (vols.I–III): *magnificent bibliophile editions, octavo or small duodecimo (Elzevir format). – Modern poetry:* Le Livre des sonnets *(1 vol.),* La Révolte des fleurs *(1 vol.) and* France *(1 vol.), by SULLY PRUDHOMME; A Mi-côte (1 vol.) by LÉON VALADE, and* Le Harem *(1 vol.) by ERNEST D'HERVILLY; finally,* Le Sang de la coupe *(1 vol.) by THÉODORE DE BANVILLE.*

Forthcoming: Une Idylle pendant le Siège, *by FRANÇOIS COPPÉE;* Works of Shakespeare (*1 vol.), translation by FRANÇOIS-VICTOR HUGO, and* Les Hommes de l'exil *(1 vol.) by CHARLES HUGO; then* Montaigne, Molière, Racine, *the next volume. – Modern poetry:* Oeuvres poétiques *of VICTOR HUGO (1 vol.);* Histoires poétiques, *by BRIZEUX* (vols. III & IV); Le Cahier rouge *(1 vol.), by FRANÇOIS COPPÉE;* Quatre octaves de sonnets (*1 vol.), by CLAUDIUS POPELIN.*

Bibliothèque **Charpentier** *(already published):* La Tentation de Saint-Antoine *(1 vol.), and* Le Candidat *(1 vol.), by GUSTAVE FLAUBERT;* La Conquête de Plassans *(1 vol.) and* Les Contes à Minon (*1 vol.), then* Les Contes pour les grandes personnes *(1 vol.), by our two collaborators, Messrs. ZOLA and D'HERVILLY;* Portraits contemporains, *by THÉOPHILE GAUTIER (a volume in the* Oeuvres complètes *of this master, of which the previous volume to appear was* L'Histoire du romantisme).

We shall postpone speaking, to the portion of our journal headed Advice on Education, *of the publications of the firm of* ***Hachette,*** *until the return of the studious to Paris: just now the* Guides Joanne *are still in everyone's hands.*

EXHIBITIONS: In the Champs-Élysées, exhibition of the ***Union of Fine Arts applied to Industry:*** *furniture, bibelots, etc., of which one group will especially interest our Lady Readers, i.e. The History of Costume, from the most ancient times to the 17th century, represented by all the graphic arts and sculpture of the time.*

Also, *in the* Salle de l'École des Beaux-arts, Decorative paintings *by BAUDRY, for the new Opéra: thirty-three canvases, some very large.*

THEATRES

Théâtre-Français: Zaire, *with* ***Sarah Bernhardt*** *and* ***Mounet Sully,*** *one of the great and beautiful successes of the season; together with other pieces in the repertoire, notably* Une Chaîne, *a revival, with* ***Favart***[95] *and Got.*[96]

Opéra: *first performances of* L'Esclave, *by MEMBREE, and the repertory, principally* Les Huguenots *and* Robert le Diable; La Favorite, *for the debut of M.* ***Manoury.***

95. Pierette-Ignace Pingaud, known as Favart (1833-1908), French actor.
96. François Got (1822-1901), French comic actor.

Odéon: *continuation of* La Jeunesse de Louis XIV, *with* ***Léonide Leblanc, Hélène Petit*** *and the actor* ***Gil Naza;*** *the appearance on stage of a real-life pack of hounds makes this one of the productions most in harmony with the season.*

Opéra-Comique: Le Pardon de Ploermel, ***Zina Dalti*** *and* ***Lina Bell; Bouhy, Lhérie.*** *The repertory.*

Vaudeville: Les Ganaches, *revival*: ***Delannoy, Saint-Germain.***

Gymnase: La Dame aux Camélias, *revival,* ***Blanche Pierson*** *alternating with* ***Séraphine***, *revival; and then* Gilberte, *a new work by GONDINET:* ***Gilberte, Mlle Delaporte.***

Variétés: La Vie parisienne, *revival:* ***Mlle Vanghel, Dupuis, Grenier Berthelier;*** *then* Les Pommes du Voisin *and the one-acter by MEILHAC and HALÉVY,* L'Ingénue, *a novelty.*

Palais-Royal: Les Jocrisses de l'amour, *revival*: ***Geoffroy, Hyacinthe, Lhéritier, Lassouche, etc.,*** *names warranted to bring a smile to the face of the gloomy and home-sick traveller, however far from Paris. Curtain-raisers.*

Gaîté: *continuation of* Orphée aux Enfers, *with a new Act, 'The kingdom of Neptune', by the beloved Master: décors by* ***Fromont,*** *costumes by* ***Grévin, Italian dancers: Christine Roselli*** *and* ***Fontabello*** *in the ballet of the ocean-nymphs, under the direction of M.* ***Fuchs.*** *The Lake, the Flood, the Storm, the Enchanted Cave, the Bottom of the Sea, the Fish Quadrille, the Awakening of Amphitrite and Atlantis (an underwater city): to think that each of these words, enough by themselves to open the door to magic, represents a complete and cunning and decorative spectacle!*

Châtelet: *continuation of* Les Deux orphelines, *which, till this theatre changes its name to 'Opéra Populaire', will continue to moisten handkerchiefs, both of lace and of linen.*

Ambigu: L'Officier de fortune, *a new five-acter, in a redecorated theatre: success in every department, in the auditorium, on the stage and in the wings, where there is a contrivance destined to become famous.*

Bouffes-Parisiens: *continuation of* La Jolie parfumeuse. ***Théo*** *– enough said! No, because even at her side, one notices* ***Mme Grivot;*** *also* ***Daubray*** *and* ***Bonnet.***

Renaissance: Thérésa *and* ***Paulin-Menier*** *(bravo! and bravo!) in* La Famille Trouillat, *which, were it even a masterpiece (and it is amusing), ought to give the place of honour on its poster to these two famous performers.*

Folies-Dramatiques: *a lecture by* ***Milher*** *on 'The Supermoral theatre', a favourite theme just now; followed by* La Fille de madame Angot. *Will* tout Paris, *having forgotten its operetta for two whole months, go to see it again? Women, whose function it is to make comparison between tenors, will, at the Folies, make the acquaintance of M.* ***Mario Widmer,*** *just as we, of the male sex, will go to compare* ***Desclauzas,*** *who has remained faithful to her role, with herself.*

Cluny: Les Bêtes noires du capitaine, *a new comedy by M. PAUL CELLIÈRES, with* ***Mme Lacressonière;*** *before that, a verse one-acter by M. DREYFUS,* Le Médaillon de Colombine, *an exquisite piece.*

Théâtre des Arts *(formerly the* ***Menus-Plaisirs):*** Les Jeunes, *with a prologue in verse;* Revendication, *in three Acts, a novelty.*

Théâtre Scribe *(formerly the* ***Athénée):*** Les Écoliers d'amour, *a verse one-acter by M. Pierre Ezéar, and* Le Vignoble de madame veuve Pichois, *in four acts: both new.*

Château d'Eau: *a novelty,* Le Treizième coup de minuit, *a lyrical fable, with real music, by DEBILLEMONT, and exquisite décors and stage-devices.* ***Mmes Jeanne Bressoles*** *and* ***Suzanne Vial.***

Délassements-Comiques *(formerly the* ***Nouveautés):*** Le Rhinocéros et son enfant, *with the maddest of texts and music by a genuine and delicious musician, M. DE SIVRY.*

Folies-Bergère: *notably the Hungarian Gypsies, an admirable little orchestra; an English pantomime (despite its title,* Madame Benoiton restera chez elle*); English acrobats, an English ballet of women pugilists – a strange and charming spectacle.*

Finally, the ***Théâtre Déjazet:*** *a new tableau in the fantastic* Les Femmes *by PAUL DE KOCK, with, as a curtain raiser,* Le Cadet de Gascogne *by Beaumarchais: both first-time productions; and at the Folies-Marigny, still* La Fille de l'air, *which will not vanish from the Champs-Élysées until the winds of autumn.*

* * *

The ***Salle Ventadour*** *and the* ***Théâtre Lyrique*** *are going to be reborn from their past, their ashes, rather than from the sleep of the summer closure, which now no longer holds sway over any Parisian theatre.*

Other places for distraction and pleasure, both day and night, after the ***Jardin d'Acclimatation*** *(animals, notably two little orang-utans and a pair of giraffes, plus flowers and an orchestra): one of those gardens which never know winter.*

The ***Cirque d'Eté:*** *where one can still see those extraordinary skaters,* ***Goodrich and Curtis.***

The ***Panorama,*** *in the Champs-Elysées, with the spectacle,* Le Siège de Paris, *by the painter PHILIPPOTEAUX.*

Robert-Houdin: *'The Maharajah's Cabinet,' by its inventors* ***Robert-Houdin the Younger and Brunnet.***[97]

97. But see *ante*, p. 39, where we learn that this famous trick is also being staged by Franconi in his Circus, though the person who mysteriously materialises within the cabinet is, in his version, not a turbaned Indian but a pretty girl.

The Théâtre-Miniature: *last performances for the 'laureates', a ticket for* Le Vainqueur de Jemappes *as first prize.*

A sweetshop, the **Salle des Familles:** *but less barley sugar is consumed here than at the preceding theatre, from which the spectators return older and wiser.*

* * *

III

RAILWAY STATIONS

Such are our renewed pleasures; but so long as the sun persists in shining under the first clouds and the greenery in not departing at the first winds there will be citizens averse to all thoughts of returning. With time on their hands, many of the casinos having closed, they take advantage of the remaining summertime Excursion Trains and go to feast their eyes, for the year to come, on mountains and fields and groves, on lakes and glaciers. Travel! They need it after the beach and before the city street. Let us specify some of these excursions, now that the season is about to close, but rapidly and in no order, without pretending (for space forbids) to mention them all or even nearly all.

First the Ligne de l'Ouest.

Excursions on the Normandy coast and in Brittany. *Return tickets valid for a month: season of 1874. Four itineraries, thanks to which no corner of interest will remain unknown to the Tourist. The first: 1st* class, *60 fr.; 2nd* class, *45 fr.; the second: 1st* class, *80 fr.; 2nd* class, *65 fr.; the third: 1st* class, *90 fr.; 2nd* class, *70 fr.; the fourth: 1st* class, *135 fr.; 2nd* class, *105 fr. (See the indicators.)*

The Ligne de l'Ouest *runs, in conjunction with the Orléans line, the* ***Excursion on the coasts of Brittany:*** *season of 1874. Return tickets valid for twenty days. Price: 1st* class, *154 fr.; 2nd* class, *115 fr. 50.*

No need to give the itinerary, which is known to everyone since the official journey in Brittany undertaken by the President of the Republic.

A beautiful and grand **reduced price excursion** *from Paris to the centre of France and the* ***Pyrenees:*** *1st* class *225 fr.; 2nd* class, *170 fr., tickets valid for a month, is one that allows us to visit winter spas and to see mountains and circuses.*

Orléans and Midi lines? The Lyons one which, before November's migration towards so many blue skies (its speciality), invites us to enjoy the magnificent ***reduced price round trip for Dauphiné,*** *Savoy, Switzerland, Burgundy, Lyons and Franche-Comté: 1st* class, *160 fr.; 2nd* class, *140 fr.*

* * *

Ligne du Nord.

Circular tours at reduced prices, *season of 1874, to visit Holland, Belgium and the Rhine; first class tickets, valid for a month: 123 fr.*

This tour is today a classic for tourists and the cultured.

* * *

We may leave the Ligne du Nord *proper to take advantage of its merging with the* Ligne de l'Est.

Circular tour at reduced price to the banks of the Rhine *and in Belgium, season of 1874: tickets valid for a month, first* class, *140 fr. 40 c.; without forgetting the patriotic pilgrimage to Alsace, announced by us in the first issue.*

In a little while we shall give you the other ***Tours and Excursions,*** *not being able to list them all at once; and as the railway companies inform us of the cessation of one or other of them, we shall begin naming holiday resorts for the autumm and winter.*

Address all ***Books,*** *and all information regarding the* ***Theatre, Tours or Fine Arts*** *to M. STÉPHANE MALLARMÉ, 29, rue de Moscou.*

The Proprietor: ***DAVID.***

CORRESPONDENCE WITH SUBSCRIBERS

Mme LA MARQUISE DE L . . . , RENNES: We greatly regret that our Specimen Number reached you stained and creased: but postmen rarely wear gloves; and, to get the journal into a letter-box, they often fold it into four and crumple it generally. What can one do? – Mlle R . . . , NANTES: We have sent you a toothed roller to perforate the cut-out patterns; it is often used for this purpose, and even more often to trace out the pattern on a fabric, which is then easier to cut. – Mme LA BARONNE DE R., NICE: We will provide you with many descriptions of new costumes, so far as space will allow; to notice such costumes everywhere, and combine them or invent them, is one of my principal preoccupations. – Mme DE C.L. NEVERS: Do not complain of the richness of our costumes: it is always possible to omit ornaments from an elaborate ensemble, whereas, in the case of a too-simple one, it is often very difficult to add them. – Mme LA VICOMTESSE T. DE C . . . , TURIN: our Paris Chronicle, as well as our Programme and Gazette for the Fortnight, will inform you of all the new theatrical productions and the worth of each new play: this, indeed, was announced in the Chronicle. You say you are very fond of the theatre, so I am happy that our journal can meet your desires. Being literary almost as much as technical (it is the first time a fashion-journal has set itself such an aim), La Dernière mode *will, in every issue, deal with Parisian plays and theatres. If other subscribers will encourage us in this new enterprise, we shall go ahead with confidence. – Mme V (Dresses and mantles at LYON): from this number onwards, being the second of the edition-with-text, the black-and-white engraving on the first page will always depict a pair of models. – Mme the DOWAGER MARQUISE DE S . . . , NANCY: It is very kind of you to interest yourself in our publication, and equally, to interest your acquaintances in it, for subscribers often come to us by recommendation. – Mme LA BARONNE DE B . . . . , TOURS: We have chosen the required article for you at the price you indicated: it will make a simply ravishing offering, and I think you will be pleased with it. Rely on us to send it, punctually, for Michaelmas eve. – Mme D . . . , TOULOUSE: Yes, Madame, you may safely trim a plum-coloured silk dress with light blue: but you must confine it to borders and* rouleautés,[98] *or the effect will be simply ugly: and it must be a very pale blue. – To several of our readers: You can obtain a second cut-out pattern every month, at 3 francs for the half year, but we must be allowed to choose the pattern (which will be of the Coloured Lithograph published the second Sunday of every month). If in addition you will let us know of a particular pattern you would like, it can be cut for you specially, at a cost of 1 fr. 25.*

98. A *rouleauté* (or *roulotte*) is a portion of material rolled round on itself.

Issue 3

TROISIÈME LIVRAISON — DIMANCHE 4 OCTOBRE 1874

LA DERNIÈRE MODE

GAZETTE DU MONDE ET DE LA FAMILLE

MARASQUIN

PARAIT LE 1er ET LE 3e DIMANCHE DU MOIS, AVEC LE CONCOURS

DANS LA MODE & LE GOUT PARISIEN

EN MUSIQUE

EN LITTÉRATURE

DE THÉODORE DE BANVILLE, LÉON CLADEL, FRANÇOIS COPPÉE, ALPHONSE DAUDET,
LÉON DIERX, EMMANUEL DES ESSARTS, ERNEST D'HERVILLY,
ALBERT MÉRAT, STÉPHANE MALLARMÉ, CATULLE MENDÈS, SULLY PRUDHOMME, LÉON VALADE,
AUGUSTE VILLIERS DE L'ISLE-ADAM, ÉMILE ZOLA, ETC.

TOILETTES DU JOUR

In her leading article on Fashion, in this issue, Mme de Ponty is at her most knowing and devious, borrowing a passage from *La Vie parisienne* about the *collier-bagatelle* but adding a touch or two of mystery to it, and flattering her Parisian readers by saying that some of what she has to report about 'Today's Taste' is well-known to them already; she is only reporting it for the benefit of those in the provinces.

FASHION

Paris, 4 October 1874.

Our last column told the world about the complete transformation that Fashion has already undergone, or will undergo, this autumn and it explained the Season's change of décor; it only remained to describe a thousand charming whimsies, indispensable extras for daytime wear, when we realised that, having depended too much on our own observations, we had quite neglected certain of such items – commonplace ones, indeed, and of course well known in Paris; but then, we are not writing for Paris alone. Today it is true, our task is (as one would say about a silk or gold embroidery) to 'fill in the background', but we must not neglect the delightful, brilliant trifles which are the finishing touches dictated by Good Taste.

Let us begin with these trifles, if only to get them out of the way! How many whimsies have seen the light of day before and during this fortnight: above all, the ravishing Lavallières, *scarves with pink buttons embroidered in contrasting colours, and others in tartan or every imaginable shade, and ones with satiny stripes, of pale blue and pink – really adorable. I award no less praise to charming little turquoise necklaces – scarves and bows for the hair which come in two colours or two shades, such as nasturtium and sulphur-yellow, blue and green, pink and blue, pearl-grey and pink, steely blue and iron-grey, etc.: all with* guipure *or Valenciennes lace. As for microscopic handkerchiefs made for the tiniest hands, I see several: one with a cockchafer embroidered in colour in the corner, with two interwined letters in pink and blue or red and bronze which is, to say the least, original. Some have a letter embroidered in green and red wool: those with a broad hem in pearl grey foulard are very stylish, perhaps more so than the ones entirely in pink or blue foulard, with pleats of the same and inserts of Valenciennes lace.*

But all these novelties, soon to be familiar to some of us, pale before one which is still, indisputably, the ornament of the moment, as it has been of the Season. Nothing has caused it to go out of fashion, neither the months spent gazing at the sea, nor the weeks already spent in the hunting field – the latter less than the former, for to the vague term 'collier-bagatelle' *the evil fate presiding over this object persists in preferring the hunting term 'dog-collar').*

What is it? I will answer quite simply: a little black velvet ribbon which goes round the neck and is fastened behind with a square buckle, through which it passes and falls. A thousand diamond letters sparkle with the captivating brilliance of a secret which is apparent but remains hidden: interlaced Christian names and surnames of her who wears the collar and of him who gave it. Legend has it that a single jeweller makes these collars and varies their mystery. Now, to reveal his address, even among women, would be an act of high treason: useless too, for it is not up to us women to buy them. However, I shall add, for those of my readers who (gifts being a chancy affair) would like to make their taste known, that these ornaments also come in coloured stones and in pearls, or even with a little diamond fringe. Even earrings of velvet ribbon are worn, with single initials repeated. London, Vienna, St. Petersburg and New York know about this; and such an almost classic ornament brings me back to some quite general matters, needed to complete last fortnight's sketch of autumn fashions.[99]

We mentioned the chapeau Berger *and the* chapeau Valois, *finding the* chapeau Lamballe *almost too well known. But it is completely new only for those of our subscribers who did not come to Paris during the holidays and have not been in Normandy. What then is the* chapeau Lamballe, *which continues to be all the rage? If a thousand letters written on blue vellum inquire of us, only then shall we reply.*

Let us speak of hair styles. The hair styling which is in perfect harmony with our hats, better than the chignon, is the Catogan: *quite a surprise, as it carries us right back to the* Directoire! *We remember the plait, or the two plaits folding back on themselves, now held by a bow in the same shade as the hat. Our grandmothers, and even our grandfathers,*[100] *wore this a century ago. The head still supports a scaffolding of little rolls, back-combing coils and plaits; while raised bands are lightly curled, showing no disorder other than prettily ruffled hair.*

A few more remarks, so that this column, along with the one in the previous issue, can constitute an all-round view of Today's Taste. Let us stress a point, at the risk of repetition: namely that Fashion, this autumn, is definitely reviving the Tunic. It can be round or pointed, with flounces or pleats, or even take the form of a scarf; or it may be squared off behind, in which case it is turned up in a roll, the two flaps being tied together with a handsome faille *bow. But the main point is that all tunics,*

99. In this passage, as Lecercle points out, Mme de Ponty is borrowing from, and playing minor variations upon, a paragraph or two in *La Vie parisienne* for 22 August 1874, about a 'dog-collar in black velvet' which was 'inaugurated at Trouville during an intimate soirée'. *La Vie parisienne* says simply that the collars are all the work of a single jeweller, and that shopkeepers refuse to give his address.

100. *A catogan* was worn by some infantry soldiers during the eighteenth century.

whatever their style, should be exceedingly close-fitting in front and very loose behind. This is as de rigueur *today as the corset fastened, or rather laced, in the back. Basques will, of course, cling closely to the hips: it will even be advantageous, to reduce them, to mount the skirt of the dress on a smooth piece of fabric, both in front and at the side.*

All this was known to me, at our great fashion-designers, before it was known at the last races in the Bois de Boulogne[101] *– seeing which latter has, all in all, only confirmed me in all my earlier opinions. Only one new point, highlighted both by the last suns of the season and the gaslight of the department stores I have visited, relates to this winter's fabrics. We extract from our notebook, at random, a note or two regarding this, already mingled with names famous in the world of fashion. 'Heavy fabrics . . . and* grosgrain, *quilted materials of all colours and patterns, especially cashmere: all styles created to clothe beautifully a well-built person. – What, no* recherché *design? No, it is the fabric itself which produces the dazzling effect. Here, what are actually furnishing fabrics are worn with grace.'*

I will add, now, that we may need to go even further, and I shall spread a rumour which is almost an echo of all I have said before. A great fashion designer (one of those whom Paris sometimes obeys) is proposing, before New Year's Day, to revive the splendid Louis XIV costumes, for which were created (it would seem) those rich, strong fabrics suddenly arriving from the great factories to the plate-glass windows of Fashion's laboratories.

We shall see what we shall see.

MARGUERITE DE PONTY

THE FIVE TOILETTES

Black-and-white engravings

First page.

1. Costume in poult-de-soie *and snuff-coloured velvet, in two shades. The lappet of the tunic lies very far back, held by a bow in the same shade of velvet. Velvet waistcoat and facings. 2. Pale blue cashmere dress trimmed in front with a satin apron of the same colour, with little flounces. Cashmere pocket and sleeves, trimmed with a satin flounce. Large bows of black velvet are placed both on the skirt and on the sleeves.*

101. The racecourse at Longchamp in the Bois de Boulogne was a fashionable rendezvous.

Middle Pages.

3. Little girl, 5–6. Dress in light brown tweed, 'Princess' style in front but with basques behind (but forming only one garment). Starting from the 'little side' in front, the skirt is fitted to the waistline with flat pleats. The first pleat is trimmed on either side with little bows of chestnut-coloured faille, *the buttons also covered in chestnut-coloured* faille, *and the buttonholes are made with chestnut braid. Around the jacket a* biais *in the same chestnut* faille *surmounting the hem, forming piping. Tyrolean hat in brown felt with a pheasant feather and a twisted plait of chestnut-coloured velvet. 4. Little boy, 5–6. Black velvet blouse, plain in front, with a double pleat at the side and back. The skirt fairly short, the waist loose, not tight, and set very low to lengthen the body. Light-grey felt hat with wide brims, only slightly turned up: a round, very narrow crown, trimmed with an artificial plume.*

MARGUERITE DE P.

For Ix, Issue 3 is an occasion to express his real preferences and his strongest dislikes in the theatre, without too much concealment. What his readers would be supposed to make of this is a question one keeps asking oneself. Though he detests vaudeville and its 'Poverty-stricken language', Ix manages, as we see, to pay a most handsome and fanciful compliment to the celebrated Pauline Virginie Déjazet (1797-1875), queen of the vaudeville theatre for fifty years. Déjazet specialised in 'breeches' roles and was still, in her seventies, 'impersonating the morning-plucked rose', i.e. playing fresh-faced young noblemen. The drift of his article, however, remains clear: that the French theatre in his day, with an occasional exception, has so little to do with literature, its language is so banal and debased, its 'period' revivals are so chocolate-boxy, that his heart goes out to the circus and the pantomime – to all, that is to say, that is wordless.

PARIS CHRONICLE

No! The electric light which turned the greenery of Esclimont blue – Esclimont, the French château visited by the Prince of Wales[102] *– will not divert me from the moonlit canvas and cardboard of our Parisian stages: that is, if any of the current plays, by their stage-moonlight, can set us dreaming. Such is not the case with* Une Chaîne, *a comedy by Scribe, which calls, above all, for the artificial glare of the footlights; indeed, during the first night at the Théâtre-Français, I wondered why its title, long pondered by the author, had not boldly been changed, to make the*

102. For the Prince of Wales's visit to Esclimont see p. 127–9.

point of the play even clearer, to Une Corde: *since critics all agree in noting that the characters 'dance on the tightrope of passion'. As for myself, that figure of speech will never quite suit, for when it comes to tightropes I only like the literal kind used by dancers and funambulists; and because I dream of that other kind of 'passion', sublime, grandiose and real, which, in these days of vaudeville and its poverty-stricken language, was displayed for us by Madame Saqui,*[103] *when, amidst the ether of the firmament, she stripped herself of her beggar's rags and appeared like a dazzling 'genie', naked and fulfilled. Yes, when will theatrical pedantry (for it exists, despite the efforts to conceal it by prodigious performers like Favart*[104] *and Got*[105] *and Coquelin,*[106] *Fèvre and Berton!*[107]*) disappear, as a ridiculous and useless fetish, disdained by true, supple, and incomparable skill?*

I shall grant, for three minutes, the metaphor I have just attributed to critics. Very well, there are those who set forth on the 'tightrope' with a sure foot, a pure flame in their eyes and chalk on the soles of their shoes[108] *(but Scribe is not one of them). But what shall we say about the others, who take pleasure, first, in fraying this rope into a thousand fine strands, nets perfectly designed* not *to catch ideas, and then, having done so, make no use of so many loose ends? The clever authors of* Gilberte, *Messrs. Deslandes and Goudinet, rather enjoy this; and one ought to see their play, if only to be convinced that it never existed, though the costumes of Mlle Delaporte – too soon carried off to the depths of Russia,*

not without the echo of frantic applause[109] *and those of Mmes. Fromentin, Helmont and Angelo, were made to last almost a whole winter. For, in this paradoxical world of the theatre, where the whole history of an empire can last the length of one well-spoken line, one may see a mere stage-costume braving entire seasons.*

103. Julie Saqui, *née* Boas (1786–1866), French dancer and tightrope walker.
104. Pierette-Ignace Pingaud, known as Favart (1833–1908), French actor.
105. François Got (1822-1901), French comic actor.
106. Benoît-Constant Coquelin (1841-1909), French actor.
107. Pierre Berton (1842-1912), French actor and playwright.
108. Presumably a practice among actual tightrope walkers.
109. See p. 96.

These are two of the current successes, and one could speak of them as two premières or as two revivals, depending whether one is thinking of the stir they made at this or that Paris theatre or of the total absence of novelty in their plots. But I shall not abandon metaphors, just because they are bad! We have had the rope, and now we shall have tow, dear to fire-eaters, who, in their heroic cheeks, set it alight and, with the wind of inspiration, puff it out in smoke (knowing that the stuff is still the same old loose ends).[110] *Quick! Find us some simple, cheerful street burlesque, with its own perfect language, to make us forget modern* Comédie bourgeoise,[111] *which only exists if it is not bourgeois and if it belongs to all time. Does it even have to exist, as comedy? Let us welcome* Le Tricorne enchanté[112] *that marvel of subtle rhymes and verve which the Odéon is reviving along with* L'École des maris,[113] *fitting in between these two exquisite and perennial masterpieces a revival – old-fashioned, faded and washed-out – of a* comédie bourgeoise *by Wafflart and Fulgence. Well, so be it! But to dig up such a play fifty years after its time, that is to say now that this genre, unknown to Racine and Aeschylus, has begun to come true,*[114] *whereas when it was written it was artificial, quaint and out-of-date! Still, what adorable costumes, both for men and for women, those of 1821, as exhibited by Porel, Richard, François or Mme Gravier! Only, what if such costumes, copied from the prints of the day take over all the Paris theatres, proving me all too prophetic? For I see them at the* Renaissance *in* La Famille Trouillat.[115] *Paulin Menier has done well and bravely to retire from the company into his solitude and his near-genius, remote from that world of joy, good humour and first-rate mockery which Thérésa,*[116] *that always astonishing woman, creates round herself (but round herself alone!).*

Personally, I enjoy these implausible and nostalgic scenes. Then there is Parisian life in La Vie parisienne *as it has been shown at the* Variétés, *since its re-opening*[117] *mad, incoherent and bizarre, even without mademoiselle Van Ghel, Dupuis, Grenier and Barthelier, who make it even more mad, incoherent and*

110. Tow is made of the loose ends of flax or hemp.

111. i.e. the inheritor of the so-called *'comédie bourgeoise'* popularised by Diderot, Sedaine and others in the mid-eighteenth century.

112. *Le Tricorne enchanté*, by Théophile Gautier.

113. By Molière.

114. Ix presumably means: when, as in the 1870s, French society has in actual fact become 'bourgeois'.

115. *La Famille Trouillat*, an operetta in three acts by Hector Crémieux and Ernest Blum. The principal roles were created by Thérésa and Paulin Menier.

116. 'Thérésa', born in 1837 as Emma Valadon and originally a dressmaker, became famous as the leading singer at the newly opened Eldorado, and later, specialising in comic songs, of the style known as *canaille*, she earned the huge salary of 233 francs a day.

117. Re-opened on 1 August with *La Vie parisienne.*

bizarre. Or again L'Ingénue,[118] *which only eight nights ago was seen by Hortense Schneider,*[119] *Marie Legault, Peschard, Grandville, Silly, Paola Marie, Zulmar Bouffar and Blanche Méry, Thèse, Delphine de Lizy, and some gentlemen whose black coats would have disappeared under the brilliance of their decorations, and their white ties under the ribbons of their orders, if they had not all come as for a family party. However when, apropos of the air from* Alceste,[120] *murmured from the throat of an ingénue still in the convent, Cécile Chaumont*[121] *said she preferred one of the less learned arias of* Orphée aux Enfers,[122] *half the audience enjoyed the joke, spiced though it was with irony on the part of Meilhac and Halévy, and they saluted Offenbach, who being an intelligent man, ignored this tactlessness.*[123] *Perhaps one should not play games with ordinary things, because no-one knows how far the game will go, nor where they will stop being ordinary: or at least, like Dumas,*[124] *one should deprive them, by wickedness, nastiness and heightened drama, of any resemblance to ordinary life, as the only alternative to frank caricature.*

This is the superiority which Pantomime pure and simple has, when it is not debased. This, indeed, is the moment for it, for here we have Pierrot and the boastful Pamphile, Colombine with her ugly mug, and Harlequin himself, brought to us on the stage by M. Maurice Dreyfus and his gift for fantasy, but above all for Poetry, who, clown-like, but always exquisite and sonorous, splits crescent-wise to the ears or closes into rosebud shape, with the smile and the laugh, short only of audible syllables, the mouth of mimes who long to speak and to speak in rhythm.[125] *However charming, on the same stage another work,* Les Bêtes noires du capitaine, *by M. Cellières. I have (alas!) this quirk of preferring, to a jewel of that expensive species – were it to cost thirty-nine francs, or fifty-nine, or even sixty and be bought at the grandest jewellers of the Palais-Royal this pinchbeck object, quarrelled over by a crazy gang of puppets, entitled* Le Médaillon de Colombine. *These are two shows opening at the* Cluny.

Where am I? I must be firm and, knowing all too well how little I have said, I must stop at this point. Yet, while aware that everything I have said about the

118. By Meilhac and Halévy.

119. The famous singer and actress (1833-1920), creator of many Offenbach roles.

120. The opera by Christoph von Gluck (1714–87).

121. Or rather, Céline Chaumont, actress and singer (1848–1926).

122. The well-known operetta by Offenbach.

123. Obviously, as a compliment to Offenbach, it would have been very ill-judged, implying that he himself rated his music higher than Gluck's.

124. Alexandre Dumas *fils* (1824–95) wrote a number of intense dramas whose highly-flavoured plots were intended to expound a moral or social problem.

125. Ix is describing the verse one-acter *Le Médaillon de Colombine* by Maurice Dreyfus at the *Cluny.*

theatre-season will scatter like leaves before the wind, I have too much in store to stop altogether. To pretend, if vainly, to cut a discussion of a single topic into three and say: 'These three portions will join up again, like an adder in the forests of Fontainebleau': well, that is my absurd duty, for I want to neglect nothing in Paris's annual resurrection by Drama, Comedy, Farce and Fantasy.

But have I deviated, even for a moment, to any other topic? By no means. The very name 'partridge' has not passed my lips, any more than 'pack', or 'stags'. Let Chantilly[126] *or Paris blow a thousand horns: for my part, I have had one thought only, that while I am talking, Books have been gathering and will occupy me more tyrannically when winter arrives. For they shall have their turn, and a lengthy one, just like the theatre. Meanwhile, what excellent things, in prose and poetry, pile up on our table – or rather, I should say, live in our memory, recollections ready to become remorse!*

Neither Nature, which has been nothing to us since last week, save for Croisette,[127] *these last evenings, inaugurating the Tour of the Lake for 1874 and 1875; nor the wonderful litle objects in the Exhibition of Fine Arts Applied to Industry (a forbidding title for such notable things and such a worthy effort); nor Mignonette, winner of the Royal Oaks, nor Perplex, of the Grand Criterium; nor Blue Boy, champion of future greyhound-races; nor the fashionable post-chaises which, by a witty fiction, appear to post direct from homes in Poitou and Touraine to the top of the avenue des Champs-Élysées; none of these has diverted me from my solemn duty, which was above all to tell Paris and Nevers that the* Délassements-Comiques, *which used to be known as the* Nouveautés, *describe themselves as The most Elegant Theatre in Paris (and announce a delightful piece entitled* Le Rhinocéros et son enfant, *with music by M. de Sivry).*[128]

126. A château to the north of Paris, famous for its race meetings. There is a vast forest nearby.

127. The 'Croisette' must be a reference to the ferry-boats on the Lac inférieur in the Bois de Boulogne.

128. Charles de Sivry (1848–99), composer.

But it is time, rather – it would make a worthy conclusion to such a chronicle – to speak, even a week late, of the unique event at the Opéra *in honour of Déjazet, with Faure, with Tamberlick,*[129] *with gods and mortals, and Déjazet herself! The most famous actresses fought for a place in the chorus or in walk-on parts – as if to show that, now that Song herself, the winged, the near-a-century-old, seems to be resigning her voice, the best of singers can do no more than add theirs to the confused murmur of the crowd, or even stay silent. But not so! For if that ever young princess (through whom, it would seem, the fairy godmother who endowed her in her cradle took on flesh and blood), is to give up her facile impersonating of the morning-plucked rose, it is because, in some place unknown to us but known to her, there stir mysterious flowerings of future talents, which she in turn must strike with her all-powerful wand – able even to command, in a few hours, a gala night worthy of the attention of Europe.*[130]

Ix

Fifth leaf

Menu for a dinner to celebrate the return to Paris
An intimate meal for twelve persons

Consommé à la Sévigné[131]
Saint-Hubert[132]

Trout à la Chambord
Fillet of lamb. Purée of artichokes
Quails in their nest
Braised chicken Saint-Lambert

Sparkling wine sorbet

Pheasant
Roasted corncrakes
Salad à l'italienne
Fresh ceps Bordelaise

129. Enrico Tamberlick (1820–89), Italian tenor.

130. The benefit night for Déjazet on 27 September 1874 was organised by *Le Gaulois*, as was her funeral, which was attended by 30,000 mourners.

131. See Carême, *op. cit.*, vol. 6, pp. 83–4.

132. Game consommé.

Mallarmé on Fashion

Ramekins of Parmesan
Crayfish à la Colbert

Praline ice
Mecca cakes

Dessert chosen by the mistress of the house
Coffee, Liqueurs from France and the West Indies
Russian cigarettes and Grand-Hôtel cigars

WINES

Grand vin ordinaire: Fleury, and Pommard (1865)
Rudesheim (1857)
Desaigne or Saint-Galmier water
Malaga
Chilled champagne

THE CHEF DE BOUCHE CHEZ BRÉBANT

The 'Sixth leaf' of the 'Golden Notebook' offers an evocative piece of *décor,* prompted by thoughts of the hunting season. It is a 'Lark-hunt', as devised – so at least it claimed – by the zoologist Alphonse Toussenel (1803–85), author of the intriguingly-titled *L'Esprit des bêtes: vénerie française et zoologie passionnelle* [The Mind of Animals: French Hunting and Passionate Zoology] (1847) and *Le monde des oiseaux: ornithologie passionnelle* [The World of Birds: Passionate Ornithology] (1852). In its choreography it is like a modern version of a renaissance masque.

Sixth leaf

The Lark-hunt, with a Draw-net

More than ever this season, ladies are hunting in the open, gun in hand, before pursuing bigger game in the forest. Some may not have a passion for gun-shot or breakneck galloping: so here is a hunt, for the fashionable world or for the family, of which the style, albeit original, is no different from that of an ordinary picnic.

An open space, situated where larks fly, is marked off between two mounds or thickets: between these two features, a long strip of net is stretched upright, at less than a man's height, to make a covert for the game. When evening comes, after an early dinner, you rise from the table, ladies and gentlemen, and go to somewhere about a thousand steps from the place, directing your eyes towards it. Groups are formed and then, hand-in-hand, everyone advances, like the ladies' chain at a ball but more spread out. Rustle of dresses over the ground (become a hunting technique) and the sound of hurrying feet: to these are added the noise of stones and reeds dragged along by cords, while the general march advances straight for the device, and the larks set off, with their low, horizontal evening flight, running their heads and wings into the wide meshes of the pantière *(that is its name), like the* verveux[133] *in a river transforming fishing into a miraculous hunt. A good bag, all things considered; and, handing the baskets to the gamekeepers or the servants, one returns, under the first stars, to the drawing-room, where dancing proper can begin its evolutions.*[134]

Would not making such a net, in a rustic shelter in the park, be an occupation for all fingers, some afternoon?

This is the charming after-dinner entertainment feasible today even for our great hostesses and their guests, which was recently proposed to us, on behalf of our readers, by one of our most delightful humorists, himself an old huntsman, whose name has lost none of its charm for our generation; for we have the good fortune to add, to this description of a little-known sport, the fact that it has been done here

according to TOUSSENEL

GAZETTE AND PROGRAMME FOR THE FORTNIGHT

From 4 to 19 October 1874

THEATRES

Our journal, which, as well a Collection on *Fashion, would like to be a journal* in *fashion, will naturally find its home on the* salon *table. To lift the cover and look at this page will become a habit for any Lady Reader in search of entertainment. The intention of this page is to compose, and group together, a picture of all the Pleasures offered during the Fortnight by Paris and to indicate, by a few more intimate words, the best choice for various evenings or for an afternoon. But it will be important to verify that no change has occurred to the Programme, which, at the moment of its publication, has, often, to combine actualities with prognostics.*

In such a case, simply consult the Theatre list in a daily newspaper.

---

133. A *verveux* is a conically shaped fishing net mounted on rings of osier.

134. The lark-hunt itself, evidently, is meant to be seen as a kind of dance.

Théâtre-Français: *The Repertoire, principally* Une Chaîne (*revival*), *with* ***Favart, Got, Delaunay and Coquelin.***

Opéra: *Inauguration, for the season, of the Special Sunday Performances. On the classic days for opera, the repertory:* Les Huguenots *and* Robert-le-Diable, La Favorite; *and* Guillaume Tell, *for the return of* ***Faure.***

Odéon: *continuation of* La Jeunesse de Louis XIV, *with Léonide Leblanc, Hélène Petit and Gil Naza, a success alternating with another:* L'École des maris *in which Isabelle is played by Mlle* ***Blanche Baretta;*** Le Célibataire et l'homme marié *by Wafflard and Fulgence, with its delicious costumes of 1821; an evening of Repertory ending with that marvel,* Le Tricorne enchanté, *by GAUTIER.*

Opéra-Comique: Le Pardon de Ploermel ***(Zina Dalti and Lina Bell; Bouhy, Lhérie)*** *is to give up some fine soirées to* Mireille. *The repertory; notably* Le Pré-aux-Clercs, *with* ***Mme Carvalho, Duchesne, Melchissédec.***

Vaudeville: Le Roman d'un jeune homme pauvre, *the last, let us hope!, of the series,* Les Ganaches, *is going to give us* ***Jane Essler*** *for the new piece by D'ENNERY,* Marcelle.

Gymnase: Gilberte, a *new piece by GONDINET. Gilberte,* ***Mlle Delaporte,*** *alas! up to 10 October; the other roles,* ***Angelo, Fromentin, Helmont,*** *all with admirable toilettes; and* ***Lesueur, Landroli, and Ravel,*** *with the whole troupe.*

Variétés: *mixed entertainment until the première (said to be for 10 October) of* Les Prés Saint-Gervais, *by SARDOU, GILLE and LECOCQ; the one-acter by MEILHAC and HALÉVY:* l'Ingénue, *and* Les Pommes du voisin, *both great novelties.*

Palais-Royal: Revival, every evening, of ancient fooleries and laughter always fresh, suggested to the reader of advertisements and journals by that illustrious name, LABICHE. Or the Repertory.

Gaîté: *continuation of* Orphée aux Enfers, *with a new Act, 'The kingdom of Neptune', by the Master: décors by Fromont, costumes by Grévin, Italian dancers:* ***Christine Roselli and Fontabello*** *in the ballet of the ocean-nymphs, under the direction of M. Fuchs. The Lake, the Flood, the Storm, the Enchanted Cave, the Bottom of the Sea, the Fish Quadrille, the Awakening of Amphitrite, the Atlantide (an underwater city): to think that each of these words, enough by themselves to open the door to magic, represents a complete and cunning and decorative spectacle!*

Porte-Saint-Martin: Don Juan d'Autriche, *the play by CASIMIR DELAVIGNE, superbly cast with* ***Dumaine, Taillade, René Didier, and Fraisier,*** *etc.; madame* ***Patry,*** *etc., and no less superbly staged.*

Châtelet: *Continuation of* Les Deux orphelines, *which, till this theatre changes its name to 'Opéra Populaire', will continue to moisten handkerchiefs, both of lace and of linen.*

Ambigu: L'Officier de fortune, *a new five-acter by MM. JULES ADENIS and JULES ROSTAING, in a theatre redecorated by* ***M. Fisher:*** *success in every* *department, in the auditorium, on the stage and in the wings, where there is a contrivance destined to become famous.*

Bouffes-Parisiens: *Continuation of* La Jolie parfumeuse. ***Théo*** *– enough said! No, because even at her side, one notices* ***Mme Grivot;*** *then* Madame l'Archiduc, *that winter-long soirée.*

Renaissance: Thérésa and Paulin-Menier *(bravo! and bravo!) in* La Famille Trouillat, *which, were it even a masterpiece (and it is amusing), ought to give the place of honour on its poster to the diva beside the title of five or six broad jests which become great songs.*

Folies-Dramatiques: La Fille de madame Angot, *Paris having, for two months, forgotten its operetta, wants above all to see it again. Women, whose function it is to make comparison between tenors, will, at the Folies, make the acquaintance of M.* **Mario Widmer**, *just as we, of the male sex, will go to compare* **Desclauzas**, *who has remained faithful to her role, with herself, or applaud Rose-Marie.*

Cluny: Les Bêtes noires du capitaine, *a charming new comedy by M. PAUL CELLIÈRES, with* **Lacressonière**; *before that, a verse one-acter by M. Dreyfus,* Le Médaillon de Colombine, *an exquisite piece.*

Théâtre-des-Arts *(formerly the Menus-Plaisirs):* Mon abonné, *a one-acter:* Revendication, *in three Acts; and* Trente cinq ans du bail, *another comedy by M. Paul CELLIÈRES: five acts, three novelties.*

Théâtre Scribe *(formerly the Athénée):* Hélène et Marcelle *(première).*

Château d'Eau: *Revival of Paris la nuit, with the Corsican brothers revealing the Quadrille des Gambilleurs.*

Délassements-Comiques *(formerly the* ***Nouveautés****):* Le Rhinocéros et son enfant, *with the maddest of texts, by M. SAINT-FARGEAU and music by a genuine and delicious musician,* M. DE SIVRY, *before* Le Vicomte de Chrysocale, *an attractive one-acter by* MM. DHARMENON *and* ESCUDIER, *with music* by E. ETTLING.

Folies-Bergère: *An English pantomime (despite its title, Madame Benoiton will stay at home); English acrobats; an English ballet of women pugilists – a strange and charming spectacle: a worthy frame for the exhibition of the Tattooed Man. When shall we have the Gymnastic Dog?*

Finally, the ***Théâtre Déjazet:*** Les Heures diaboliques, *first performances in a separate auditorium, so as not to interrupt the latest success, refurbished during the night: Beaumarchais,* Le Cadet de Gascogne, *first performances, with Donato and the whole theatre all gold; and at the Folies Marigny:* Mimi Chiffon, *first performances, the summer of Bougival transported to the autumn of the Champs-Élysées.*

The ***Salle Ventadour*** *and the* ***Théâtre Lyrique*** *are going to be reborn from their past, their ashes, rather than from the sleep of the summer closure, which now no longer holds sway over any Parisian theatre: the one on the 15th with a very* *famous Italian troupe, orchestral conductor, Vianesi, and later, a French troupe, conducted by Constantin: the other, in November, with the* Jeunesse du roi Henri, *and musical preoccupations. Our best wishes to MM.* ***Bagier*** *and* ***Castellano.***

* * *

Other places for distraction and pleasure, both day and night, after the ***Jardin d'Acclimatation*** *(animals, notably two little orang-utans and a pair of giraffes, plus flowers and the last orchestra): a promenade which will acclimatise the sun in wintertime.*

The ***Cirque d'Été:*** *where one can still see those extraordinary skaters Goodrich and Curtis.*

The ***Panorama,*** *in the Champs-Élysées, with the spectacle, Le Siège de Paris, magnificently evoked by the painter PHILIPPOTEAUX.*

Robert-Houdin: *'The Maharajah's Cabinet,' by its inventors Robert-Houdin the Younger and Brunnet,*[135] *and how many other things!*

The ***Théâtre-Miniature:*** *last performances for the belated 'laureate', a ticket for* Le Vainqueur de Jemappes *as first prize.*

A sweetshop, the ***Salle des Familles:*** *but less barley-sugar is consumed here than at the preceding theatre, from which the spectators return, older and wiser, to applaud authentic premières and genuine debuts.*

CORRESPONDENCE WITH SUBSCRIBERS

4 October 1874

Mme LA COMTESSE S . . . , MILAN. – It is a cushion that you need, Madame: they no longer tend to make them in tapestry; the fashion today is to embroider them with coloured material upon black. A sample, with all accessories, costs from fifteen to twenty francs at our Special store for Women's Needlework, Au Sphynx.[136]

Mme L . . . , TOULOUSE. – Have a dress made, Madame, of black cashmere trimmed with English crêpe *or* crêpe *impératrice: the latter, though of as high quality as the English* crêpe, *is less expensive. You will be well aware that you cannot wear ready-mades from now on, the shawl and long veil being* de rigueur *for three months; but what is less widely known is that earrings should be in hardened wood rather than in jet. You will wish me to go on? For you will be glad*

135. But see ante, p. 39.

136. See their *carte de visite*, p. 46.

to question me on the strict etiquette of mourning: black cashmere and crêpe *during the first six months, black silk and smooth black* crêpe *during the six which follow; finally, grey, violet or black during the last six weeks. Yes, one wears mourning for a father-in-law just as for a father.*

Mme de B . . . , FONTAINEBLEAU. – You are right, dear Reader, a sewing-machine is indispensable in a household such as yours: if you do not use it yourself, you will have your femme de chambre *do so. Many manufacturers give lessons free of charge if you purchase from them; otherwise, they have to be paid for. I assure you that in seven or eight lessons, or even less, your* femme de chambre *will be able to do whatever is needed. Send her here, and we will introduce her to a well-established firm, who will supply her with a machine guaranteed for a number of years. She will be perfectly capable of making Childrens' Costumes, of which we would send you the patterns. As regards these, be sure to give me exact measurements, since all five-year-olds do not have the same waistline or breadth of shoulder.*

Mme La Comtesse S . . . , SEVILLE. – We have seen at Frainais & Cramagnac's[137] *Indian cashmeres in the region of a thousand to twelve hundred francs; they are pretty without being expensive, which would be an extravagance these days. Let us know, Madame, whether you would like yours long or square; our ignorance on this matter is all that has prevented us from choosing you one. But we would recommend a square one, shawls no longer coming to a point. As soon as we hear from you, the garment, in its box, will be sent to you on receipt of payment.*

Mme LA DUCHESSE DE LA T . . . , MADRID. – Madame, if you have only two girls, dress them the same; if you have three you will not do this, or they will look like a boarding school. No, the same hat will perhaps not be suitable for the two sisters; as for coiffure, *choose different ones to suit their faces.*

Mme B . . . , TAILORESS, BRUSSELS. – The costume for a Young Girl which we gave in the last issue would perfectly well suit a Young Woman; only, you need to trim the velvet skirt with flounces or puffs, or even both.

Mme LA MARQUISE DE C.L . . . BEAUVAIS. – You want to confide your child only to nuns, Madame, otherwise we would ask you to glance at the carte de visite *opposite, from an excellent* pension *that we would recommend; or we would consult our invaluable adviser on all educational matters. It remains for us to prove our maternal experience and, as you request, suggest the best plan for four years of youth. It is a simple matter: in your city of Beauvais is there a house of the order of the Sacré-Cœur? Place your dear child there for two years, to make the separation less cruel and prepare you for the greater one entailed by two further*

137. Specialist in shawls, 82, rue Richelieu.

years in the Mother Houses in Paris, among some of the greatest names in France. The same system of education is provided in all the Houses of this order, so the instruction will not suffer. Need we say that these ladies will give their charges a perfect education and fill their young hearts with praiseworthy feelings. This is well known, and I am reminding you of what you know better than I; but one likes to have one's private thoughts confirmed by someone in whom one has confidence. We need only insist on one point: that, though education is pushed to its limits in these pious sanctuaries, needlework is not neglected, nor are social accomplishments. To interest young persons just as much as to edify them: that is the motto.

Mme BRENC . . . , NANTES. – The Capulet[138] *can be worn by young girls; this very simple garment completes their outdoor or visiting costume.*

Mrs M.Y., LONDON (or WILTS). – Yes, real flowers are very pretty in the hair, but they hardly stand up to the atmosphere of a ball; after an hour or two at the most they have faded. That is why, for your coiffure *at this festivity (an official one and quite out of season) I would prefer artificial flowers, which can be most marvellous in their workmanship.*

No more letters. Now we shall speak to all our lady readers. First:

BARGAINS

Toys, novelties, even villas and châteaux during the spa season; bargains in the Shops or at the Auction-rooms, or exchanges among people of fashion. But to give this chapter its full interest we must wait for the return of connoisseurs. Ladies and Gentlemen, the city calls you, and the sudden brilliance taken by window-displays in the first bad weather: we mean, tomorrow.

ADVICE ON EDUCATION

The express trains of all lines and at all hours are bringing back parents and their children. For parents who, wanting to keep their children at home, would not choose for them any of the educational establishments recommended by us in the adjoining cartes-de-visite, *yet would hesitate for them to be educated entirely in isolation, by means of tutors or governesses (two of the latter, by our mediation, put themselves at the disposition of families: one from abroad, who speaks almost all the northern languages as well as French, the other French and a remarkable musician, but more in the nature of a* dame de compagnie), *we would mention a celebrated Course for Young Ladies. Truly, we hardly need to remind parents*

138. Originally, a Pyrenean woman's cap or hood.

(except of the fact that it is now preparing for its 24th reunion), of this group of mothers, teachers and young ladies, the Cours Lévy Alvarès, *which flourishes in the rue de la Chaussée-d'Antin and, simultaneously, in the place Royale*[139] *in the Marais. The girl and young person receive there all the instruction that a woman can and should acquire and mingle it with the teaching they receive at home. What is charming is that more than one mother, interested in questions she has forgotten since her childhood and reminded of them by the Course, becomes a fellow-pupil of her daughter. No need to go into any details here, for the Director (Officer of the Academy) will send parents a prospectus on request.*

Books for the new term? We are ready to recommend all the good works addressed to Monsieur S.M., 29, rue de Moscou, by authors or booksellers, as requested by families; but nevertheless leave complete liberty of judgement. The only exception we make to this impartiality is the books published by the House of Hachette, which, at this moment, is enlarging for the school year of 1874-5 its vast catalogue of works, prescribed almost officially and recommended by the Council for Public Instruction before being so here. The note on education in every one of our issues could be filled with praise of the vast efforts of those publishers to keep abreast of current syllabuses and thinking.

Let us bring to an end this special discussion, the proportions of which, somewhat extensive compared with the space devoted to Bargains, prove our eagerness to master such a prime subject for a Gazette, which gives news not only of the world but of the family.

139. Now called place des Vosges.

Issue 4

QUATRIÈME LIVRAISON — DIMANCHE 18 OCTOBRE 1874

LA DERNIÈRE MODE

GAZETTE DU MONDE & DE LA FAMILLE

PARIS — Directeur : MARASQUIN — FRANCE

Paraît le 1er et le 3e Dimanche du mois, avec le Concours

DANS LA MODE & LE GOUT PARISIEN

EN MUSIQUE

DES PRINCIPAUX COMPOSITEURS

EN LITTÉRATURE

DE THÉODORE DE BANVILLE, LÉON CLADEL, FRANÇOIS COPPÉE, ALPHONSE DAUDET, LÉON DIERX, EMMANUEL DES ESSARTS, ERNEST D'HERVILLY, ALBERT MÉRAT, STÉPHANE MALLARMÉ, CATULLE MENDÈS, SULLY PRUDHOMME, LÉON VALADE, AUGUSTE VILLIERS DE L'ISLE ADAM, ÉMILE ZOLA, ETC.

TOILETTE DE VILLE & TOILETTE DE GRANDE VISITE

The transvestism of the hunting-field versus the seemliness of the nuptial; the tug-of-war between the *château* and the Town, and between the Right Bank and the Left: Madame de Ponty's thoughts, this fortnight, run all upon antitheses.

FASHION

Paris, 18 October 1874

Autumn has begun, as this Journal has truly done, with this season. The last two of our columns have sketched, in general terms but not without some detail, the more or less astonishing transformation Fashion had made by that date. To study Paris life in its pleasures and its duties everywhere, on the public scene and in private – such is our aim, as even an inattentive reading of our Journal will reveal. Celebrations simply for their own sake? Yes, and because they are an excuse, and an occasion, for dressing up. 'Go there', and 'Here is how you should go': these words will constantly be found in our column, and 'Madame, with such-and-such a toilette *you could well stay at home, saved from the tedium of the long hours by this silk or that lace, enchanted and as it were made new to yourself'.* Toilettes, *and more* toilettes, *in colour or black-and-white, separate or as part of the text or sometimes simply created by words. Here they are, ordered from our dressmakers yesterday, and to be ordered again tomorrow, by the guests of the long-drawn-out weeks of* château *life.*

Am I speaking of party dresses? No, of hunting costumes; and in order to judge them, and bring out their attraction, one has to imagine as background, not a drawing-room or a street, but the greenery of a park. Two sketches, the first of them made at one of our great fashion houses, when the garment, with the name of a great lady upon it, was en route for a princely, nay almost royal, hunting-lodge. A short skirt, enough to show a hazelnut-coloured boot, laced with a green ribbon. A bodice fitting very closely and outlining the bust. A little nut-coloured felt hat, pierced with a green feather. Its material? Autumn-coloured cloth, dark green or almost brown. Shall we compare, with this actual costume, one we have imagined for ourselves? Breton trousers, closed and frilled at the knee with elastic; soft boots in natural deerskin. Short skirt in navy-blue cloth, trimmed with silk braids. It is lifted up at the back of the waist by pleats, in a nun-like manner, but flat in front. Jacket of navy-blue cloth, double-breasted and buttoning over a waistcoat of the same; silk trimmings on the pockets and sleeves. A Tyrolean hat in natural grey felt with navy-blue velvet and artificial plumes.

Which would you choose, Mesdames, while there is still time and the huntsmen have barely sounded their first summons? The first of these costumes, as simple and practical as the other, has the advantage of taking its style from one of our great beauties; the second, of having been worn by no-one. But now, mainly to distinguish the glamour essential to the Theatre from the sobriety which more befits the Town (even when the Town is the Forest!), I must describe the hunting costume, which our noble absentees were not in Paris last week to applaud, of an actress now preparing to display it in St. Petersburg. (I am referring to ***Mademoiselle Delaporte,*** *who appeared in* Philiberte *at the Variétés.) A skirt in bronze silk with little flounces. Tunic in light grey wool, striped with gold, silver and bronze braid. Grey felt hat trimmed with grey feathers, and a bronze-coloured scarf, with a gold and silver tassel at the end. To brave the open air is impossible for this costume, which needs the glare of footlights. But what the Diana of the Tuileries*[140] *herself, goddess though she be, would not be able to procure, should she step down from her marble pedestal – to go, not to a theatrical costumier, but to a fashionable tailor or dressmaker, to be transformed from huntress to 'sportswoman' – is the jewellery almost indispensable to hunting dress today. Steel? Jet? No. Amber or coral? Certainly not. No, but rather the crosses of orders bestowed by foreign courts on ambassadors, wives, or ladies of immemorial ancestry, meant to be worn on the bosom on formal occasions: the order of the Star of Austria, of St. Elizabeth of Portugal, of Maria Luisa of Spain, St. Anne of Munich and the other St. Anne of Wurzburg, with St. Elizabeth (all from Bavaria), and the Ribbon of St. Catherine of Russia.*[141]

With this charming paradox of masculine dress, and the insignia of official merit, worn for an hour by feminine beauty and nobility, let us compare the traditional woman's dress par excellence, *the white and filmy one worn at a wedding. Could the contrast be more complete? I have just seen a delightful vision at La Trinité Church,*[142] *which prompts me to add, after a quick impression of its lace and flowers, some notes on contemporary etiquette relating to our presence at the ceremony. A wedding dress is not meant to impress. One simply accepts it as it is: mysterious; following fashion and not following fashion; tempering contemporary taste with vague reminiscences of the distant past; and hiding brand-new details under the conventional, as with a veil.*

The costume was as follows: a white satin underskirt covered with a tarlatan skirt, each flounce finishing with a ruche; there were at least twenty on the train, but I only counted four on the front. Tunic pleated crosswise and attached to the skirt; on the bottom of the tunic, a fringe decorated with white pearl. A broad satin

140. The statue of Diana, by E. Lévêque, now stands in the north-west corner of the Tuileries gardens.

141. The image is nicely caught by Morin in his cover-design: see Frontispiece, p. v.

142. This church, completed in 1867, was situated in a very grand part of Paris, and was noted for its socialite atmosphere.

sash to one side, falling on to the tunic and attached to the train with a bow: this bow was itself attached to the skirt with a crown of orange blossom with a train. The bodice was high and had basques, completely lined with satin, as were the sleeves; and all the trimming of the basques consisted of an ample chicorée[143] *and a bouquet of orange blossom, placed to one side, towards the shoulder. A veil of* tulle illusion *and orange-blossom skilfully intertwined in the hair. Everything at once worldly and virginal, and giving no hint of a ball gown, which would have been a grave fault of taste. No, somehow rich and yet light and suggestive of reserve. As for the women guests at this ceremony, Fashion retains its full 'kingship of a day' over them, though subject to customs which alter over the years. So long as Society has not yet resumed its sway over the Town (and at present, we note, aristocratic weddings still take place in the private chapels of* châteaux*), the law for this winter remains uncertain. We are, thus, still under the summer rule which, I take it, you know? The rule for weddings is double, like Paris herself, divided by her river. Left Bank:*[144] *no deviation from the traditional ceremonial. The costume is special: white hat, and light-coloured dresses with a train, set off by a lace cape. Right Bank (by contrast): the visiting-dress in fashion at the moment. This is the rule, though it applies to both in one particular: the wonderful earrings worn during the day give way (and will continue to) to diamond studs.*

This column of mine grows almost unlike itself. For, though dedicated to entertainments, it has been dealing only with solemn ceremonies, or with quite out-of-the-way pleasures. Its role, though real, very real, in the system of the seasons, is to sound the note of fantasy. A piece of news, completing today's bulletin, brings home this fact supremely. 'What is it?' you may ask. It is the announcing of an emblematic Butterfly, which, huge and magnificent and made from light and delicious fabrics, will, my dear Ladies, lift its motionless flight to one or other of your cheeks, replacing, with its fantasy, the historic ruff of these late years. Your curled coiffure will let fall its ringlets between its two wings. It is (surely?) a brilliant invention, recalling the metamorphoses – a woman's face joined to the gauzy wings of insects – in Grandville's[145] *old albums. But no, it springs from the genius of another magician, no less extraordinary, and master, not of vignettes, but of the sublime and daily-renewed pageant of Paris, of Vienna, of London and St. Petersburg: the great Worth.*[146]

MARGUERITE DE PONTY

143. A ruche in the shape of the chicory leaf.

144. By 'Left Bank', Mallarmé is referring to the very conservative Faubourg Saint-Germain.

145. The fantastic illustrations of Grandville (pseudonym of Jean-Ignace-Isidore Gérard, 1803–47) often portrayed his contemporaries as animals.

146. See p. 124–5.

After the amusements of transvestism, Mme de Ponty comes to the attractions of narcissism. 'Madame, with such-and such a *toilette* you could well stay at home, saved from the tedium of the passing hours by this silk or that lace, enchanted and as it were made new to yourself.' Ix has already broached the same topic, though less drastically, in Issue 1: 'For, indeed, what does it signify, Madame, that in your salon, the scene of your triumphs, the pier-glass is carved with a tragic or comic mask, a flute and paint-brushes, and a text half-unrolled, since all this bygone French style (still in fashion!) does no more than frame a mirror where you encounter yourself? . . .' There is a great coherence in Mallarmé's ideas, and one remembers how central narcissism is to his poems. For instance in the great apostrophe of Hérodiade:

O miroir!
Eau froide par l'ennui dans ton cadre gelée
Que de fois et pendant des heures, désolée
Des songes et cherchant mes souvenirs qui sont
Comme des feuilles sous ta glace au trou profond,
Je m'apparus en toi comme une ombre lointaine,
Mais, horreur! des soirs, dans ta sévère fontaine,
J'ai de mon rêve épars connu la nudité![147]

But not only to the poems. It is central also to his theory of poetry. 'As for me', he wrote in 1867, 'poetry stands in the place of love because it is in love with itself, and its pleasure in itself falls back deliciously into my soul'.[148] There is here a sort of definition of the *Symboliste* poem.

As for the everyday narcissism condemned by moralists, Mme de Ponty and Ix recommend it to their women readers without compunction. It is in this sense that Mallarmé's fashion magazine is a commentary on fashion magazines – not so much to pass judgements as to shake every ounce of meaning out of the word 'fashion'. The imagined reader can be thought of as part of the *décor* that Mallarmé is constructing. As Judy Kravis writes in her *The Prose of Mallarmé,* 'the reader virtually becomes the book, and the book itself is but an ornament in a world of ornaments'.[149]

147. O mirror! Cold water frozen in your frame, how many times, and for hours, desolated by dreams and seeking my memories which are like leaves in the deeps of your ice, I appeared in you like a distant shadow, but, horrors! at evening, in your severe fountain, I have known the nudity of my scattered dream.

148. To Henri Cazalis, 14 May 1867.

149. Judy Kravis, *The Prose of Mallarmé: the Evolution of a Literary Language* (1976), p. 87.

Black-and-white engravings

First page.

1. Town Dress. – Black velvet skirt. Natural white cashmere tunic, trimmed with a fringe of the same: the arangement repeated three times. A fitted basquin *in black velvet, with Japanese buttons.*

2. Formal Visiting Dress. – Overskirt in grey Russian faille, *piped with satin. A tunic-scarf of the same shade, with velvet and satin stripes; this tunic attached to the train with a bow is trimmed with a stylish fringe. A little shawl; a pleated cape over the shoulder, in fact attached, but looking as if thrown back.*

Middle pages.

3. Chapeau Lebrun. *A model hat from Mme Moreau Didsbury. Broad curved rim, very low crown covered with black velvet, a plume of black feathers with an aigrette at the side: under the brim, a crown of broad black velvet bows with a big bouquet of red roses, a ribbon fluttering behind.*

4. Comb and coiffure 'Virgil'. This hairstyle is made with an 80-centimetre plait, the placing of the comb allowing the intertwining of the locks. The addition of three tortoiseshell balls would make this an enchanting style for a dinner-party.

In this Issue we meet for the first time Mme de Ponty's ingratiating, supposedly English, colleague, 'Miss Satin'. Her role is said to be to speak for the foreign colony in Paris and for fashion and highlife everywhere. In fact, however, as we soon find, her function is to bring news of the great Parisian dress-shops and beauty-experts, especially those who have a visiting-card in the magazine, and to undertake commissions for correspondents. By this she allows Mme de Ponty's meditations to remain unsullied by commerce.

On her first appearance, Miss Satin extols the hatmakers Mmes Moreau-Didsbury for their *chapeau Helena Fourment* and their Virgil comb (with a passing gibe at correspondents who ask, in their innocence, 'Who is Helena Fourment?'). In Issue 5 she will eulogise the 'blue-of-dreams' dress of the great Charles Frederick Worth and in Issue 6 eloquently evoke the artificial flowers from 'Louise and Lucie', made by their 'fingers like morning roses, but an artificial morning, one which opens calyxes and pistils of cloth'. In the final issue she will imagine a new régime for perfumes. The exquisite beauty-preparations (with their exquisite names, *Crême-neige* and *Lait d'Hébé)* of Messrs. Pinaud and Meyer should not, she will write, be banished to the bathroom but, filling porcelain flasks and Bohemian glassware, should give out their scent in the boudoir.

'Marasquin', in a retrospective synopsis of the magazine in Issue 6 (pp. 156–7), reveals that, after all, 'Miss Satin' is not English, her name being merely a pseudonym for a well-known Parisian lady.

THE FASHION GAZETTE

My first chat

'My first chat'. Three very simple words, but already several hundred subscribers are quite worried. There are those among you, Mesdames, who dislike anything new. 'Her first chat', you ask; 'so there are going to be a number?' Then you add, 'What a pity! Our journal was so complete, so artistic, so well edited!' Eventually, La Dernière mode *drops out of your hands altogether: you have looked at the bottom of the page and seen a foreign name, exclaiming, 'An Englishwoman!'*

To tell the truth, Ladies, that is what I expected. This word 'Fashion', this signature, this intrusive half-page in place of a description of the Five Costumes: it was not likely it would be received with enthusiasm. Yet, in your own interest, I must persevere.

The management has commissioned me to make a confession. It shall be brief and loyal.

In your Journal, we had forgotten the Ladies of the foreign colony in Paris, and indeed foreign Ladies everywhere: forgotten them all!

We were so preoccupied with yourselves, Ladies, that it was as if the festivities in London or Moscow or Vienna did not exist. In consequence, what a shower of letters there has been, bearing bizarre postage-stamps and delicately hinting that susceptibilities have been injured!

Nor is that all. The ladies of Paris were soon sending us requests for new kinds of information. Here is one, opened at random, which asks to know the origin of the Rubens-style hat known as the 'Helena Fourment', and adds, 'Who was Helena Fourment?' To help us in our researches, we are told that this remarkable hat was first worn by a Lady at a party this autumn.

A second letter asks how to obtain the 'Virgil' comb which, so delightfully, binds the blond tresses of the Honourable Mrs P--.

There is a touch of the American here; it is a little hard to credit. But what such letters reveal is the need for a rapprochement *between all members of High Society, whether belonging to Paris, the home of all elegances, or to other, perhaps far-flung, centres of fashionable life.*

The management of La Dernière mode, *eager to satisfy this need, means to anticipate such demands by announcing a 'Fashion Gazette', designed to keep French ladies abreast of developments abroad.*

Now it only remains for me to reply to the requests concerning the 'Helena Fourment' hat and the 'Virgil' comb.

Helena Fourment was the second wife of the great Rubens, and the hat which he most admired was exactly the one which had such success among Lady —'s set. It comes from the workrooms of Mmes Moreau-Didsbury (23, boulevard des Capucines); and these ladies are also the creators of the new model which you find illustrated on the back of this page, facing the fashionable hairstyle with the 'Virgil' comb (24, rue de la Chaussée d'Antin).

'Helena Fourment' hat, 'Virgil' hairstyle: Art and Nature.

To reconcile you to the 'Fashion Gazette', Ladies, be assured that it will often ask you to turn the page, thus directing you to the illustrations, which will reproduce, as often as possible, the latest creations of Paris's fashion houses; for the English word 'Fashion' means the same as 'La mode' with which it is the Gazette's mission to occupy itself.

MISS SATIN

Ix, in this issue, is characteristically needling about the Philistine seductions of *château* life, with its *charades,* and its gossip about so-called 'brilliant' titled amateurs; also equally needling about the commercial theatre. Of the friends and genuine writers whom he mentions, the poet Ernest d'Hervilly contributed a sonnet ('At home') to the present issue and Catulle Mendès a short story *(La Petite servante)* to Issue 5.

PARIS CHRONICLE

Theatres, Books, Fine Arts, Echoes from the Salons and the Seaside

*I am not one of those who believe that producing fine books or stage-scenarios is the prerogative of professionals alone; and were one to divide authors of all periods into amateurs and professionals, one would find amongst the former some of the geniuses who have fired the world with enthusiasm – from King Solomon to Baron **** or *******. However, as I know none of the manuscripts of the day, signed with names made famous by birth or wealth before being so by a masterpiece (a topic of conversation from the shores of the ocean to the leaf-strewn terraces of noble desmesnes) I shall wait till such masterpieces, stamped by the bookbinders of the rue de la Paix with Japanese imaginings and coats of arms no less imaginary, make themselves known. I shall be content to speak of plays, if not of music. by ordinary authors, circulated before the winter to actresses, actors and prompters. What a precious exchange, if, upon studying the titles I am about to list, one of my Lady Readers would graciously write to me with others preserved in her* *memory! It would be such a boon that I would then promise that this third chronicle of the theatre-season should not be my last.*

But what am I saying? I am forgetting that no woman, at this moment, has time to write even the briefest of notes, given that the opening of the Season (officialdom having commanded in vain that Amusement should begin), will be late, very late, this year, not till after the private gaieties staged, on non-hunting days, all over France. Tableaux vivants,[150] *and perhaps even* Tableaux parlants, *with their charm and their sophisticated elegance, will outshine the commoner doings of the Theatre. Here is how men, keeping to themselves their verses and their symphonies, and women, depending on mere appearance and gestures, on their smile and beautiful eyes, will supplant the ancient collaboration of poet and actor. But not without a struggle! For if the return of the Theatre, this year, has been marked more by old-style verve than by richness in its ideas, nothing is lost. At the Théâtre Français, where a slight illness of the delicious Sarah Bernhardt has caused a temporary interruption to* Zaire, *we shall have Alexandre Dumas'* Le Demi-monde, *and maybe later his* Le Fils naturel. *Both these are revivals; but* Joseph Balsamo,[151] *that great play only just completed, altogether modern and not even translated from the* Book of Judges *or* Deuteronomy: *who knows, maybe we shall see it?*

Monsieur Nicole, Le Roi des faiseurs, Pièges à loup, *three titles forming one play, by AUGIER. This is an event in the green-room as well as in the auditorium; and both actors and playgoers are eager for the revival of the same dramatist's* Philiberte, *in which the charming Mademoiselle Broisat will make her début.*

Is that all? No, not even there, for there is also Cadol's La Grande maman. *But what is on elsewhere? Sardou's* La Haine *at the Gaîté, to be seen for the sake of* **Lafontaine and Mesdames Marie Laurent and Lia Felix:** *also of* **Rubé, Chapron, Cambon, Cheret, Lavastre and Desplechin,** *who have conjured up, from their magnificent dreams, the settings for five acts, while six hundred costumes designed by M. THOMAS will evoke, bringing these costumes to life, strange and very beautiful personages as well as voices charged with emotion: for there is a drama*

---

150. A craze for *tableaux vivants* had already begun in the last years of the *ancien régime.*

151. *Joseph Balsamo* (the real name of Cagliostro) was originally a *roman-feuilleton* by Alexandre Dumas *père,* published in 1846–8.

somewhere in all this, a stirring one. Without counting the fact that that musician![152] *the organiser of the splendours of this place,*[153] *forgetting the number of days in that half of the calendar known as Winter, risks, with dazzling irony, to put on, on the heels of his* Orphée, *his* Geneviève de Brabant! *But* we *are not to speak here of music, even with* ***Patti*** *at the French Opéra! a sad privation for a day. Let us forget all that, and the other Opéra too, the Italiens, with their classic staircase.*[154]

Meilhac and Halévy recently gave *a reading of their* La Veuve, *at the Gymnase,* ***Desclée***[155] *being absent, but with* ***Blanche Pierson*** *in her place, in a different costume for each Act – black and grey and parti-coloured, nuances through which the varied talents of that actress will find the way to shine. When shall we see it? Wait first for the return* of La Princesse Georges, *though* ***Desclée*** *will not appear in this either, but rather* ***Mademoiselle Tallandiéra.*** *For they are trying their hardest to get rid of* ***Desclée,*** *but it would be simpler to mourn her genius: to give equal applause to a celebrated actress and to a young woman of great originality, all set to become one. We do not know the date, but we know for a certainty the coming, of* La Parisiane *by M. BARRIÈRE, at the Vaudeville, which will try with this, as it did with MM. Denery and Brésil's* Marcelle, *to dispel the veil of somnolence and oblivion behind which, for the last four months, so many worn-out and merely ghostly characters have moved: and this, in the most delighfully modern of houses!*

Everyone is determined not to fall asleep, even on a chest full of gold; for, in the midst of the success of L'Officier de fortune, *and in spite of the chase across the ice and the escape from the revolving pavilion – those strokes of genius – and of the play's own actual worth, the Ambigu is to begin active rehearsals of* Cocagne, *by FERDINAND DUGUÉ and the late-lamented and so-talented ANICET BOURGEOIS; after which they are already contemplating* Cromwell, *a work by VICTOR SÉJOUR, who, to his recent crown of 'everlastings', will see fresh flowers added and three or four leaves of green laurel. Thus, at the moment when Paris is seeing, at the Porte-Saint-Martin, not without a certain interest, the exhumation, to be followed by a careful reburial, of plays by the 'distinguished' Casimir Delavigne,*[156] *beginning with* Don Juan d'Autriche, *it also knows that, extraordinary if*

---

152. i.e. Offenbach.

153. i.e. the Gaîtê theatre.

154. Ix seems to be referring, in his usual manner, to that scene of fashion, the theatre or opera-house staircase.

155. Aimée-Olympe Desclée (1836–74), French actress. She made a hit in Meilhac and Halévy's *Frou-Frou* and appeared in several plays by Dumas *fils,* dying suddenly, more or less at the height of her fame.

156. Casimir Delavigne (1793–1843), French poet and dramatist.

only for the expense (150,000 francs) involved, the Voyage autour du monde, *that fairy play, that drama, that living geographical atlas, joins to all the other names the popular ones of DENNERY and of the inimitable JULES VERNE. Enough! For each new reference reminds us of a hundred omissions; and our aim, in the hope of attracting new discoveries, was only to mention – with the exception (but we do not even discuss Dance!) of the ballet* Les Djinns, *interpreted by the Opéra Populaire, with music by JEAN TROUBETZKOI, an* attaché at *the Russian embassy in Paris – the reception at one of our great legitimate theatres of a historical drama,* Le Devoir *(this must mean civic duty), signed with the name (it is the only indiscretion known to us), not of a nobleman but of his* château. *Of the guesses at the author whispered behind fans, surmises based upon the* Almanach de Gotha *or the* Stockbrokers' Annual,[157] *I caught no more than a charming murmur, fresh and frivolous but insufficient for historical truth. But do you ask for still more names, to complete this already ample bulletin? To enforce my victory as an exact chronicler I have kept back the ones most dear to me, those of collaborators in this magazine and other friends. M. CATULLE MENDÈS is giving, at the Théâtre-Lyrique, now a 'legitimate' theatre, a vast drama, of great power and lucidity,* Les Mères ennemies. *After a curtain-raiser,* La Jeunesse du roi Henri, *and, at the* ***Théâtre des Arts,*** Justice *(another swift-moving play, no less revealing the hand of a master), following a performance by* ***Mademoiselle Rousseil.*** *The* ***Cluny*** *is rehearsing a piece by GUSTAVE FLAUBERT, written in collaboration with LOUIS BOUILHET; and at the* ***Odéon***, *if the triumphant run of* La Jeunesse de Louis XIV, *by DUMAS PÈRE and DUMAS FILS (with the actor* ***Gil Naza and Léonide Leblanc!***), *ever comes to an end, we shall see the adorable little Japanese comedy,* La Belle Sainara, *by ERNEST D'HERVILLY, of which Paris knows the success it gained, this summer, with a few hundred Alexandrines and a 'romance' by ARMAND*

157. A free rendering of Mallarmé's original, which reads: 'le Mémorial nobiliaire ou la liste des agents de change près la Bourse de Paris'.

GOUZIEN, at the home of Charpentier the publisher, before an audience of 'princes of the mind'. So it happens that, even for those forgetful people who would neglect, equally, the attractive verse one-acter, L'Ilote, *by M. CHARLES MONSELET and ARÈNE, at the* ***Théâtre Français,*** *and an admirable piece of foolery by M. ZOLA at the* ***Cluny*** *(see above), plus I don't know what else, it is still (Muses, you shall not deny it!) poets who write plays and musicians who write music. It is all just as in the past (the future of our winter is now revealed), and it was not of the king of amateurs (though that is what he is!) but of the most indefatigable of visionaries (as he proved himself to the age of seventy by his stream of pamphlets and new editions), that M. Falguière was thinking when he raised that fine statue of Lamartine,*[158] *accepted the other day by a jury of artists and compatriots.*

Ix.

Ix, as will be seen, is here beginning a quiet vendetta, maintained for several more issues, against Sardou's *La Haine*, a drama about Guelfs and Ghibellines in Siena in 1365 which was forthcoming at the Gaîté. The play, with its wildly lavish décor and enormous cast, was receiving much advance publicity, and Ix assumes that his readers will be eager to hear about it. We begin to perceive, however, that he thinks it will be too appalling actually to go and see.[159] His comment on it in Issue 7,[160] which begins 'La Haine, by Sardou, which we shall only just have seen when this Programme appears', is somewhat ambiguous; and something in the wording of his review in the next issue, though more elaborate and adding that 'So much *faste* (extravagance) has perhaps never transfigured a stage-scene of wood and canvas!', suggests that maybe he never saw it. It may be added that, though the first night (3 December 1874) was a glittering affair, this enormously expensive production did very badly, and Sardou asked for it to be taken off after ten or so performances. The theatre manager consoled himself with the reflection that the medieval armour, which had cost 160,000 francs, might come in handy for a revival of *Geneviève de Brabant*.

158. Alexandre Falguière (1831–1900), sculptor. The poet Alphonse de Lamartine (1790–1869), best known for his *Méditations poétiques* of 1820 and for his role in the Provisional Government at the time of the 1848 Revolution, produced a lot of educational and historical hackwork in his later years. The statue is in Mâcon.

159. In this Bernard Shaw, twenty years later, would be much in sympathy with him. 'Of course', writes Shaw about Sardou's *Madame Sans-Gêne*, 'I admire the ingenuity with which Sardou carries out his principle of combining the maximum of expenditure and idle chatter with the minimum of drama; but I have admired that so often that it is beginning to pall on me.'

160. In the Gazette and Programme for the Fortnight.

Seventh leaf

MENU FOR A FAMILY DINNER

Potage Germiny[161]

Butter, Prawns, Anchovies and olives

Cod à la Hollandaise
Haunch of saltmarsh mutton à la Bretonne
Sweetbreads in tomato sauce

Roast partridges – Escarole salad

Fresh cucumbers in cream
Little ramekins of chocolate soufflé

Dessert chosen by the mistress of the house – Pâtisseries

Coffee and brandy, Authentic liqueurs by the Widow Amphoux
Russian cigarettes au Dubèque aromatique[162] *and Havana*
(Grand-Hôtel[163]*)*

WINE
Ordinaire: Île Verte and Côte Rotie

THE CHEF DE BOUCHE CHEZ BRÉBANT

The 'Eighth leaf' of the 'Golden Notebook' is a recipe for Chicken Gumbo, *à la Créole,* as supplied by one of the journal's *Maisons de Confiance:* a delicatessen shop, named *Le Propagateur,* in the boulevard Haussmann. Here, as in the succeeding 'leaf', Mallarmé is evidently remembering the claim that *La Dernière mode* is a 'Family' journal as well as a 'High-life' one.

---

161. Sorrel soup.

162. An aromatic cigarette, favoured by Des Esseintes, the hero of J.K. Huysmans' decadent novel, *À rebours.*

163. Imported cigars could only be obtained from the Grand Hôtel, 12, boulevard des Capucines, and two other locations.

Eighth leaf

Chicken Gumbo
(An excellent bisque)

Bring to to the boil 1/2 litre of stock, and add 1 lb of okra cut in rings; while they are cooking, brown 125 gr. of ham in lard, and add it to the okra, 1/2 roast chicken cut in pieces and a red pepper chopped finely; let it simmer for 2 hours. Half-an-hour before serving, add 125 gr. of shrimps, 1/2 lobster, 3 crabs and 12 oysters; failing oysters, 1 litre of mussels previously opened in a pan; add the juice of a tomato and a few drops of lemon juice. Serve with a dish of Rice à la créole.

Let me add to this recipe for okra (an excellent vegetable, shaped like a gherkin but ribbed) the information that our readers owe it to the proprietor of a restaurant offering exotic fruits, liqueurs and dishes, which is to open at 56, boulevard Haussmann, under the patronage of the Parisian colonies from South America and the East. All the fashionable customers of the neighbourhood are preparing to bring their native traditions, to make them better known; and more than one of these ladies intend, for their amusement, to come to supervise the preparation of dishes in person and actually take a hand in it. For ladies wishing to taste the gumbo before attempting to cook it themselves, let me tell them that it will be prepared on Thursday 22 October.

That is why this recipe, which, like some future ones, is owed to the kindness of the 'Promoter' of exotic produce and cuisine, bears the signature,

A CREOLE LADY

* * *

Ninth Leaf

A movable false ceiling for a rented apartment

Not everyone, even of those endowed with Taste, owns a town house, and we know of more than one condemned to the misery of flats. In these places the obstacle to the realising of many a dream is inevitably the ceiling: for the wall, with its wallpaper, is hidden, and doors can be painted; but white as a sheet of paper without a poem, only larger, or veiled with cloud on a sky-blue background at so much the yard, is the Sky offered to the tenant's eyes, as he looks up from his armchair, instead of an allegory in the French style, or a fine coffered ceiling from the country.

One can go some way to imitate this latter at a very moderate cost.

A large deal panel, covering the whole expanse, hides the plaster surface and its 'rose'. Lengthwise, i.e. from the doors to the windows, there run flat and neatly squared off strips of wood, ornamented along their middle, in the same direction, with a rod sunk in a groove, and placed at intervals equal to three times their width. Crosswise, slender joists, ornamented in the same manner but (according to your fancy) three or five or seven times further apart, and made more prominent. So what of the panel, as a background? It should be painted, between the beams, in a flat, dull vermilion, and all the framework in black lacquer (Japanese varnish or carriage paint), except for gold on the rods. Can you picture this ceiling; rich, exquisite and unusual, and set, with its edges and the curving end of its intersecting beams, above the commonplace cornice of the wall (disguised with black paint and gold on the mouldings)? Doors, window-frames and mirror-frames, as well as the overmantel: all disappear under the same paintwork, or under fabric in two shades, black and madder, enhancing each other; likewise frames of wallpaper enclosing great fragments of antique tapestry. A dining-room, the stamped leather of its chairs harmonising with the gold and dark vermilion above; or, to complete the effect, a Study and a Library containing many books, their morocco spines stamped with gilt titles. Lit by a Dutch chandelier, the scene (thanks to the lowness of our rooms) is simple, handsome, enclosed and solitary, a little suggestive of a luxurious ship's cabin.

Here is a furnishing scheme which its moderate cost – 400 francs, or even half of that – allows us, if we cannot remove it, to bequeath it to a landlord, to compensate him for any objection he feels to dark paint and unaccustomed gilding applied to lath and plaster.

According to MARLIANI
Interior decorator

* * *

GAZETTE AND PROGRAMME FOR THE FORTNIGHT

From 18 October to 1 November 1874

THEATRES

Théâtre-Français: *The Repertoire, principally* Une Chaîne *(revival), with* ***Favart, Got, Delaunay and Coquelin:*** *while waiting for the reappearance of Sarah Bernhardt in* Zaire.

Salle Ventadour: Opéra: *Having sung* Les Huguenots *in our language, the marquise de Caux*[164] *cannot, without singing* Faust *again on Sunday 18 and Wednesday 21, desert the public which used to acclaim Patti; and* ***Italiens:*** *opening of the season with* Lucrezia Borgia, *with* ***Mme Pozzoni,*** *that débutante in Paris famous in all the countries bordering the Mediterranean: fashionable and dilettante Paris hangs on the bow raised for the first time by M.* ***Vianesi.***

Odéon: *Hundredth performances of* La Jeunesse de Louis XIV, *with Léonide Leblanc, Hélène Petit and Gil Naza, a success alternating with another:* L'École des maris, *in which Isabelle is played by Mlle* ***Blanche Baretta;*** Le Célibataire et l'homme marié *by Wafflard and Fulgence, with delicious costumes of 1821; an evening of Repertory ending with that marvel,* Le Tricorne enchanté, *by GAUTIER.*

Opéra-Comique: Le Pardon de Ploermel ***(Zina Dalti and Lina Bell; Bouhy, Lhérie)*** *is to give up some fine soirées to* Mireille, *given with the fragments previously cut at the Théâtre-Lyrique, and always and very happily with* ***Mme Carvalho.*** *Repertory, notably* Mignon, *for the return of Mignon – no, I mean of* ***Mme Galli-Marie,*** *it's the same thing.*

Opéra-Populaire: Les Parias *by MEMBRÉE, an unknown opera, then* Les Amours du Diable by *GRISAN, a forgotten opera, then a new ballet by MASSENET; add the conductor MATON, the singers Nicot, Mme REBOUX and the unbelievable luxuriousness and modest price of these evenings: sum total, success.*

Vaudeville: Jane Essler *in the new piece by D'HENNERY and BRÉSIL, and* ***Mlle Barthet,*** *are, certainly to be seen, one close beside the other: let us go to* Marcelle, *if only to delay a repeat of* Le Roman d'un jeune homme pauvre *and the series* Les Ganaches.

Gymnase: Gilberte, *transported to St. Petersburg in the* toilettes *of* ***Mlle Delaporte,*** *who has exiled her talent there, is succeeded by* La Princesse Georges, *revived this time, alas!, without Desclée, though with the very beautiful* ***Mlle Tallandière.***

Variétés: *Let us leave in today's Programme, if only to hasten it, the* première *of* Les Prés Saint-Gervais, *by SARDOU, GILLE and LECOCQ, which we announced last time; meanwhile* ***Schneider*** *features in the playbill, and in* La Périchole*!*

Palais-Royal: *Beautiful* soirées, *with that mad foolery* Le Roi Candaule *and that gay piece* Doit-on le dire? *MEILHAC and HALÉVY, LABICHE* and *DURU:* ***Brasseur,*** **Hyacinthe, Geoffroy, Gil-Peres** *and* **Lhéritier**.

Gaîté: Orphée aux Enfers, *with the new Act, 'The kingdom of Neptune', immortalises itself with the trains of pleasure-seekers from the seven corners of Europe; and now it is Parisians who come to see the dazzling* première *given in their absence.*

---

164. i.e. Patti.

Porte-Saint-Martin: Don Juan d'Autriche, *that historical play by CASIMIR DELAVIGNE, superbly cast with* ***DUMAINE, TAILLADE, RENE DIDIER, and FRAISIER,*** *etc.; Madame* ***PATRY,*** *etc., and no less superbly staged.*

Ambigu: L'Officier de fortune, *by MM. JULES ADENIS and JULES ROSTAING, in a theatre redecorated by* ***M. Fisher:*** *well-deserved success in every department, in the auditorium, on the stage and in the wings, where there is a famous contrivance.*

Bouffes-Parisiens: *Continuation of* La Jolie parfumeuse, *with* ***Théo*** *– enough said! No, because even at her side, one notices* ***Mme Grivot;*** *then* Madame l'Archiduc, *that winter-long soirée.*

Renaissance: Thérésa *in* La Famille Trouillat, *which, were it even a masterpiece (and it is amusing), ought to give the place of honour on its poster to the diva, who makes great songs out of six trifles.*

Folies-Dramatiques: La Fille de madame Angot, *Paris, having forgotten its operetta for two whole months, wants above all to see it again. But* ***Mario Widmer, Declauzas,*** *and that new Clairette,* ***Mlle Perant*** *will not stem till the frosts of winter our impatience to see* La Fiancée du roi de Garbe, *by LITOLFF, in which* ***Mlle Van-Ghel*** *will appear.*

Cluny: Les Bêtes noires du capitaine, *a charming new comedy by M. PAUL CELLIÈRES, with* ***Lacressonière;*** *before that a one-acter lent by the Théâtre-des-Arts*, 35 ans de bail.

Théâtre-des-Arts *(formerly the* ***Menus-Plaisirs*****):** La Closerie des Genêts, *a fine old play, before* L'Idole *with* ***Mlle Rousseil.***

Château d'Eau: *Revival of* La Fille du Diable, with *the* ***Dorst*** *brothers, those clowns, no, those convulsionists, no, those performers of a strange quadrille, called by a calm and aggravating name, the Frétillants [Wrigglers].*

Délassements-Comiques *(formerly the* ***Nouveautés*****):** Le Rhinocéros et son enfant, *with the maddest of texts, by M. SAINT-FARGEAU and music by a delightful musician, M. DE SIVRY, followed by* Le Vicomte de Chrysocale, *an attractive one-acter by MM. DHARMENON and ESCUDIER, with music by M. de Sivry.*

Folies-Bergère: *Everything: The Birds, the Tattooed Man, Lira and Neni, Les Martinettes, the Gypsies and the Gymnastic dog; what shall I say? an operetta, a tightrope walker; the elements of a five-act play, remaining, oh joy! in its elemental state.*

Finally, the ***Theatres Déjazet:*** Les Heures diaboliques, *first performances in a separate auditorium, refurbished during the night so as not to interrupt the latest success: Beaumarchais;* L'Abîme *and the theatre all gold; and at the Folies-Marigny:* Mimi Chiffon, *first performances, the summer of Bougival transported to the autumn of the Champs-Élysées.*

* * *

Other places for distraction and pleasure, both day and night, after the ***Jardin d'Acclimatation*** *(animals, monkeys up their painted poles, all of them: Hamadryas, Chaemas and Papions, plus prolonged flowers and prolonged orchestra, a promenade which will acclimatise the sun in wintertime.*

The ***Cirque d'Été*** *with a septet of prodigies, those mountain-dwellers from the Appenines drawing the voice of doves and of women from earthenware gourds; great success of the season like that, now winter has come, of those extraordinary skaters Goodrich and Curtis.*

The ***Panorama,*** *in the Champs-Élysées, with that bad dream,* Le Siège de Paris, *magnificently evoked by a painter, PHILIPPOTEAUX.*

Robert-Houdin: *'The Maharajah's Cabinet', by its inventor Brunnet, and how many other miracles!, in the boulevard des Italiens; whilst those of the boulevard Saint-Denis are, at the same hour, accomplished by M. LITSONN at the* ***Cercle fantastique.***

The ***Théâtre-Miniature:*** *with* Le Pied de Mouton*: décors, costumes, everything display a magnificence only restricted by its dimensions.*

The ***Salle des Familles:*** *where drama sometimes gives way to marvellous and instructive scientific spectacles etc. for children. Monday, Wednesday and Friday evening, and Sunday afternoon.*

* * *

RAILWAY STATIONS

Such are our pleasures, now restored to us; save for lovers of the hunt and guests of the château, our fellow-citizens no longer rebel against returning. Travel! The word was filled with magic yesterday, and today one wonders what it can have meant.

But how many exceptions all the same!

At the end of October, in NORMANDY, served by the Ligne de l'Ouest, *and in BRITTANY*[165] *and the ARDENNES, served by the* Ligne de l'Est, *there is shooting and the chase, not to mention in the splendid country on the banks of the LOIRE, and bordering part of the SOLOGNE and the CHER, on the route of the* Ligne d'Orléans. *TOURAINE, on the same line as the rich BORDEAUX REGION, and BURGUNDY, on the* Ligne de Lyons, *keep their hold on their great proprietors and attract to their fair domains a succession of guests, not yet acclimatised to the City and its new winter. There they are – if you add the excursions of incorrigible dreamers in quest of autumn in the Paris environs, FONTAINEBLEAU* (Ligne

165. Mallarmé has made a slip. Brittany was served by the Ligne de l'Ouest.

de Lyons, *return ticket), COMPIÉGNE* (Nord) *or VERSAILLES and SAINT-GERMAIN* (Ouest) *– the last expeditions, before the definitive journeys of the cold season. Note the Races from the 22nd to the 25th at CHANTILLY and LAMARCHE* (l'Ouest), *and the REGATTAS of the 25th at ARGENTEUIL, so exciting last year: finally the traditional PILGRIMAGE to the tomb of SAINT-DENIS* (Nord); *so as not to desert Paris, so brilliant, so stirring, for more than a few hours.*

Important Note: The Winter Service is about to begin on almost all the lines.

Farewell to the ***Excursions and Journeys*** *of which we have not space to list the most recent. As the Lines inform us of their closure, you will see here the name of one or other of the Autumn and Winter resorts.*

* * *

CORRESPONDENCE WITH SUBSCRIBERS

18 October 1874

TO ALL OUR SUBSCRIBERS. – Our Journal is a de luxe publication; and, according to the usual practice of booklovers, each issue, after the half-year or the year, should be bound up with the cover. Having on its recto the marvellous frontispiece by Morin, and on the verso the summary of contents and explanations of the Toilettes, *it is an inseparable part of the journal. We urge our subscribers, before receiving further instructions, to keep the cover in perfect condition. As for creasing in copies posted to the provinces or abroad it will disappear during the binding.*

Mme L MARQUISE DE C . . . , BRUSSELS. – I do not know the water you speak of, dear Madame; it may be excellent for preventing hair loss, but I prefer the one recommended to me by Doctor Gendrin, for you can make it yourself. Take a bottle and simply put in fifty grammmes of liquid tar: fill it up with ordinary water and you will have lotion for strengthening the hair. One word more! Be careful not to leave any undissolved tar in the water, for it is a sticky stuff and would be difficult to get out of the hair.

Mme LA DUCHESSE DE C . . . , MADRID. – You make us blush, Madame, by your compliments about our journal; we can thank you only by trying always to deserve them.

Mme LA COMTESSE DE LA P . . . LE MANS. – I can almost venture to promise you some NEEDLEWORK PATTERNS. The administration of LA DERNIÈRE MODE is seriously considering such an adjunct, which is common in Fashion magazines of a different character though an innovation for ours. It will not in any way diminish the high-life quality of our journal, for it will be a separate plate, like the cut-out patterns, and, above all, it will come from the MAGASINS DU

SPHINX,[166] *known throughout fashionable Paris for their marvellous creations in this line.*

Mme R . . . , TOULOUSE. – I have sent you, Madame, the cut-out pattern for the last model (no. 26) (Coloured lithograph of 20 September). Please notice that, for the Polonaise to make the effect of novelty, it must close behind and not in front, where there will absolutely need to be a seam, and it is the back, with a little pointe, *which must be laced. The front of the tunic must be separated from the breadth at the back, forming two distinct pieces. Yes, I can supply you with cut-out patterns in muslin, mounted and trimmed, as well as mounted on paper.*

Mme LA PRINCESSE K . . . , ST.PETERSBURG. – We have received the sum you sent us, Princess; the boxes will be sent on the 29th of this month, containing: a Costume for everyday wear in cheviot gisèle, *another very simple one in Persian cloth with jade trimming, a* Toilette de Visite *in slate-grey velvet and satin trimmed with curled feather, another in pink cashmere with bands of white gauze embroidered with flat silk; then a Ball Gown in blue* poult de soie *with* tulle illusion, *white jet and a garland of pink convolvulus. The three* Toilettes *for a young girl will be very simple: for at fifteen one is still practically a child: Navy-blue Costume, black velvet* Toilette *with a pink satin sash and a Dress of white Chambéry with blue bows. The coiffures or hats to go with these different Costumes and* Toilettes *will match.*

Mme B . . . , MÂCON. – Madame, we have found out the price of the grey waterproof, with hood, and cape (in front only); it costs fifty francs and is of the highest quality.

Mmes DE S . . . , SAINT-BRIEUC and COMTESSE DE C . . . , AVIGNON. – Your two letters, Mesdames, which arrived by the same post and asked me the same question, with the difference that one concerns the now far-distant toilette *worn by mademoiselle Gravier in* Gilberte, *and the other the still-to-be-seen* toilette *of Madame Gravier in* Le Célibataire et l'homme marié, *praised in our last PARIS CHRONICLE, will receive a single reply: for two Parisian ladies momentarily in exile cannot but take an interest in what is going on at the Odéon and the Gymnase; in both theatres the actresses, dresses, 'period' as well as modern, are governed by the surest taste. The Japanese* Toilette *worn by Mademoiselle Delaporte in the second Act was in Paris, and will be in St. Petersburg, a veritable miracle! Overskirt of leather-hued satin embroidered with tortoiseshell peacock feathers. Underskirt: straw-coloured brocade with tortoise-shell embroideries, like those of the skirt, and a border of lace, feather-stitch and tortoiseshell. Mauve satin lining. A great Japanese sash, blue and embroidered with flowers and chenille in all colours, knotted round the waist. Earrings, coiffure and bracelets: all Japanese. The* Toilette *of Madame Gravier, in the first Act, in the Friday repertory nights, is*

166. See their visiting card on p. 46.

reproduced from Restoration engravings. Dress of blue cashmere, high-waisted; sash in black velvet pearled with jet, three little ribbons of black velvet pearled with jet at the bottom of the skirt, flat collar also in velvet and jet, fichu of black tulle with jet, hat in the Directoire *style in white silk trimmed with red daisies and coloured plumes. Well . . . by no means ugly! Admittedly, it was worn so well!*

GOOD WORKS

A crèche is being founded in the 10th arrondissement, near the Hôpital Saint-Louis.

May our readers who did not know of last Sundays's meeting, in the winter-garden of the Vauxhall Tivoli, not regret missing the moving verses recited by Madame Richaud, and the music, the fanfare and the choral societies, the solos both sung and acted, and the salon *comedy, indeed everything, it being such a pretext to dress up and come (I would have liked to note the costume of Madame Rattazzi,*[167] *were it not my intention to aim straight for the end of this Correspondence!).*

As for the collection made by the charitable Ladies, which reached the handsome figure of more than four hundred francs, it could be increased (and by you, Mesdames) by gifts in money or in kind, made to the President, the widow Duval (21, rue de Rome), the Treasurer, Mme Courcel (7, passage Parmentier), the Mayor of the 10th arrondissement, or the curé *of the Eglise Saint-Joseph (172, rue Saint-Maur).*

We have several times announced in this very place, the 'Correspondence with Subscribers', the participation of LA DERNIÈRE MODE in good works; and it is a satisfaction to us to begin with this particular form of charity, the crèche, a matter of interest to all women. Toilettes *and alms: there is between these two things a mysterious link, and particularly in this instance. The muslin of an evening, a miraculous Ball Gown, could equally well be cut to make clean white curtains.*

Madame de Ponty's blandly misogynistic equating of toilettes and alms is, as one notices, entirely characteristic.

ADVICE ON EDUCATION

A Professor in one of the Paris Lycées offers us his enlightened cooperation whenever is a question of recommending a new educational work, of interest to

167. See p. 196.

mothers, an educational method, or even a male or female teacher; through this stroke of good fortune we can claim to be in touch with university thinking.

Briefly, there being so much to choose from or to praise, we urge mothers of families to spend a day, which they themselves will find instructive, exploring the great Educational Bookshops, which, at this moment of the Return to Paris, become an important Parisian rendezvous. The House of ***Hachette,*** *before all, and then* ***Delagrave:*** *from which more than one carriage will be taking, beside childrens' classics, magnificent dictionaries for the mothers themselves; here Littré's dictionary of the French language, there Dezobry's dictionary of history and geography. General reading must also not be neglected, and* ***Furne and Hetzel*** *in the same quarter and* ***Lemerre*** *in the vicinity of the Italiens offer, as well as strictly scholastic textbooks, recreational reading of a serious kind, for Thursdays and Sundays or evening leisure-time in Colleges and Pensions.*

Madame De P.

Issue 5

CINQUIÈME LIVRAISON DIMANCHE 1er NOVEMBRE 1874

LA DERNIÈRE MODE

GAZETTE DU MONDE ET DE LA FAMILLE

PARIS	DIRECTEUR :	FRANCE
Un an . . . . 24 f.	MARASQUIN	Un an . . . . 30 f.
Six mois 13	9, Rue de Châteaudun, 9	Six mois . . . 14

Paraît le 1er et le 3e Dimanche du mois, avec le Concours

DANS LA MODE & LE GOUT PARISIEN

DES GRANDES FAISEUSES, DE TAPISSIERS-DÉCORATEURS, DE MAITRES QUEUX DE JARDINIERS, D'AMATEURS DE BIBELOTS ET DU SPORT

EN MUSIQUE

DES PRINCIPAUX COMPOSITEURS

EN LITTÉRATURE

DE THÉODORE DE BANVILLE, LÉON CLADEL, FRANÇOIS COPPÉE, ALPHONSE DAUDET, LÉON DIERX, EMMANUEL DES ESSARTS, ERNEST D'HERVILLY, ALBERT MÉRAT, STÉPHANE MALLARMÉ, CATULLE MENDÈS, SULLY PRUDHOMME, LÉON VALADE, AUGUSTE VILLIERS DE L'ISLE ADAM, ÉMILE ZOLA, ETC.

TOILETTE DE VISITE & TOILETTE DE RÉCEPTION

Madame de Ponty, now that the Season is in full swing, rhapsodises over the glorious new materials available and reports, dizzyingly, on changes in fashion 'over the last few evenings'.

FASHION

Paris 1 November 1874.

I resume – after an interruption caused by the Festivities, as will happen more than once during this winter – the normal subject of this page, that is to say Fashion: or to be more precise, the Taste of the Season. These fortnightly articles, for those who study them later, should form an exact and complete history of the Variations in Costume over the period of a year; but I should be failing in my duty as historian of toilettes, *and the caprices which vary them, if I did not discuss other matters also, such as the rules prescribed by High-life for the wearing of these* toilettes *in country or in town, or the choice of materials on offer in the Stores.*

Tissues, and the nuances of *these tissues: all that we have already announced, in somewhat mysterious tones, as novelties in the great fashion houses, or as still in embryo, is now common knowledge among women and reported throughout France on the back page of newspapers. In the lavish abundance of six or seven famous window displays there is nothing not already hinted at by me a month ago; and if I examine this profusion now, it is to reduce my conflicting impressions to a certain order. At the leading 'Exhibitions' (that is the term they like now), where one can arrive at one's own judgements, and in their Catalogues (many of them as exquisite as books for bibliophiles), where one can, above all, dream, there are – dear Walker or Reader – things to trouble you! A profusion of diverse materials, and a string of new terms, some well-chosen, some merely bizarre.*

But do not be alarmed. Let us chat about it!

Rich door-hangings and Levantine rugs, which you are free to handle or simply to look at, not without a certain satisfaction that these, the sole product of the weaver's art suited to our floors or our walls, are making themselves at home there: you must make haste to see them! Profusion is not confusion. Listen, why do we not consider these materials, from the very start, from the point of view of our double existence, out-of-doors and indoors?

Outdoor Costumes: a charming series of twills for girls is the first thing on offer, in every pastel shade; and then traditional cashmeres, but also in every colour: light demi-draps, *tweed, or tartans, striped or with a single band of colour or a simple check pattern like mattress-material: finally, all the coarse materials, woven from animal hair. English velvet excellent for rainy November and February days, but it must be of the best quality; warm and silky paddings, suited for making cuirasses and polonaises,*[168] *allowing one to do without an overcoat: these are the broad selection from which to make one's choice. Then, as well as materials, one has to consider colour. The shade still most in vogue for out-of-doors is tinted havana – known as 'cachou' yesterday, and from this morning onwards as 'gyzèle'. We can also list the following (combining well-known hues with quite new ones): peacock green, garnet blue, lees-of-wine,* suresne, *regina, otter, iron-grey, tile-grey,* gris mode, *'holland' brown, and other less useful terms for the same colours.*

It would be silly to try to enumerate these last.

Indoor Costumes: Lyons offers us her fayes *and her* failles, *her* poults-de-soie, *her satins, her incomparable velvets, her gauzes and tulles and her* crêpes-de-Chine, so *completely naturalised that one day she will be exporting them to the land of tea: and finally gold and silver lamé, a most sumptuous revival.*

But the most exquisite of all the new fabrics, so smooth, so kindly, and destined (I give you my word!) to reign for more than a single season, is light-coloured cashmeres, which have been adapted now (better than failles *or* poults-de-soie) *for evening wear. They come in pink and tea-rose, blue and sky-blue, corn-colour, mignonette, forget-me-not, cream and moonlight grey. Dresses of such cashmere, garnished either with gauze or with embroidered tulle and with edging in white jet and feather, with jet fringes, indeed with all the ornaments of a ball-gown, are now the wear for the Theatre or a Grand Dinner-party or a little Supper; but square-cut at the neck, never* décolleté.

Given our neat classification, Mesdames, the vast profusion of materials need no longer bewilder you; you will be able to look ahead, with fair confidence, for two months or more – no short span when it comes to Fashion.

So what, you ask, are you to do with those materials? You are to create masterpieces. As for me, though perhaps I cannot aim so high, I feel this instant the urge to sketch a costume made from one of those delicious cashmeres.

Costume for a Dinner-party: in cashmere: I picture it as pink, but you may imagine it as blue. The Apron of the overskirt is decorated with many a horizontal flounce on either side, these being piped with satin and themselves resting on a flounce. The train is ornamented with seven little pleated flounces. Eight scarves, each with an insertion of white gauze, embroidered with flat silk, form a tunic and are knotted high up on the train. Bodice with round basques, laced behind (hence the name robes-corselets) *and also enveloped in gauze. Ruff of* tulle illusion *with a neck of cashmere lined with satin and puffed sleeves with cuffs.*

To the first of my Readers to wear this costume shall fall the honour of baptising it: for there is a pretty custom, some days old by now, that a dress shall be named

168. A polonaise is a frogged *redingote*.

after the woman who, by her deportment, charm and distinction, gains it a Reputation in Society.

But, inevitably, we shall return to the subject of the splendid social gatherings of the hour, in the grand salons of noble residences or in the opera-house.

I have noted on my ivory tablets a word on a part of Costume which, undeniably, has given it great distinction in the early days of this Season: I mean the Apron. Sometimes it is simple and meant for home wear, not really forming part of the costume and slipped over any dress whatever: it will have lace frills or pleats and be secured round the shoulders by rich bows, of different sizes, falling loosely over the skirt. Sometimes, on the other hand, it is resplendent, fabulous, superb. It is adorned with embroidered flowers in brilliant colours, or with velvet bows and attachments, and is decorated with pearl braid. Note, however, that this pearl passementerie *has, over the last few evenings, become something different from the white or black jet or blue or white steel we predicted in our first report: jet, yes, but scintillating now, like all the precious stones of the earth assembled into one: shimmering and glittering and paling in Queen of Sheba style. This talisman, on an opera-gown or a grand Evening gown, gathers to itself the whole richness of the* toilette *and the first glances of admirers.*

MARGUERITE DE PONTY

Black-and-white Engravings

First Page.

1. Formal Visiting dress. (Chapeau Figaro). – *Skirt of dark violet* faille *with a large flounce, high on the train and low in front. – Tunic in dark violet velvet, trimmed with very pale blue feather and brandenburgs in dark violet passementerie. Sleeves decorated with slashes of pansy-coloured satin.* Chapeau Figaro *in dark violet velvet.*

2. Toilette de réception. – *Skirt of garnet-coloured* faille *with a flounce only in front and with flat pleats. – Tunic* in matelassé *of the same shade, trimmed with black lace; garnet-coloured scarf in satin of the same hue.*

Middle pages.

3. Little girl, 7–8. – Polonaise *pleated skirt raised high behind and decked with little blue* biais. – Boots *in glacé goatskin, and stomacher and sleeves in cambric.*

4. Little boy, 7–8, in tweed costume. – Jacket and waistcoat, both with pockets. – Skirt pleated except in the front, where it is plain with little fixed bows, of the same shade as the material. – Sailor-suit collar in Irish linen; little boots of polished goatskin.

Miss Satin, appropriately, devotes her column in this issue to her compatriot, the great Charles Frederick Worth (1825–95), who, 'alone, has the art of creating a *toilette* as elusive as our own thoughts'. Worth was born in Lincolnshire and trained in Swan and Edgar's store in London, then in 1845 went to Paris, and twelve years later he set up an independent business as a dressmaker, attracting the patronage of the Empress Eugénie and coming more or less to dominate the Parisian world of fashion.

THE FASHION GAZETTE

Which should one believe, one's eyes or one's ears? The question at issue is whether shopping is flourishing in Paris or, as one hears it said, is in decline. Certainly, judging from the great crowds just now in the Galéries du Louvre, or the Bon Marché[169] *in the rue de Sèvres, one would might think the whole of Paris determined to make the fortune of these stores. With what zest, moreover!*

Go to M. Worth's establishment in a two-horse carriage, attracted by the news of that Master's three new creations; or to the Malle des Indes for cashmeres – thyme-coloured, otter-fur or heron-hued; you will find the same crowd, quite desperate to spend money.

There are some, it is true, who greatly dislike this filling of the pockets of rich manufacturers, and insist, obstinately, that things in Paris are going to the dogs. This is a problem for gazetteers like myself, but one must listen to the discontented too. Not everyone is lucky; not everyone can buy 'blue-of-dreams' (and 'chaos' and 'Infanta') gowns, nor otter-fur-coloured tunics of pure Tibetan wool.

So now I have named them, those three famous gowns; and, angry though the envious may be, I want to describe at least the 'blue-of-dreams' one.

We have all of us been dreaming of that gown, without knowing it. M. Worth, alone, has the art of creating a toilette *as elusive as our own thoughts.*

Picture (you can if you try) a long skirt with a rep train, of the most ideal sky-blue silk – that blue so pale, with gleams of opalescence, that one sometimes sees, like a garland, round silvery clouds. The front of the skirt is in faille *and furnished with a profusion of pleats; the panels at the side are decorated, all along their length, with pompoms lined with straw-coloured silk; and from one side to another, under a grooved* pouff, *there passes a serpentine sash in blue and primrose-yellow. The bodice is medieval style, with straw-coloured slashes; the sleeves are garnished with pompoms. The rich folds of the* fichu *are in spring-like*

169. The great Parisian department store (the first of its kind), founded in 1852 by Aristide Boucicaut and imitated in many other parts of the world. The Grands Magasins du Louvre occupied the ground floor of the Hôtel du Louvre, on the rue de Rivoli.

colours. Here you have a toilette *for grand occasions such as any young woman should wear, in preference to those red or yolk-of-egg affairs that other great designers are favouring.*

For cashmere dresses, and for all the heavy camel's hair and goat's hair fabrics in vogue at the moment, La Dernière mode *has just come to an arrangement with the first fashion House in Paris, allowing us to send samples to our readers gratis and by return of post.*

MISS SATIN

Ix, this fortnight, finds two new fields to which to apply the aesthetics of Fashion. First, funerals, cemeteries and burials. It has some piquancy that the creator of the great *tombeau* (tomb) poems for Edgar Allan Poe and Verlaine writes, in the person of Ix, that tombs seem to be going out of fashion, in favour of urns. Secondly, Ix sketches an artistic rationale for day-to-day or fortnightly journalism. Whereas poetry aims at eternity, journalism is to acquire beauty by running to the very opposite extreme: to the ephemerality of '*tulle illusion* or artificial roses, imitating roses and clematis'.

PARIS CHRONICLE

Theatres, Books, the Fine Arts; Echoes from the Salons and the Seaside.

Neither the Theatre, past and future, which up to now has filled this column, nor Books, which are always put off 'till the next issue', which becomes the issue next but one, are to concern us in the present causerie. Bouquets, yes, but not the sumptuous ones hurled from theatre boxes on to the stage, but pious and yellowing crowns of immortelles.[170] *Phantoms, yes certainly, but not the brilliant and imaginary ones the reader is led to conjure up by the latest novels, but rather those real and beloved shades we seek to recapture from the year's tombs, and the tombs of other years.*

All Souls' Day.[171] *Everyone knows how much for Paris (a living city* par excellence) *the memory of the departed means on this date. Thoughts about those who, in the common phrase, have 'passed on', dwell on three necropolises:*[172] *on the*

170. Crowns of *immortelles,* artificial flowers or pearls were traditional at French funerals.

171. 2 November.

172. Mallarmé seems to be at fault here. There were three major cemeteries in Paris apart from the new one at Saint-Ouen: Père Lachaise, Montmartre, and Montparnasse, none of them being particularly on a hilltop or down on a plain.

hill-top, or down in the plain, and, alas!, on that other bare, desolate and far distant one to which people, in their sense of death as a deportation, have given the horrible name of Cayenne.[173] *Who knows if we are not seeing it for the last time, the touching procession this afternoon and the following day, with all its ancient usages? May not the railway-train, with its furious speed and whistle, and the promiscuity of mourning in its carriages, disturb its intimate calm. So long as the question of railway stations and cemeteries (of Méry-sur-Oise and Wissous or Massy*[174]*) is not resolved, there is a sort of embarrassment in the air about funerary matters. Who knows indeed whether, with the increasing dominance of the Urn, for ashes, the Tomb may not come to be considered an outmoded curiosity? What a world of impressions, and I might add of familiar feelings, of the human race, changed for new feelings and different impressions and as-yet-unknown methods of expressing grief!*

But if the duty of a Family Gazette has been to speak with sympathy about a melancholy custom, it is the duty of a journal of High-life not to neglect even what is frivolous.

At all events, what is it safe to say, given that it is almost certain that this Issue, enclosing the picture of a Ball-dress, will lie on salon tables till a fairly distant date, at least the day after tomorrow? A dress, designed according to principles meant to rule through a winter, is not so soon useless and stale as a Chronicle, even a fortnightly one. To have the permanence of tulle *illusion, or of artificial roses imitating roses and clematis: that is one's dream for every sentence one writes, not for a short story or a sonnet, but about the news of the day. Let us chroniclers be vague and null and almost insignificant: it is easy enough always, for a variety of reasons, but a little because Paris, given over to its annual theatrical resurrection, cuts no very definite figure to the eye of the observer. The great festivities take place outside the city, in the* châteaux: *their* salon *transformed, by means of a screen, into a private stage, for*

173. Cayenne was the site of a penal settlement in French Guiana..

174. In 1874 the municipal administration of Paris decide to purchase a large plot of land at Méry-sur-Oise and provide a railway to serve it, but the scheme was not carried through.

the performing of 'proverbs,'[175] *and their park (an inspired idea) making its lawns and spacious views into a track for private horse racing. Under the ceiling, and under the sky, there is a double distraction for those outside the city and unwilling to return to it – save just for an hour to acclaim* **Patti,** *swaying amid the bravos, the flowers and her own emotion, but continuing to sing, in French, twice each,* Les Huguenots *and* Faust, *evenings already historic! It is all there has been: so much so that that observer of Paris we have mentioned is reduced to wondering: 'Is it because the* beau monde *has still not decided to return that nothing notable happens: that there is nothing elegant demanding our attention, for lack of aristocratic eyes as witness?'*

It is a problem, a problem; and, though it recurs every year, one would like to put it to the subtle-minded Hamlet, if Hamlet had not other things on his mind. For there were those who said 'He means to leave us', and others, 'No, you see, he means to stay'; and the prince of Denmark, that is to say **Faure** *(who, as a great singer and actor, is the only man who could play such a character) is soon to perform again as Don Juan for us. I shall not dwell even for our Peruvian readers, on the recent awkwardness*[176] *involving Europe and the Grand Opera; thanks to helpful third parties, thanks to the virtuoso himself, and thanks to the wise Director, it is all over and forgotten. Only there is something to be learned, once and for all, by people too quick to complain of 'unreasonableness' or 'hurt vanity'. The truth is, when an artist considers himself offended, it is not primarily his own dignity that he is defending. No! it is everything that he represents on behalf of Art: that is to say, in the present case, passion, gravity, knowledge, intuition, incomparable nobility and genius.*

A 'Mastersinger' was wanting to leave; meanwhile royal guests arrived on our soil. We note especially the excursion made by post-chaise from Esclimont to Rambouillet by the Prince of Wales, who passed by Dampierre; but these equipages and these four-in-hands, raising a whirlwind of autumn leaves in their gallop, were of course pursued by a cortège of reporters, eye at the window and pencil at the ready. The daily press has supplied all the details, day after day, and has been read in every far-flung village and hamlet.[177] *As for me, I come late in the day; and, though it is my duty to comment, who will read my comments, in this France which*

175. Plays illustrating a proverbial phrase, such as Alfred de Musset's *On ne badine pas avec l'amour.*

176. Faure's absence from Paris during 1870–71 was regarded as unpatriotic, and there were hostile demonstrations on his return to the Opéra in November 1871, causing much resentment on his part.

177. This visit by the Prince of Wales to a string of *châteaux* belonging to ardent French monarchists was much disapproved of by Queen Victoria, who tried to get Disraeli to dissuade him from it, and it got him into hot water with the radical press, both in France and in Britain.

is no more than a vast Paris traversed by rivers, woods and mountains?[178] *I will only venture one comment, on the unanimity of my colleagues (great, small, and middling) in praising his Highness's visible love of children. To my delight, indeed: but what did they base it on, this trait of his that is already becoming legendary? On this: that in the great* château *of Dampierre,*[179] *where the very masterpieces seemed to want to pay him homage, the illustrious visitor bent down to the seven-year-old Duc de Luynes and (I quote) 'regaled him with cakes'. A praiseworthy gesture, we must agree; but for my own part I cannot conceal that, sumptuous as were those pastries, taken from a plate of ancient and emblazoned porcelain, they – two pineapple meringues and a tartlet – did not represent a gift so very different from the one I sometimes bring, from a famous* pâtissier, *for my own friends' children. Yes, for high-flying journalism it was perhaps a slightly feeble example of princely generosity to the young. The simple-minded, among whom I include myself, for whom the notion of a queen's son, even in the face of reality, persists in evoking a thousand dazzling possibilities, will be sad to give up the supposition they cherished while reading. I mean, that the prince would have given the child one of the diamonds (crystallised by some technique known in Lahore or Singapore) with which he was no doubt covered, on his hands, his clothes and his feet – sole sweetmeat fit for a sovereign, if only a future one, to bestow on the scion of one of the most magnificent families of a friendly nation.*

But no! Far from living continually, and so sating themselves, in the extraordinary pomp of their décor, these princes, like ourselves, feel the need, after the day's hunting and before the galas, after Chantilly[180] *and before Heilles-Mouchy,*[181] *to go to a fairy-play in the theatre. In the course of my peregrination*

178. He means, perhaps, that France has become Paris because everyone in France reads the same newspapers.

179. Dampierre [Dompierre] was the residence of the Duchesse de Luynes, widowed daughter of the Duc de la Rochefoucauld.

180. The racecourse.

181. Among the Prince's hosts were the Duc and Duchesse de Mouchy at Mouchy-le-Chatel (Oise).

in Paris, I saw the heir to the throne of England, the other day, at – Orphée aux enfens! *In a box, he, who had just seen seven* châteaux *and the space between them appear and disappear in the course of three days, applauded the changes now happening before his eyes (and which with the aid of canvas, gaslight and* paillon *took only three seconds). The previous evening, or two or three evenings earlier, I encountered the Grand Duke Constantine*[182] *studying the* Folies-Bergère. *Who knows whether, in his great overcoat buttoned over his badges and orders, he did not envy the authentic magnificence of the Tattooed Man,*[183] *made handsomer than all his fellow men by the insignia stamped on his very skin, and the only man marked indelibly with the symbols of chiefdom?*

Ix

* * *

Tenth Leaf

Menu for a Grand Dinner

Soup
Purée of partridges Chasseur
Pearl barley soup à la Princesse

Oysters: Marenne, Ostend, Imperial

Hors d'oeuvre
Prawns, Canapé of Caviar
Herrings à la Russe, Smoked salmon

Relevé
Trout à la Régence
Fillet of beef à la Godard

---

182. The son of Tsar Nicholas I.

183. The Tattooed Man was a certain Georgius Konstantin, born in Albania about 1831. In 1862 he and twelve companions ventured into Chinese Tartary in quest of gold and were unwise enough to stay on during a popular uprising and sell arms to the rebels. Nine of his companions were massacred by government forces, but the remaining three, including Konstantin, were condemned to the penalty of tattooing – a ferocious process by which every square centimetre of the body was covered by figures and signs. His companions quickly died under the treatment, but Konstantin survived and escaped to France, becoming a leading attraction at the *Folies-Bergère*. Experts were continually trying to prove him a fraud, but never succeeded.

Rabbit puddings à la Lucullus

Entrées
Chicken à l'Écossaise
Grenadins of veal à la Maréchale
Ravioli timbale à la Monglas

Champagne sorbet

Roast game à la Véron
(Partridges, quails, ortolans, snipe)

Cardoons with marrow
Asparagus tips in cream

Hazelnut ice cream with wafers

Dessert selected by the Mistress of the House
Coffee, Liqueurs: Martel Cognac or Veuve Amphoux, or other authentic liqueurs or cognac
Russian cigarettes, little canons roses[184] *au Dubèque aromatique*
Cigars 'Regalia de la Reine Figaro' (Grand-Hôtel)

WINE
Madeira [sic] Pichon Longueville
Grands-Soussans and Thorin in carafe
Romanée Conti Piper iced, White Latour
Imperial Madeira
St. Julien, Larose, Richebourg
Veuve Clicquot (chilled)

THE CHEF DE BOUCHE CHEZ BRÉBANT

* * *

184. Little pink scented cigarettes.

Eleventh Leaf

Applying of leather on leather: an afternoon occupation.

'Interior decoration for women' is the wording in our rubric. We gave you, a fortnight ago, a precious suggestion for an apartment (a false ceiling), the construction of which would be a matter for the master of the house; but here today is something which can be done by women, as a simple manual occupation. The Golden Notebook's suggestions may seem to occur a little haphazardly, not always offering something timely as well as new. Well, so much the worse for them!

The plan, Mesdames, is for you to go to the shoemaker or if you prefer, to the leather-shop – and buy some large pieces (squares or oblongs) of leather, thin and supple and in their natural colour. You will also need hundreds of small scraps of leather: red, blue, green and silver. For the bright-coloured ones, go to a bookbinder; for more muted ones, go to an antique dealer for spines and covers of books and fragments from Spanish or Flemish wall-hangings.

That is all you will need, plus your thimble.

But now imagination will be required; or at least some memory of those vague flower-pieces our grandmothers would embroider for Louis XIII chairs. You create your bouquet or sheaf or garland (these are better than a pure arabesque) by applying leather on leather, using all your scraps in simple or fantastic contrasts.

This you will do by sewing, with a strong needle, having first trimmed with a knife the outlines of each many-coloured flower, bird or butterfly, with its border of fine silk, securing it to the background by a 'blanket stitch'.

Leather on leather: the effect is superb. The oblong pieces will for instance serve for a chair-back, and the square ones for a chair-seat (a Louis XIII chair, as I picture it). I am not supposed to say it, since furnishing is not my province, but a set of chairs decorated in this way would be ideal for a dining-room; that wooden chests could be covered by this method, in the antique fashion, and the golden nails used on such chests would help not only here but on other kinds of furniture; and that wall-panels made in this manner would look beautiful when framed, like marquetry, in rare woods; for it is, above all, marquetry that this rich, this plain and simple, this noble and artistic and elementary décor, *resembles.*

I have seen this done in the provinces (but with coats-of-arms, not flowers), and I present it to you here

according to A BRETON CHATELAINE

PROGRAMME FOR THE FORTNIGHT

Nothing about books: our next Chronicle will be devoted to them; nor about EXHIBITIONS: see our last Programme; nor TRAVEL: we are preparing a study of wintertime emigrations. It is all the fault of the THEATRES, which, during this exceptional fortnight, are rich with a hundred premières.

THEATRES

Théâtre-Français: *Premières (rue Richelieu) of* Le Demi-monde *by ALEXANDRE DUMAS FILS, stolen from the Boulevard:* ***Delaunay, Got, Febvre, Thiron, Croizette, Nathalie, Tholer and Broizat;*** *this will give you an idea of these magnificent soirées. Repertory:* Zaire *(or* ***Sarah Bernhardt).***

Salle Ventadour: Opéra: *performances by* ***Faure*** *in* Don Giovanni*; Ottavio, the tenor Vergnet. Zerlina, a débutante. When shall we see the ballet for* ***Sangalli*** *(rumour says* Sylvia ou la Nymphe de Diane*) and* Le Comte Ory, *already announced? Ordinarily, the repertory: notably* Les Huguenots.

Italiens: *opening of the season with* ***Mme Pozzoni,*** *that débutante in Paris famous in all the countries bordering the Mediterranean;* ***Mlle Sebel,*** *a Swede like Nilsson;* ***Mme de Belocca, MM. Verati and Padilla.*** *Premières every evening:* Lucrezia Borgia, La Traviata, Il Trovatore, Un Ballo in Maschera, the Barber, Martha, Violetta, Crisino et la Comare, La Somnambula, *etc. Fashionable and dilettante Paris hangs on the bow raised for the first time by M.* ***Vianesi.***

Odéon: *Will the vogue of the first performances of* La Maîtresse légitime, by *POUPART DAVYL be balanced by that of* L'École des maris *in which Isabelle is Mlle* ***Blanche Barett,*** *and of* Le Célibataire et l' homme marié *by Wafflard and Fulgence, displaying the delicious costumes of 1821. This evening of Repertory ends with that marvel,* Le Tricorne enchanté, *by GAUTIER.*

Opéra-Comique: Le Pardon de Ploermel ***(Zina Dalti and Lina Bell; Bouhy, Lhéerie)*** *is to give up some fine soirées to* Mireille, *given with the fragments previously cut at the Théâtre-Lyrique, and always and very happily with* ***Mme Carvalho.*** *Repertory, notably* Roméo et Juliette.

Opéra-Populaire: *Opening (I persist in believing it!) with* Les Parias *by MEMBRÉE, a new opera, then* Les Amours du Diable *by GRISAN, a forgotten opera, then an unpublished ballet by MASSENET; add the conductor MATON, the singers Nicot, Mme REBOUX and the unbelievable luxuriousness and modest price* of *these evenings: sum total, success.*

Vaudeville: *Failures are no less interesting to lovers of the theatre than successes, for one has time to study the latter, whereas with the former one must hurry. Seeing* Berthe d'Estrée *as one has seen Marcelle and* ***Mlle Barthet*** *struggling their* *best with ill-fortune, like Jane Essler, above all after* Entre deux trains, *that novelty, and before other single-acters, made a pretty sight.*

Gymnase: Gilberte, *transported to St. Petersburg in the* toilettes *of* ***Mlle Delaporte,*** *who has exiled her talent there, is succeeded by* Gilberte, *which is still with us in the hands of* ***Mlle Délia,*** *who is gifted with the most beautiful dresses and a charming talent. Soon to come:* La Veuve, by *MEILHAC and HALÉVY, and* ***Fargueil*** *and her three dresses, and her talent no less varied than them.* La Princesse Georges: *a revival, alas! without Desclée, but with* ***Mlle*** *Tallandiére – very curious.*

Variétés: *Let us leave in today's Programme the première of* Les Prés Saint-Gervais, *by SARDOU, GILLE and LECOCQ, announced by us last time and the time before last; for it will last more than two fortnights or even two months. The name of Mlle Z. Bouffar changed for that of* ***Peschard:*** *there is the only change to our notice of something near to a popular success.*

Palais-Royal: *There are two kinds of laughter, that of a hundredth performance at the Palais-Royal, releasing an accumulation of ancient merriment, and that of premières: thus* Le Roi Candaule *is succeeded by* La Boule, *thereby exhausting both varieties of Parisian joy.*

Gaîté: Orphée aux Enfers, *with the new Act, 'The kingdom of Neptune', immortalises itself, drawing trains* of *pleasure-seekers from the seven corners of Europe; and now Parisians come to see the dazzling première given in their absence.*

Porte-Saint-Martin: Le Tour du monde en 80 jours *will perform the Tour of the Paris year; from Suez to Liverpool from October to July. What can we say? You will have to see it: the Cave of Serpents, a Suttee in India, the exploding and sinking of a Steamer, an attack on a train by Dawnie*[185] *Indians: magical titles, but they are put into the shade by the real thing, by which I mean fairy-theatre!* ***Dumaine, Lacressonnière, Alexandre and Vannoy, Mlles Angèle Moreau and Patry:*** *for there is a drama somewhere in this spectacle by* ***d'ENNERY and JULES VERNE.***

Ambigu: *why, in the midst of great success, interrupt* L'Officier de fortune? *if not to stage* Cocagne, *by FERDINAND DUGUÉ, which we spoke of in our previous chronicle? But what that did not mention was the superb playing of Fargueil.*

Bouffes-Parisiens: Madame l'Archiduc, ***Théo*** *departs,* ***Judic*** *arrives: should we sigh, or should we rejoice? Ovations, bouquets (which, in this sweetshop of a theatre, could well be crystallised flowers); diamonds in their looks and on their shoulders; a fabulous première due to continue right through the winter. Dazzled, fascinated, I shall name no-one else: yes I shall, though: that other charmer, Grévin, for his costumes for the Trumpets of the Grand Duke.*

Renaissance: Thérésa *in* La Famille Trouillat, *which, were it even a masterpiece (and it is amusing), ought to give the place of honour on its poster to the* diva, *who makes great songs out of six trifles.*

---

185. In error for 'Pawnee'?

Folies-Dramatiques: *Première of* La Fiancée du roi de Garbe, *by LITOLFF: what can compare with the inspired buffoonery of a grave and sublime artist? How I wish not to have had the exquisite* ***Mlle Van-Ghel*** *so continually before my eyes, so that I could remember more of the marvellous music; but who can tell if that would suit me either?*

Cluny: Madame Mascarille, Le Mage, *pleasant pieces by young authors; and that marvel of loud laughter* Les Héritiers de Rabourdin, *a four-act play by ZOLA which one ought to hear and to read: one of the masterpieces of the day!*

Théâtre-des-Arts *(formerly the* ***Menus-Plaisirs****): The new play by MM. CRISAFULLI and STAPLEAUX has great qualities, above all of being interesting: what is there left to say after the* feuilletons *of the day after or Monday of the tragic, ardent and noble performer,* ***Mlle Rousseil!***

Château d'Eau: *Revival of* Paris la nuit, *with the* ***Dorst*** *brothers, those clowns, no, those convulsionists, no, those performers of a strange quadrille, called by a calm and aggravating name, the* Frétillants. *Their place is in the* Revue, *first of all because they appear as one of the extravagances of the year: but will they know how to imitate themselves?*

Folies-Bergère: *The Birds, the Tattooed Man, Lira and Neni,* Les Martinettes, Ka-kin-ha *and* Les Fausses Almées *and the Gymnastic dog. What shall I say? an operetta, and the three Horizontal Bars: that is what a thousand posters, blue, green, red and yellow tell you in Paris. Three premières a week (Tuesday, Thursday and Saturday): it is the work of Harlequin, dispenser of public happiness.*

* * *

Other places for distraction and pleasure, both day and night, after the ***Jardin d'Acclimatation*** *(animals, monkeys up their painted poles, all of them: Hamadryas, Chaemas and Papions, plus prolonged flowers and prolonged orchestra, a promenade which will acclimatise the sun in wintertime).*

The ***Cirque d'Ēté:*** *with a septet of prodigies, those mountain-dwellers from the Appenines drawing the voice of doves and of women out of earthenware gourds; great success of the season like that, now winter has come, of those extraordinary skaters Goodrich and Curtis. Let us not forget the* ***Davenne*** *family (the English gymnasts), who, acclaimed every evening, are (despite what the poster says) not beginners any longer.*

The ***Panorama,*** *in the Champs-Élysées, with that bad dream,* Le Siège de Paris, *magnificently evoked by a painter, PHILIPPOTEAUX, attracts us in the beautiful afternoons of the season; after pausing to see the* Ouvrages Militaires, *etc., in relief, of the same siege at the Summer Garden of the Alcazar.*

Robert-Houdin: *'The Maharajah's Cabinet', by its inventor Brunnet, and how many other miracles!, in the boulevard des Italiens; whilst those of the boulevard*

Saint-Denis are, at the same hour, accomplished by M. LITSONN at the ***Cercle fantastique*** *(especially recommended: distribution of flowers and sweets and reduced price tickets at the same time, which is veritable magic).*

The ***Théâtre-Miniature*** *does not content itself with* Le Pied de mouton – décors, *costumes, everything, displaying a magnificence only restricted by its dimensions. It has also summoned* **M. Veille** *from Hungary and makes him evoke* Spectres and Table-rappings! *But what is certain is that, in that deliciously refurbished theatre, the ghost of Mr. Punch will never be absent, for he enjoys an indestructible and charming life.*

The ***Salle des Familles:*** *where true premières sometimes give way to marvellous and instructive scientific spectacles for children, etc. Monday, Wednesday and Friday evening, and Sunday in the afternon.*

For children also, exquisite matinées at ***Frascati,*** *on Sundays. The season for making friendships in squares and parks is over, but here is a winter Garden which allows lonely children to meet, a precious opportunity.*

Literary Matinées *everywhere, at the* ***Porte-St-Martin,*** *soon at the* ***Gaîté*** *(people also mention the* ***Ambigu*** *and the* ***Renaissance****); and there, as here, one finds clever troupes brought together the previous evening and eloquent lecturers at the very moment. No need to speak to Parisian families about this Sunday institution; but what should be known by families in the provinces who have children in Paris or, on the other hand, are afraid to send them because of the freedom of a Paris Sunday, is that there is a well-established system for enrolling them for these classic occasions and the serious and inspiring lectures that they offer.*

The Programme for the ***Porte-Saint-Martin*** *is: Sunday 1 November,* Le Chevalier à la mode, *a comedy in three acts by DANCOURT, with a talk by LAPOMMERAYE.*

Sunday 8 November, Le Véritable Saint-Genest, *a five-act tragedy by ROTROU, with a talk by M. ARBOUX.*

At the ***Gaîté,*** *opening of these literary and musical festivities by a prologue in verse, a jewel, by COPPÉE.*

The ***Salle des Capucines*** *also re-opens, announcing all the names most honoured by its audiences; travellers come from the four corners of the earth, without their books, to speak about literature, and scholars who are also men of the world.*

But the altogether original innovation will come on the evening of Monday 9 November, the Feuilleton parlé *by M. DE LAPOMMERAYE, the much-loved critic and* causeur. *You have been to the Theatre this week? You have not? Come all the same: to appreciate, to learn. How many new complexities, of high literary taste, these Monday lectures promise, with the author himself joining in the praise or blame and, who knows? tempering the one and approving the other.*

The ***Concerts Populaires,*** *with choirs as well as orchestra, each eighth Concert being devoted to an Oratorio, have been mingling their discreet announcement* *with the flamboyant posters of the Theatres.*

Sunday, 1 November: Schiller, March by Meyerbeer; Symphony in D major by Beethoven; Air de Ballet, by Th. Dubois (1st performance); Concerto in G minor by Mendelssohn, played by ***Mme Zael;*** *Violin sonata by Leclair (1720); Overture to* Tannhäuser *by Richard Wagner.*

Sunday 8 November: the programme will be annnounced on Tuesday or Wednesday before the concert.

The national ***Concerts*** *at the* ***Châtelet*** *open on 8 November, under the baton of M. COLONNE (each series including a choir audition). A glorious afternoon, which we will leave to surprise our lady readers.*

In the evening, at ***Frascati,*** *several times a week, LITOLFF brings together amateurs eager to hear the music of the masters and his own conducted by this master.*

CORRESPONDENCE WITH SUBSCRIBERS

Mme R . . . , MONTARGIS. – We will very shortly send you, Madame, our price-list for life-size cut-out patterns: the Administration of the Journal agrees to supply you with a sleeve, or a corsage, a polonaise and even a complete dress, mounted and trimmed. Do you prefer patterns in muslin, such as many dressmakers ask from us, though the cost is a little more? Their great advantage is that they can be tried on by the client.

Mme L COMTESSE DE B . . . , TOURS. – Madame Charles, the expert Parisian who purchases on behalf of LA DERNIÈRE MODE, *puts herself entirely at your disposal for your purchases and commissions: she has already sent you, as you requested, samples of cashmeres from the Malle des Indes. When you have made your choice, please return a piece of the cloth, marked with its price, with your order. Your cashmere, with its trimmings, also chosen by our buyer, will be sent you within twenty-four hours of receipt of your letter.*

Mlle LUCIE H . . . , TOULON. – For you also, dear Reader, when you and your Mother have decided on the shade of your dress, we will order it. It will be enough as before to send a corsage for size, no need for a skirt as well. All we need to know about the latter is it length. We shall not trim the Costume with feather, unless you ask for it: a young woman does not wear feathers.

Mme LA MARQUISE DE G . . . , NICE. – The chapeau Figaro *which Mademoiselle Baillet created recently will suit you wonderfully, Madame la Marquise; that is why we chose it. I hope you will be as pleased with it as with as the last one, the* chapeau Valois.

Mme De R . . . , MONTARGIS. – We have found out the price of the Book of Hours, which is sixty-five francs, with a painting on vellum. If you would like this work of art, dear Subscriber, would you kindly notify Madame Charles direct? Payment should be by postal order, made out to Monsieur Marasquin, the Director, to be sent with your order.

Mme R . . . , SAINT-ÉTIENNE. – You are right, dear Madame, trimmings are very complicated these days; but simple toilettes *can still be fashionable. Everything depends, as we both know, on the good taste of the dressmaker.*

Mme B . . . , BERLIN. – As there is no postal agreement with Germany, Madame, you can send cash by registered letter addressed to Marasquin, the Director.

Mme L . . . , NANCY. – A cashmere tunic, pearled with jet, is nowadays an essential part of a woman's Toilette*: it is indispensable in a variety of circumstances.*

Mme LA VICOMTESSE PAUL . . . , ALGIERS. – Madame, the Maison d'Ouvrages Artistiques pour Dames[186] *are augmenting their collection with heraldic tapestries, Japanese embroideries on linen, broadcloth or satin, etc. 'And old-style slippers?', you ask. Heavens! they are not entirely forgotten; they are best suited as an afternoon task for very young children, who find it hard to work with satin or broadcloth but must be kept occupied. What is charming, though it has become a little commonplace now that commerce has taken it over, is to embroider leaves and flowers and fruit, in wool, upon basket-work: mothers' work-baskets, etc., rather than wastepaper-baskets, which have been replaced in elegant interiors by a Dutch bucket in repoussé copper. Quick and small-scale works – often the most precious mementoes for husbands and brothers – include tobacco-pouches, Moroccan style or oriental, in cloth initials in cut leather or cigar-cases. Apart from these novelties (which they are not really) one will of course do Venetian embroidery and make Irish lace and* guipure*: though it will be for the pleasure of it, for otherwise how compete with the cheapness of such work in multiple stores, who obtain them from prisons? All in all, and to sum up, apart from the occupation (very popular with elegant ladies in public gardens, especially the Parc Monceau*[187]*) which consists in pearling festoons of guipure or tulle, etc., with jet, to decorate tunics, aprons or toilettes, there is nothing very striking, in this moment of new styles and fabrics, to report: indeed the last-named pastime is only indulged in by walkers as a distraction and for the pleasure of wearing clothes one has made oneself!*

Having taken all our notes in the great stores on what will be worn, we shall pay a visit to Sphynx *(Ouvrages de Dames) to see what will be emerging there this winter. As for today, content yourself, Madame, and all of you, dear Subscribers, with the marvellous work suggested, as a curiosity, in the Golden Notebook, by a Breton Châtelaine.*

---

186. i.e. Au Sphinx, 55, avenue de l'Opéra: see their visiting card.

187. See note on p. 36.

ADVICE ON EDUCATION

We learn, with great satisfaction, that M. Armand Lebrun, the author of the interesting illustrated English-German-French Dictionary, published by the House of Furne and Jouvey and praised by us in one of our articles, has been appointed by the Minister for Public Instruction, on the strength of this work, as an Officer of the Academy. This consecration by the University is a good moment to repeat our recommendation of this excellent work, a book as well as an album, on which an international public has bestowed the first of all sanctions, success.

All the publishers of classics, indeed – I will first mention Hachette and then Delagrave, Delalain and Belin – rival one another in good taste and intelligence in the production of English and German textbooks, free from outmodedness and stuffiness and the superfluous and pedantic annotation characteristic of such books in the past. The new programmes, it must be said, have followed the catalogue of these foreign collections; the great classics, certainly, but in fragments, which makes them less of a burden on the memory of beginners; likewise with modern authors, such as Walter Scott (excerpted by M. Battier) and Miss Edgeworth (excerpted by M. Mothère), or, again, M. Sevrette's select passages from English literature, which is both juvenile and truly literary, a rare combination! All these works are immediately interesting by virtue of their familiar tone in dialogue or discourse. Here is one of the happy novelties of the day in the field of books for the young.

It is Books, rather than Masters, that we are talking about today, but nevertheless all courses and private lessons are beginning again. Let us mention, though really there is no need of any recommendation, the lessons in French language and literature, and of Greek and Latin, which a sometime laureate of the Grand Concours, a man of the world and a writer, is about to begin for the young of both sexes. Whether they wish their young families to attend his lectures in formal groups or prefer the master to come to their own homes, I recommend our Subscribers to apply for information to one of our friends, M. Wiener, Professor at the Lycée Fontanes, 11, rue Saint-Lazare, who is responsible for these courses and lessons.

Here is good news in the sphere of education, and La Dernière mode is *the first to bring it.*

Madame de P.

Issue 6

SIXIEME LIVRAISON — DIMANCHE 15 NOVEMBRE 1874

LA DERNIÈRE MODE

GAZETTE DU MONDE ET DE LA FAMILLE

Directeur : MARASQUIN, 9, Rue de Châteaudun, 9

PARIS		FRANCE	
Un an.	24 f.	Un an. . . .	20 f.
Six mois	12	Six mois . . .	14

Parait le 1er et le 3e Dimanche du mois, avec le Concours

DANS LA MODE & LE GOUT PARISIEN

DES GRANDES FAISEUSES, DE TAPISSIERS-DÉCORATEURS, DE MAITRES QUEUX DE JARDINIERS, D'AMATEURS DE BIBELOTS ET DU SPORT

EN MUSIQUE

DES PRINCIPAUX COMPOSITEURS

EN LITTÉRATURE

DE THÉODORE DE BANVILLE, LÉON CLADEL, FRANÇOIS COPPÉE, ALPHONSE DAUDET, LÉON DIERX, EMMANUEL DES ESSARTS, ERNEST D'HERVILLY, ALBERT MÉRAT, STÉPHANE MALLARMÉ, CATULLE MENDÈS, SULLY PRUDHOMME, LÉON VALADE, AUGUSTE VILLIERS DE L'ISLE ADAM, ÉMILE ZOLA, ETC.

TOILETTE DE PROMENADE & TOILETTE DE VISITE

Créées par Madame de Ponty

CHAPEAUX DE MARIE BAILLET (35, RUE DE LA CHAUSSÉE D'ANTIN)

In this issue, Madame de Ponty devotes herself, magisterially, to the ball gown and to what she identifies as its cardinal principle: the antithesis between the 'vague' and the 'definite' – between a 'fleeting mist' of *tulle illusion,* in a hundred shades of white, and the taut and close-fitting armour of the body that it veils. Whether or not the new style comes from the Orient, she says, the despots (in other words the couturiers) who impose it can expect unquestioning obedience. As always, however, she also detects hints of the fashions of the future.

FASHION

Paris 15 November 1874.

As two threads, one of silk or even of wool and the other of gold, crossing and interweaving, so, in their yearly cycle, the changes in the Season's fashions alternate with its 'occasions'. No very marked changes in costume during the last fortnight, or which are not already apparent in ball dresses, the subject of our study here. Dresses for these great occasions are sheer fantasy, sometimes daring and terribly advanced, though developing out of ancient traditions. To look at them is to see, amidst the satin, and under the gauze, the tulle and the lace, secret symptoms of what is to come. Here is my definition of the tradition which, more or less, all ball gowns follow: it is, for that more heavenly way of walking called 'dancing', the giving of lightness, filminess and airiness to the goddess who walks in their cloud.

As for particular features which seem to be prescribed at the start of this winter – a time still without great parties of pleasure, save belated ones in the châteaux *and the first gaieties of officialdom – here they are (at least what I have managed to glean, a little from ourselves, a little from others, and a great deal from the great couturières or their male rivals).*

First and sole rule:

Whilst the classic materials of ball gowns aim to envelop us in a fleeting mist, of a hundred shades of white, the dress itelf, on the contrary – both the bodice and the skirt – is moulded more closely than ever to the body, a delightful and scientific opposition between the vague and the (of necessity) definite.

An example of this rule, which comes with the authority of too many monarchs of fashion not instantly to be followed by a thousand infatuated subjects, is: that the bodice fits closely along its whole length, modelling the hips, with a skirt flat in front, this latter confining the former at mid-waist; and over all, a scarf. Has Europe not learned this new taste from the East?

To this sole, or at least first, rule, which we must write down, for meditation, on our mother-of-pearl tablet and only erase, along with the names of last year's partners, on the afternoon before the ball, I add two or three details, diverse but not contradictory.

1. Silk skirts are no longer made with puffs for evening wear but are frilled at the top, and the frill is repeated five or six times (covering a space of about thirty centimetres). As for trimming, at the foot of the garment there should be flounces or gathers, and further up (or very much further up) there should be gauze scarves, set very high over the apron and secured to the train by a bow.

2. Waists are made with little rounded basques, or else rounded points resembling basques.

Those are some of the novelties of the beginning of the season; especially to be seen at the princely receptions of the end of October.

A thousand exquisite combinations, familiar or quite new, may spring to the imagination of a Reader impatient for the first ball of winter; but the very choice of a material to send to the dressmaker is too intimately bound up with these for us to separate them.

Fabrics and trimmings, and even certain important arrangements intrinsic to the outfit, not simply decorating it, must all be considered simultaneously. In this thoroughly practical advice only one distinction is essential: between dresses for girls and dresses for young women.

Girls, I speak first for you.

Your dresses will be made of tulle illusion *of every shade, but especially white: scarves, with pleats or gathers, attached to the train or at the side by a posy or bunch of flowers – or by a garland, which is quite the latest style. Satin underskirts are, generally speaking, to be preferred to ones in* faille, *being more shimmering under tulle or gauze. Lovely Chambéry gauze does not easily get torn in the dash of a dance but* poult-de-soie *to my mind is more suited to a dinner dress than to a ball-gown. Will you try it? It should be trimmed with a lot of* chicorée, *resting on pleating fringed on either side. This ragged edge gives a charming illusion of feathers.*

Now Ladies, it is your turn.

For you, satin or faille *dresses for the dance-floor, veiled with white* tulle illusion *and enhanced graciously at the side with masses of flowers; or dresses entirely trimmed with real feathers or lace (Brussels lace or point d'Alençon). Let me add: always have plenty of blonde lace encrusted with 'white jet', or embroideries of dull silk on tulle. A thousand ravishing effects can be obtained from these trimmings, reproducing flowers from the world of dreams or from our flowerbeds: sometimes like frost-flowers, all white!*

Shutting my eyes to enchanting designs, which tempt me to describe them, I shall be brief and severe, as always.

Butterfly bows placed, with a happy lack of symmetry, as a finish to spaced-out flounces and narrow pleats; flower-patterns allowed to branch or to meander; here we have an ordinary, even an easy, form of luxury. But the genius which transforms woven fabrics into butterflies and flowers must be humble beside the pure and simple splendour of the fabrics themselves: white tulle threaded with silver against bands of white satin, or powdered with gold like the dust of many-coloured precious stones. In this case, no superfluous ornamentation, no useless additions, other than the thousand complications caused by the very design of the skirt: the flounces and frills set here, set there, at the top, at the foot. Nothing beyond this intricate and elusive glamour.

That is enough, and – although this may surprise you, dear Readers – I shall not offer you positive instructions: they are what you have the right to expect from a Fashion column, but only after it has described the march of Taste. On this subject, we have hardly begun: and it is only as a marvel of eccentricity that we cite the following, glimpsed at a famous ladies' dressmaker's. A dress of white tulle, trimmed with pleats of pearled blonde,[188] *the whole embroidered with the oddest greenery – artichokes, stem and all: an ornamental motif favoured in architecture and, it would seem, in Fashion. Baroque? No, decidedly not. It was even beautiful. But what did it mean (if it is true, as poets say, that a dress means something)? Really! to go to the vegetable patch, when you have the garden and the greenhouse!*

All very well for you, dear Readers, who are preparing for a ball, but I know others, mothers several times over, who would be happy to be present at the triumph of a daughter, of a daughter-in-law, or perhaps – charming thought – a grand-daughter. Which reminds us of a needful commonplace: that the shade (for we are now on the subject of colours) must correspond to a person's age or looks; not to mention – something very commonly forgotten – that we have to reckon with the colour or the shade of the wallhangings, that is to say with our background in any drawing-room. After my listing of fabrics a fortnight ago, I shall only mention one or two special ones. I choose (remembering the dazzling spectacle above) silvery grey tulle and, ignoring all the other colours, black tulle entirely sewn over with jet. Those other colours would be: pastel mauve, yellow, twilight grey, tsarina grey, scabious blue, emerald, golden brown . . . but enough is enough.

MARGUERITE DE PONTY

* * *

188. Blonde is bobbin-lace made from raw silk.

Black-and white Engravings

First page

1. Plum-coloured walking dress, chapeau Lamballe. – *First skirt in cashmere, flounces of the same, alternating with flounces of* faille. – *The tunic is rounded in front but has square flaps behind; trimmed with a cock's feather. – Bodice with rounded basques, buttoned down the front. – A fitted jacket, long in front and short behind.* – Chapeau Lamballe.

2. *Visiting Dress in garnet-red satin and velvet. – A satin apron, extending far back, the top gathered and the foot trimmed with velvet and lace flounces. The train made with a very deep triple fold. Jacket in garnet-red velvet edged with fur (choose your own fur).* – Chapeau Fleur-de-thé.

Middle pages

1. – Fourteen-year-old young girl. – Blue velvet dress trimmed with satin biais. – Grey felt hat.

2. – Fourteen-year-old young girl. – Tweed dress. The foundation is plain, and all the biais *as well as the sash is in striped tweed. The tunic is made up of three aprons, one above the other. Hat of the same, trimmed with feathers (choose your own feathers).*

* * *

A hat is a 'shape', which is very often the absence of a shape, writes Miss Satin. 'Make something out of that, even with flowers, feathers and my words!' The deliberate hint of *Symboliste* poetic theory is not to be missed (though one can suppose that, by many of her readers, it very possibly *was* missed.)

THE FASHION GAZETTE

Dresses are all very well: a fashion column has to describe them right down to the train. Everyone, from the dressmaker down to the skilful housemaid, can read our descriptions and more or less cut out a bodice or a tunic, a skirt or an apron. But a hat is something else! There is velvet or silk, there is felt or a 'shape' (which often is the very absence of shape), and I could go on for an hour. Make something out of that, even with flowers, feathers and my words! Inevitably, dear Readers, unless you have a very special imagination, you will make straight for a famous milliner.

There are, again, a thousand accessories which ladies need advice in buying – corsets, gloves, or shoes – and these few lines will deal with them.

Of all the model hats I have glimpsed in the last few days, in the Bois, in the theatre, everywhere, none were so enchanting as Marie Baillet's[189]*; one might with difficulty find her equal, but she cannot be surpassed. Skilled in the matching of shades, where others are more haphazard, and in the use of flowers both common and rare, she applies them to shapes not merely eccentric but, better still, Parisian, and being Parisian, queening it over the world. Foreign capitals have borrowed from us the* chapeau Lamballe, *which is most fetching and suits all young women, even if they are not pretty (are there any such?), for it serves as a face in itself. As for the* chapeau Figaro, *it is delightfully original but too well known to describe here; also it appeared in one of our engravings a fortnight ago.*

I can and must also praise the current speciality of Louise and Lucie: these are wonderful flowers, made by themselves, with which they create equally wonderful hairstyles. You could say of these ladies that they have fingers like morning roses – but an artificial morning, one which opens calyxes and pistils of cloth. Speaking of roses, I especially noticed in this new collection a garland of that flower, too underestimated these days, backed by gleaming gold foliage: also a trimming of purple geranium with lovely trailing greenery, again of velvet.

Did we say gloves, shoes, etc.? No, this time it must just be corsets. Choose the Elegant Corset, made by Madame Gibert (187, rue du Bac). It is specially modelled, all in one piece, and so perfectly made that it is a pity to hide it under a dress! This garment is indispensable when worn with a fitted dress, as they all are nowadays. Fashion everywhere recognises Madame Gibert's talent, and I might add, her obligingness: a point to remember, for she visits her clients in person, prepares, views and tries on. A word in the post a few hours before is all that is needed.

These details have already been very clearly stated on one of the visiting cards on our cover, and, as with mademoiselle Baillet, we are merely expanding on it.

MISS SATIN

Ix at last keeps his promise to write about Books, and to very odd effect. There is a species of calculated absurdity in his lavish praise of the poetry of Théodore de Banville and Emmanuel des Essarts, and it is not too plain what the point of the game is. Certainly, Mallarmé himself, though he was extremely fond of des Essarts as a person, detested his writing (though, out of loyalty, he included a poem by him, 'Le Veilleur de nuit', in Issue 5). He writes to Eugène Lefébure on 18 February 1865 about des Essarts' *Élévations*:

---

189. See the list of *Maisons de confiance, p. 46.*

The content is loosely expressed and degenerates into clichés and, as far as the form is concerned, all I see is words, words which are frequently chosen haphazardly: 'sinister' which could be replaced by 'lugubrious' and 'lugubrious' by 'tragic' without altering the meaning of the line. You do not get any new sensation when you read these verses. The rhythm is very cleverly handled and that compensates for so much mediocrity and gossip, but so what? You will tell me that I am being unkind to a friend? No, not at all. Des Essarts is one of those rare people whom I love very much. However, and it is most unfortunate, I cannot stand his poetry, which goes against everything that Art stands for as far as I am concerned.[190]

PARIS CHRONICLE

Theatres, Books, the Fine Arts; Echoes from the salons and from the seaside.

To think that these lines, traced before the pendulum of a little rococo clock, which marks them, has shown a hundred of them (or even twice that!), could encompass a week, and on top of that another week, of Paris: a vain imagining. The wisest thing would be to to forget the town and its winter and to speak of something else; but is there anything else? All the first nights of plays without music (our next chronicle will be dedicated entirely to music, of which we have a foretaste in the present issue in Mlle Holmes's admirable melody) conspire in vain against our urgent desire to open books, and read them, and tell you their titles: nothing shall distract us. La Veuve?[191] *But we reported its success at the* ***Gymnase*** *a month ago, as well as the magnificence of* Le Tour du monde,[192] *incredible settings, drama and crowd scenes; and we have sent greetings in advance to the* ***Théâtre Lyrique,*** *which has raised its curtain again for the first time with* La Jeunesse du roi Henri, *by the late PONSON DU TERRAIL. Since this journal began, books have piled up on our table, their pages uncut; let us wield the mother-of-pearl knife, and our eyes too, and let nothing distract us.*

Mlle Rousseil in L'Idole *at the* ***Arts,*** *though revealing herself each night as the greatest tragic actress of our time, will extract only a couple of words from us. To banish all obsession with her, there is only one way: to unfold the grey vellum of a friend's letter which describes, in detail, her costume. (Despair, despair!) I quote: 'A long* faille *train, the colour of toast, lined with straw-coloured taffeta; the front of the skirt has a thousand straw-coloured flounces, made very tight around the*

190. Translated by Gordon Millan, in his *A Throw of the Dice: the Life of Stéphane Mallarmé* (Farar, Straus, Giroux, 1994), pp. 108–9.

191. By Meilhac and Halévy; see Issue 5, p. 133. But it is described there as forthcoming.

192. Jules Verne's *Round the World in 80 Days.*

body, with bands sewn diagonallly representing huge dark-orange flowers; straw-coloured sleeves can be seen under a sleeveless waistcoat, brown like the train.'

At the **Cluny** *(M. Weinksheink's other pleasant auditorium)* Les Héritiers de Rabourdin[193] *leaves us, themselves, without comment; though, in the misunderstanding which seemed to have developed between the public and M. Zola, the admirable novelist who wrote this play, what a temptation to interject our own humble opinion (in a different spirit from a section of the press, which wants to make matters not better but worse). But a work of this importance deserves enough commentary to swallow up our whole Journal, cover and all; for with it the question raised, last season, by Flaubert's* Le Candidat *at the* ***Vaudeville,*** *arises again, perhaps never to be settled.*[194]

So now to Books.

The pious offering that, in the sad days of memories and flowers, the genius-made-man of our century consecrated to the memory of his dear lost ones, is a book! Victor Hugo has given us, on the twin Parisian tomb of his sons[195]*, some honest, serene, loving and luminous pages, which will also serve as a preface to their works, soon to be republished. The freshness of our emotion – ours, like everyone else's, is at hearing the voice of Victor Hugo once again; but also at hearing him speak of Charles and François-Victor Hugo.*[196] *He alone had the right to proclaim aloud, regarding those two young men so gloriously set apart (and not even just by their death) what for long we have been feeling in our hearts. But still, unconsciously, we confused their brilliance with their father's; and now their father has come to us to distinguish their*

193. Zola's *Les Héritiers de Rabourdin*, a comedy based on Ben Jonson's *Volpone*.

194. Flaubert's play, a political satire, had its *première* on 11 March 1874 and received so disastrous a reception that he took it off after the second performance.

195. The tomb is in Père Lachaise cemetery in Paris.

196. Charles Hugo (1826–71), a radical journalist and novelist, in 1848 became secretary to Lamartine at the ministry of Foreign Affairs. François-Victor Hugo (1828–73) produced a translation of Shakespeare. They followed their father into exile in 1851.

glory from his and to say, with finality: 'No, this is Charles's ray, that is François-Victor's glow'. All mothers, with sad admiration, will understand such a gesture and will follow it with their eyes.

From the solemn and unforgettable past – fable, legend and history – where such prodigious figures once flourished, Théodore de Banville,[197] *in his volume* Les Princesses, *has resurrected the body and soul of Semiramis, Ariadne, Helen, Cleopatra, Herodias, the Queen of Sheba, Mary Queen of Scots, the Princess Lamballe and the Princess Borghese. All the cruelty, pride, luxury and generosity inherent in woman, as revealed over the long ages before his own time, has been brought to life again by the poet, who alone can accept such treasure, in a gallery of extraordinary sonnets! His poetry, challenging the paintbrush and the chisel, has accomplished a miracle of evocation; and, in the hands of those who perfected it or in those who first created it, it never displayed more mastery, more vigour and heavenly freedom. Ladies, you must plunge your eyes into these pictures, deep as mirrors, where, as always, you will be gazing a little at yourselves. Not a single girl, on a bench at boarding school, but shares a drop of that immortal royal blood which made the princesses of bygone days.*

Harmonious, enthusiastic and wise – the work of an age of enthusiasm, bathing in the flood of the past, and of an age of science, soaring to the high heavens – M. des Essarts'[198] *book (he is a poet and one of today's most eloquent teachers) opens with a group, artfully composed, of 'Searchers after the Ideal', and finishes with another, under the invocation 'Excelsior'. Symbols and tableaux; the melancholies and joys found (and found only) in imagination: these, as in his earlier volumes, form the living substance of* Les Élévations. *Life's solemner, if still adventurous, hours, already tempered by recollection, are the ones this book will charm.*

Le Harem. *The title which M. d'Hervilly*[199] *has given his latest volume may be a shade 'warm' for some French ladies, But let no fans flutter: for this 'gynaeceum', so long as the volume which imprisons it remains on your bookshelves unopened, can safely come and go, and laugh and chatter, in an assortment of climates, free to frolic among ice-needles and banana-trees and rose-red obelisks. By a law superior to that by which, among barbarous nations, women are immured within actual walls of cedar wood or porcelain, the Poet (his visionary authority being as great as that of any despot) disposes of all the women in the world by thought alone. Yellow or white or black or copper-skinned, their grace is at once commandeered by him when he goes to work. It is the source of those apparitions which give life to books, and do so notably to this cosmopolitan album, which we owe to a much-travelled man (who, above all, has journeyed from the new Opéra*

197. Théodore de Banville (1829–91).
198. Emmanuel des Essarts (1839–1909).
199. Ernest d'Hervilly (1839–1911).

to the first lake in the Bois de Boulogne).[200] *A secret is now divulged, dear readers: the meaning of those hours that suddenly, and for no reason, seem blank and void; those quasi-absences from yourselves to which you sometimes yield in the afternoon. Somewhere a rhymer is thinking of you, or of your style of beauty.*

To this volume, which predates the return to Town (but was that its proper time, or was it merely holding itself in readiness for the beginning of the Season?), I must add Le Cahier rouge, *which has not yet been published while I write but will perhaps already be in its place in the bookshops when you read this. Many of the pieces in this forthcoming collection by François Coppée have been applauded by aristocratic or philanthropic hands at charity meetings (real ladies' clubs) before, as printed pages, enchanting the eye under the friendly glow of the boudoir lamp. The sympathy is the same: for if the popular young poet's verse strikes home at once and for ever by the precision of its tone, it feeds reverie and breathes, both for those who question and ponder it, and those who let themselves be carried away, a whole atmosphere of rarefied feeling. It is a double, almost contradictory, gift of truly perfect works: immediate applause, and lasting attraction! I have charming memories of the seaside and of fashionable parties, the imagined backgrounds of the new poems which this friend read to me one evening last May; and it was indeed from a Notebook bound in Red! Alogether intimate and casual, this detail explains a title which will surprise some of you at first but which will soon spring to the lips as naturally as 'Intimacies' or 'The Humble', as the book establishes its charm.*[201]

As it was once the delightful habit of certain very rich and sensitive persons to wear round their arm, in a nineteeth-century setting and mounted among precious stones, an attractive series of antique medals or cameos, so, beside the absolute

200. Ix's remark here is somewhat baffling.

201. François Coppée (1842–1908), author of the collections *Intimités* (1868), *Poèmes modernes* (1869) and *Les Humbles* (1872), was a well-known and successful poet of the day. His play *Le Passant* was one of Sarah Bernhardt's early successes.

and definitive works of André Chénier,[202] *it has commonly been the custom to print his unfinished poems, sometimes rough-hewn but always heavenly and revealing the outline of a half-formed conception. The re-issue of his works in one duodecimo volume, a jewel in itself, by the publisher Lemerre (to whom we owe all the poetry publications just discussed) makes available many of such little-known fragments: we may fairly describe this as a literary event.*

What! Have we come to an end before the rococo clock, mentioned at the outset of this article, has struck even one of those unwonted hours to which the first balls of winter extend? Brought to a stop by our paper – only by paper! – we have managed to speak only of poetry (with the exception of Mes fils, *those pages of prose by the Master of Masters*[203]*). So be it! Next time we shall begin with novels.*

Ix.

* * *

Twelfth leaf

Menu for an Ordinary Luncheon

Oysters: Marennes, Ostend
Prawns, Lyons sausage, Prevalaye butter
Little pigs' trotters stuffed à la Duthé (hot)

Provençal mutton chops au gratin
Sauté chicken Bourguignon

Roast thrushes
Celery remoulade

A buisson of crayfish in Rhine wine

Dessert: Camembert, Hymettus honey
Fruit and gâteaux

Coffee liqueurs: Jamaica rum and 'the widow Amphoux'
Russian cigarettes au Dubèque aromatique (Bureau

202. André Chénier (1762–94).
203. i.e. Victor Hugo.

Spécial) or Havana (Régie)[204]
Cigars: Partagas and Cabanas (Grand Hôtel)

Wines
Chablis Mouton
Grands vins ordinaires: Île verte (Médoc) 1870 and Moulin-à-Vent
Malaga G. Dorr

THE CHEF DE BOUCHE CHEZ BRÉBANT

There follow another exotic recipe from *Le Propagateur* and two 'home' notes.

Thirteenth leaf

Coconut jam

Everyone has been tempted to pick a coconut from a stall and, not knowing why one has bought it, does not know what to do with it. This classic foreign fruit remains – amid the pomegranates, the oranges and the pineapples – a curiosity for Parisians. Here is one of the best colonial delicacies in which it is the main ingredient.

Put 500g sugar and half a glass of water in a copper basin; when it is at the small crack degree add 1 grated coconut into the sugar, stirring with a wooden spatula. After 15 minutes put 2 egg yolks and a few drops of water in another basin; add the cooked coconut, stirring constantly in the same direction. Flavour with vanilla, cinammon or orange-flower water. Cook for 5 minutes, cool for another 5 minutes, and then pour into a jam dish and serve cold with arrowroot biscuits.[205]

Fresh coconuts, which arrive almost daily, can be bought, as well as herbs and spices and arrowroot biscuits, at the Buffet de dégustation des produits et des mets créoles ou orientaux, *56, boulevard Haussman. You can, if you like, write to that address from the provinces.*

This second exotic recipe is quite unknown, and we owe it, like the earlier one, to the tireless Propagateur *whom we have already introduced. Let us add that our*

204. All tobacco was manufactured by the State and sold at 'Débits de la régie'.

205. This recipe appears in *The Alice B. Toklas Cookbook* (1954) where it is ascribed to Mallarmé, but with the caveat that the timing is wrong and produced an excellent candy 'long before it was time to add the yolks of eggs'.

contributor can offer this treat all prepared, at lunchtime (if our readers simply drop him a note in the morning) just as it is given here and as he has it from

ZIZY, a mulatto maid from Surat.

Fourteenth and Fifteenth leaves

A Syrup to cure a cold

We have two doctors on the editorial board, one allopathic and one homeopathic; and their twofold consultation, signed with well-known Parisian names, will not be one of the least surprises provided by our Journal, when, in the case of an epidemic, it is offered on facing pages of the Golden Notebook, to followers of the two therapies.

Meanwhile, the only scourge is winter, season of pleasures though also of certain minor ailments and aches and pains. No call for the white tie of either of our doctors, save at parties.

So let us speak without them: first of all, about colds.

If you do not want, Madame – whether your cough be a light or a heavy one – to upset the party planned for three days hence, or to disturb your own household, then take: Corsica moss (a gelatinous lichen); Iceland lichen; root and flower of marshmallow; ground ivy; maidenhair fern; and red poppy (altogether, 5 francs' worth at the herbalist). Put it into a pan, with a lot of water; bring to the boil and reduce; add a good quarter of a kilo of sugar, and reduce it further until it goes from gelatinous to syrupy.

Take it off and, when cold, pour the syrup, which will have the colour of blackberries and the good taste of cough medicine, into the pot of your Dresden tea-service or a Venetian or Bohemian flask. Here ends my advice.

Take a spoonful from time to time, possibly hourly.

A difficult remedy? No, simple; whereas a 'simple' cold is often complicated.

Ointment for chilblains

Keep some oyster shells after dinner.

Why? To put them on the fire. Why? To heat them till white hot. Why? To have the ashes.

Mix this remainder, which you have pounded smooth, with lard. That is all.

Spread this ointment on the swelling or the cut (as you like, with a piece of cloth etc.) – one day, two days, three days – and it will be healed.

I recorded these two popular traditions (were they ever written down before? they have certainly never been published before) in my travels to a damp country, Holland, and a cold country, Norway.

Are they both old wives' tales, these prescriptions? Of course: and the worthy person who dictated them to me, practised as they had been for generations in her family, would have liked them to be called so; though a respectful remembrance requires me to sign myself, because of her,

A GRANDMOTHER

* * *

NOTICE

One of the novelties introduced by the Management into La Dernière mode *consists in fixing the day of publication, not at the start of the month or on the fifteenth, but on the first and third Sundays of each month. To await our publication till the day of family reunions, or at least of leisure, instead of being taken by surprise by it on an inconvenient weekday, is a favour we obtain for our lady readers, particularly those not in Paris. However, this arrangement suffers from one difficulty. Once every three months (i.e. in the month with five Sundays) it means leaving a three weeks' gap between issues.*

The magazine, losing its freshness (anyway its freshness of interest), will have to linger longer on the salon table: so let it linger on the piano!

A new piece of music, by one of the celebrated composers[206] *of the day, will keep it interesting. Deciphered, played and played again, sung by every musical visitor, it will save the issue from oblivion.*

Disappearance of the Programme for the Fortnight? *Yes, for there is no fortnight this time and the pleasures it would list, as always in advance, would be over and past. Similarly the CORRESPONDENCE WITH SUBSCRIBERS will disappear every sixth issue, giving way to a résumé of the past three month's issues.*

206. Augusta Holmes (or Holmès as she was spelled in France) (1847–1903) was a French composer of Irish parentage, a pupil of César Franck and greatly admired by the *Symboliste* poets. She had an affair with Catulle Mendès and bore him three children, though they did not marry. There is a poignant account of her in later years in Ethel Smyth's *What Happened Next.*

OUR SIX INITIAL ISSUES

TEXT

SIX NEWS-BULLETINS ON FASHION (the first of them devoted to Jewels) *have reproduced, over the signature of* Madame de Ponty, *a woman of the world who is also a distinguished writer, the fruit of up-to-the-minute consultations with leading dressmakers:* Costume and Accessories at the beginning of Autumn and Winter *(two articles),* Materials of the Year *(one article),* Festivities in Country and Town, Hunting Costume *and* Ball Gowns *and* Advice on Weddings, *etc. (two articles).*

No Journal gives more attention to good taste and loyalty in advertising: La Dernière mode *has introduced the use of VISITING-CARDS, on behalf of established firms, for this purpose. The News bulletins on Fashion remaining a purely disinterested analysis of changes in taste, they make no reference to (what is nonetheless valuable) the names of shops or dressmakers; and to relieve this Leader of Fashion, peculiar to our Journal, of all extraneous or commercial preoccupations, and at the same time amplify the brief information in the visiting-cards, I have now added a special article, THE FASHION GAZETTE, giving our Readers all the practical information they need. Have full confidence, Mesdames, in the foreign pseudonym of a well-known Parisian lady: Miss Satin.*

The CORRESPONDENCE WITH SUBSCRIBERS, which reports all purchases made on their behalf by the Administration, is a rich source of information.

Fifteen Leaves from the GOLDEN NOTEBOOK comprise:

Two Grand dinners, an ordinary Luncheon and a Family Dinner, a Picnic by the Sea, and two Hunt Luncheons. These menus emanate (I need say no more) from the Chef de Bouche chez Brébant.

Two recipes for exotic dishes and side-dishes, supplied by a Creole Lady and a Mulatress from the French Indies: these are certainly unknown in Europe.

Two Prescriptions, hygienic rather than medical, for the first cold days, gleaned from traditions of the North.

Let us draw to the attention of readers who have only seen this number the two decorative schemes, for an apartment and a garden, communicated to us by specialists, namely Marliani, the well-known tapestry-designer, and the chief gardener of the City of Paris. See, finally, a charming Sporting Sketch, the fruit of a conversation with the wonderful naturalist Toussenel.

The CHRONICLE, after his own introduction and from behind his mask, interests the Reader in the fantasies of our causeur *Ix, whose identity will be revealed one day. He has dealt with the first phase of the theatrical season, in three causeries; in another, 'Things of the Day'; and in his last one, 'The first books of winter', which every distinguished woman, intellectual or otherwise, needs to have read.*

Shall we call The PROGRAMME FOR THE FORTNIGHT, which is a necessary complement to the PARIS CHRONICLE, an advertisement? No. A causerie? No. It is both and passes judgement in a brief word on the AMUSEMENTS AND SOLEMNITIES OF THE HOUR. Five Programmes have appeared.

Then the literary Collaboration: brilliant, grave and always Parisian, the first such to grace a Gazette of Toilettes and Festivities. Does the list, which included only illustrious or much-loved names, contain any unkept promises? None.

All the early flowers of the day have here put forth their most exquisite bloom.

MARASQUIN

Issue 7

SEPTIÈME LIVRAISON — *DIMANCHE 6 DECEMBRE 1874*

LA DERNIÈRE MODE
GAZETTE DU MONDE ET DE LA FAMILLE

Un an . . . . 24 fr.
Six mois 13

DIRECTEUR :
MARASQUIN
9, Rue de Châteaudun, 9.

FRANCE
Un an . . . . 20 fr.
Six mois . . . . 14 fr.

Paraît le 1er et le 3e Dimanche du mois, avec le Concours

DANS LA MODE ET LE GOUT PARISIEN
DES GRANDES FAISEUSES, DE TAPISSIERS-DÉCORATEURS, DE MAITRES QUEUX
DE JARDINIERS, D'AMATEURS DE BIBELOTS ET DU SPORT

EN MUSIQUE
DES PRINCIPAUX COMPOSITEURS

EN LITTÉRATURE
DE THÉODORE DE BANVILLE, LÉON CLADEL, FRANÇOIS COPPÉE, ALPHONSE DAUDET,
LÉON DIERX, EMMANUEL DES ESSARTS, ERNEST D'HERVILLY,
ALBERT MÉRAT, STÉPHANE MALLARMÉ, CATULLE MENDÈS, SULLY PRUDHOMME,
LÉON VALADE, AUGUSTE VILLIERS DE L'ISLE ADAM, ÉMILE ZOLA, ETC.

Toilette de Bal et Toilette de Théâtre ou de Concert.

There being, according to Mme de Ponty's forecast, no great change in fashion to be expected over the next fortnight, she turns her attention to children's clothes. Her rules regarding them are, as always, very complicated and very definite, though she airily gives licence to ignore or break them. Here and there, among the illustrations, children in elaborate get-ups are depicted in stately postures.

FASHION

Paris, 26 December 1874

Laws, decrees, projects, pronunciamentos, as gentlemen say: everything has been settled now regarding fashion, and no new message from that great sovereign (who is indeed the whole world!) will come to surprise us over the next fortnight or two.

So, without rags or ribbons to occupy their mind, what will women be left to dream about? Children? There are mothers anxious to beautify their family as well as themselves, and such are the readers of La Dernière mode. *Has not this Journal, from its very first issue, devoted its most beautiful page to costumes for children or the young, enlivening the chronicle of Parisian affairs with the familiar image of these charming creatures? So is the present column a mere diversion? By no means, but rather a belated endorsement of a long-established tradition – or rather its complement, and what is owed to the pencil by the pen. For we shall not attempt to handle so vast a subject as mothers and their dreams; to deal with it in vague and general (and in consequence somewhat banal) terms is not what is called for today. But in this ancient and conservative sphere there are certain embellishments, due to the taste of the day, which we may report on.*

With what joy, only equalled by the inborn coquetry of the baby, does the young mother prepare the layette of the newly born, even before its birth, often herself making the 'brassières'[207] *and the underbonnet, which, from generation to generation, invariably follow the same pattern. Altogether different is the overbonnet, so laden with ribbons today that it cannot be covered by a hat: also, expressly for this purpose, we need one absolutely plain, and, in front, ornamented simply with two rows of ruched* petit tulle *with lace interspersed with white ribbon. The hat is always in the form of a hood, turned up at the brim. It is crowned with a great pompom of ribbon or a white feather and the effect is completed by braid or embroidery, especially when the pelisse is of the same workmanship. This, again,*

207. The *brassière* is the baby's first sleeved shirt.

can be bordered by wide bands of satin, wadded and quilted, although the current passion is for curled feather. It is costly, because it is white; and because it is white, easily dirtied: but what does the trouble of such a costume matter to mothers, compared with its charm? Who can say that such soft down has not been taken from the little new-born angel's own wings, to edge its costume – for this is the true and authentic, and nearly the only, use of this spotless luxury!

The baptismal robe always takes the form of an apron, with a white belt or a butterfly bow. The simpler and more convenient form, which goes under the pelisse, needs to be decorated only at the bottom, with two embroidered insertions, separated by Valenciennes lace. The ensemble is completed by ample lace, an immense smooth cloud of material, emphasising the exquisite tininess of the beloved creature. The specifications are: for the dress, 1 metre, 35 centimetres from the shoulder to the lace extension; for the pelisse, which is shorter, 1 metre, 25 centimetres (for we are already having to apply human measurements).

At eight or nine months, or at the latest ten, the baby goes into a short dress and a warm douillette.[208] *This can be embroidered or braided, or garnished with satin or feathered edging. The hat also changes, becoming a round felt one, coming very far down on the neck, with rosettes of ribbon and frills to protect the ears. (The shape subtly differs as between girls and boys). A swansdown boa encircles the neck, whilst the little gloved hands are kept warm by a swansdown muff, tied round the neck with a ribbon. This is what all mammas and grown-up sisters know as well as I. Up to the age of two the costume is prescribed by tradition and never varies, except as regards the colour of the belt, which may be blue or pink or red.*

Between two and five, little girls wear abundance of 'princess' dresses, these being the best for all-round protection. For Jeanne and Marguerite and Noémie must be free to wrestle and roll on the carpet without tearing their clothes or looking a disgrace. Their bright blue or navy-blue cashmere is set off by a matching dress. Pure white is the dream of all young mothers, but how many, nevertheless, will choose blue for everyday wear, as being less delicate? They have my full permission. In full dress costume white boots are de rigueur, *for blue ones would suggest the convent. They can be either of cloth or of glacé leather; but they must never be black, for fear of spoiling a tender and naive harmony.*

Dresses for everyday. I recommend deep-blue demi-drap, *perhaps with a tress of white wool, which years of success have consecrated as classic and as everybody's favourite. There is nothing better really, above all with a sailor-suit collar, dark-blue stockings and, this time, black boots. The hat, for smart occasions, must be of white felt with white feathers; and, for everyday wear, deep-blue felt with a pale blue or white feather, or an artificial plume. The same colour at that age for*

208. A child's padded coat.

little boys; but skirts entirely pleated, and the pleats always running the same way. A very long top piece with little basques with cutaways. The overcoat reaches down almost as far as the dress and is split at the back and the side. Fitting closely, it has pockets low down at the back. The hat is round, in blue or white felt as dictated by the rest of the costume.

Little girls of five to eleven can wear all the various tunics employed for women, ornamented with pleats or gathered flounces, belted jackets and basques at the waist, the skirts with flat pleats but no bouillons, *which would cramp the freedom of the little body. The elaborating or simplifying I leave to you, Mesdames; and since I would not want to seem competing with you as regards good taste or imagination, my only addition to our usual illustrations shall be a description of certain models which have happened to catch my eye.*

For instance the costumes of two little girls, seen descending from a landau adorned with a celebrated coat of arms, in front of a town-house in the Champs-Élysées. (I shall give a detailed description of the first costume, which was half-mourning, as a help to any family in similar circumstances). A paletot *blouse in white cloth with a sailor-suit collar in the same material, the costume lightly secured at the waist by a wide sash of black* faille, *knotted at the side. No trimmings, and simple white mother-of-pearl buttons to fasten the garment, under which, a hand's breadth longer, appeared a black cashmere skirt with flat pleats. A Tyrolean hat of white felt edged with royal velvet, with a white plume at the side, letting fall a flood of* faille *over the curls. Her companion, who was not in mourning, was dressed in the same way, except for the dress and for the belt, which was pale blue instead of black.*

Another model, enforcing the point that natural feather suits this particular age just as much as it does infancy and later girlhood. I made the sketch at a nuptial mass at Saint-Philippe du Roule.[209] *Two sisters were wearing dresses of grey Russian cashmere, with pleated skirts which only just covered the knee, and loosely fitting coats, of nearly the same length, in blue plush trimmed with natural feather. A little grey toque, a velvet pin with a band of natural feather and a blue artificial plume.*

My observation of these twin costumes suggests something important, on which Fashion seems to insist: that all through this winter we shall see many loosely fitting paletots *in grey broadcloth with natural feathers; and this garment, always very long, will be worn over all dresses.*

For little boys of six to eleven, a costume in grey-blue broadcloth or black velveteen, jacket and waistcoat, and trousers buttoning on the knee. A man's paletot. *A felt top hat, with its brim turned up, like those gentlemen were wearing*

---

209. An fashionable eighteenth-century church in the rue Saint-Honoré.

in the last châteaux *of the season, but enlivened at the side with a bouquet of cock feathers.*

I have told you everything or nothing. For the only reason to know these precepts is to be able to forget them; and I give my blessing to what is better, the rebellious fancies you will have been nursing even as you read.

* * *

Black-and-white Engravings

First page

1. Ball-gowns. – Underskirt in taffeta or white satin, veiled by a second very long skirt in tulle illusion. *A flounce in graceful folds, above which a garland of red roses entwines with bronze foliage. –* Cuirasse *in white satin, laced from top to bottom behind: the drapery of the bodice, like the second skirt of* tulle illusion, *is pinned here and there by a rose and foliage.*

2. Toilette *for the theatre or a concert. – Skirt in pale blue* faille, *tunic in black lace, pearled all over with jet. Bows of* faille *on the front connect the two parts of the tunic.*

Middle pages

1. Little boy, 5–6. – Pale blue cashmere dress, trimmed with white silk lacings. – A skirt pleated only behind. – A flat corsage secured at the waist by a large sash, knotted at the back. – Blue sailor-suit collar with two biais *of white satin.*

2. Little girl, 7–8. – A 'princess' dress in bright blue matelassé. *The flounces, punched in bright blue* faille, *are edged all round with a little fringe of gold lace points, secured by a button.*

MARGUERITE DE PONTY

* * *

THE FASHION GAZETTE

Not a day passes without one of our Subscribers asking us: where can I get such-and-such a material? where can I find the trimmings for it? Our reply (given here so as not to invade the Correspondence columns) is this: there are two ways of dressing: either put yourself completely in the hands of a great dress-designer or couturier, or give instructions to your chambermaid. In the one case, the material, with its trimmings, is all supplied, together with high Parisian taste; in the other, the elements for one's creation will have to be found in one or other of the four or five great Parisian stores. For it can be said that, nowadays, certain 'universal' establishments contain, separate or in boxes or even in finished form, the whole dream of Parisian womanhood. Thanks to these famous emporia, there are now in Paris, almost as in the provinces, places where everyone meets everyone and where one knows, quite simply, that it is here (or here) that one needs to go to satisfy one's needs.

No more long hours or days hunting for a particular ribbon! It is not just chance that makes us write down, before all others, the name of the Bon Marché. We have a deep conviction that the Lady Reader who, when she gets into her carriage, utters the words 'rue du Bac' or 'rue de Sèvres', will not return dissatisfied either with our advice or her own journey. To mention each successive enlargement of this noble bazaar, which expands each new season (so eventually one will find here all the riches of the world, in true oriental style) might seem unnecessary: but no, not so. It will be our only way to satisfy so many amiable enquiries coming all at once – yours, Madame, yours, Mademoiselle, and those of all you Mademoiselles and Mesdames.

Something very important to remind our readers of – what am I saying? – to bring to their notice for the first time (for the other day two of the three details given in our lines on 'Elegant corsets' were wrong) is the new establishment of Madame Gibert. It is certainly in the 'rue du Bac' but No. 106 (not 187) is the correct address for ordering from this accomplished and gracious corseteer.

Consult also our 'Visiting cards' on the cover, which often (and for instance twice today) may well be commented and expanded upon in 'The Fashion Gazette'. Such is the unity – a true, loyal and complete one – which presides over our Journal.

MISS SATIN

Ix devotes his column in this issue to a sore subject, already hinted at in his earlier causeries and theatre reports. It is that music (that 'adorable scourge') is taking over all the Paris theatres, at the expense of poetry and the spoken word. It is sometimes said that the huge success of the operetta *La Fille de madame Angot*, with a score by Lecocq, was the first real proof of Paris's resurrection after the events of 1870–1. It had many imitators; and by November 1874 Lecocq himself had two more successes on the stage, the opéra-bouffe *Giroflé-Girofla* at the ***Renaissance*** and the operetta *Les Prés-Saint-Germain* (text by Sardou and Gille) at the ***Variétés.*** In the year of *La Dermière mode*, moreover, Offenbach, recently taking over as Director of the huge ***Gaîté*** theatre, was still at the height of his fame, his operetta, *Madame l'Archiduc*, opening in October at the ***Bouffes-Parisiens.***

If one studies the 'Gazetteer and Programme for the Fortnight' in this and the next issue (see pp. 201–3), one will see that Ix's complaint is by no means imaginary. Paris has four if not five opera-houses in action; there is operetta at the ***Gymnase,*** the ***Variétés,*** the ***Bouffes-Parislens*** and the ***Renaissance,*** and something of a musical nature at the ***Vaudeville,*** not to mention the ***Athénée,*** which, according to Ix, is planning an operetta, and the ***Folies Bergère,*** which offers a Gypsy orchestra.

Ix, who has been particularly rude about the ***Vaudeville*** all through the season, says he hopes it will follow its present programme with a 'success in simple prose or in verse . . . literary and not musical'. He finds, however, a very characteristic, blandly ironical, defence for this musical take-over: that music attracts the most marvellous specimens of feminine beauty and fills the stairs and vestibules of theatre with dazzling *toilettes*.

His dig at the behaviour of 'Society' at concerts, where the listener may 'fix her gaze for minutes at a time on a blank spot in the ceiling . . . smiling in silence', puts one in mind of Proust's Mme Verdurin in the concert-hall, her face entirely buried in her hands. 'Did the Mistress wish to indicate by this meditative attitude that she considered herself as though in church, and regarded this music as no different from the most sublime of prayers? Did she wish, as some people do in church, to hide from prying eyes, out of modesty or shame, their presumed fervour or their culpable inattention or an irresistible urge to sleep?[210]

PARIS CHRONICLE

Theatres, Books, Fine Arts; Echoes from the Salons and from the Seaside

Perhaps, mesdames, you have already seen* La Haine[211] *when you open this journal? Nevertheless, as if it were still for ever postponed, I shall write instead on the topic I promised before.

Scarcely a century old,[212] music today reigns over every Soul. A religious cult for some of you, who are completely under its sway, and for others simply a pleasure, it has its catechumens and its dilettantes. Its prodigious advantage is to stir, by artifices reputedly denied to words, the subtlest or the most sublime reveries; and furthermore to entitle the listener to fix her gaze for minutes at a time, smiling in silence, on a blank spot in the ceiling, bare even of painting. The whole

---

[210] *Remembrance of Things Past*, vol. III, p. 253.

[211] The play by Sardou, see *ante*, p. 105.

[212] It is a puzzle what Ix can mean by saying that Music is barely a century old, even if he is referring to music in the Paris theatre (i.e. opera and operetta). It might be a reference to the foundation of the Paris Conservatory.

life of 'Society' is summed up there: the care it takes to hide the finer emotions, for which the imagination was created, or even (sometimes) to pretend to have them.

Who would dare complain that music, that incorporeal Muse, made up of sounds and sensations, that goddess – no, that nimbus, that adorable scourge – should invade the town's theatres one after another. For it attracts around it, in these worldly centres of its glory – in boxes, in the balcony, in living reality! – the most marvellous types, and most perfectly attired specimens, of feminine beauty. They are dazzling, these occasions, and are repeated every day and everywhere; not to mention the Théâtre Italien, resuscitated with full traditional splendour, behind the footlights as well as beneath the chandelier, by the sole person capable of this miracle, M. Bagier. He summoned from the shores of Africa the intrepid and brilliant Mme Pozzoni,[213] *who performs new works every evening to an accompaniment of bouquets and 'bravo's; he brought back from the limpid springs of classical art (such as nymphs drink at, on frescoed ceilings) that impeccable maestro Vianesi,*[214] *and finally (supreme magic!) he has contrived, after an interruption of three years and on the very first evening, to recreate in all its old magnificence the array of silks and satins, of jewellery, coiffures and elegant poses, which floods the stairs at the Italiens while the carriages arrive. This might seem enough for him, the accomplished provider of one of the great joys of Paris. But no, he is only waiting, to continue the work on behalf of modern music of the old* ***Théâtre Lyrique*** *(seemingly, alas! abandoned by the recent* ***Opéra-Populaire****), for the hero of the day, M. Halanzier,*[215] *to vacate the* ***Salle Ventadour*** *where, thanks to a miracle and to the Marquise de Caux and Faure, the Imperial Academy of Music*[216] *has survived for a year – and move to the Palais, the Temple, or the new Theatre to be inaugurated in 1875.*[217] *What good fortune it would be, my dear composer friends,*

213. Antonietta Pozzoni (1846–1914), Italian soprano.

214. Vianesi (1837–1908), Italian conductor, later naturalised French. He was at Covent Garden 1870–80, where he conducted *Lohengrin* and *Tannhäuser.*

215. Hyacinthe-Olivier-Henri Halanzier-Dufresnoy (1819–96). He managed the Opéra and installed it in the Salle Ventadour in 1873.

216. Otherwise the Académie nationale de musique. Another name for the Opéra.

217. i.e. the new Opéra.

if the ***Châtelet*** *of M. Fischer, should rediscover, to its own glory, one of the compositions that, in discouragement, you have allowed to gather dust; and another work, reserved for the conductor Colonne,*[218] *as the former would have been to the conductor Maton, should arise to consecrate the third Parisian Opéra.*

As for 'stars',[219] *they will appear at your first notes, as the sky at evening lightens at the sound of the young shepherd's flute. The subject of all conversations of the hour, having a few months ago been the mysterious comings and goings of M. Halanzier ('He is returning from Naples,' the whisper ran, 'from London, from Vienna . . . or perhaps from St. Petersburg?'), is now, not a question of performers but of a work! As for performers, one may guess it will be Faure and Nilsson, and perhaps Sanghalli; but in what? In a foreign opera already known and acclaimed in Paris? No, for, thoroughly cosmopolitan in spirit though the new* ***Opéra*** *is to be, this solution would hardly suit the moment of its inauguration. Otherwise the answer would be obvious: to go, without hesitation, for* Tannhäuser *and, by a supremely glorious gesture, wipe out the stain to France's name of earlier stupidities.*[220] *But this would be impossible, even more so than before, after invading armies, after Alsace, after bloodshed! Dreamed of, as soon as the first stone was laid, as one of the sublimest ceremonies of the century, this simple act of taking possession of the site can, as things stand at the moment, scarcely be the occasion for universal rejoicing. It is under a sky veiled not only by wintry clouds but by a certain palpable sadness that the bronze Apollo raises his golden lyre.*[221]

The idea bequeathed years ago by the ingenious architect, to whoever would exploit it, was a vast fairy entertainment, to occupy the stage while the audience feasted their eyes on the auditorium. The pièce de circonstance *devised by M. Armand Sylvestre, and printed in the newspapers, followed this plan, with somewhat less magnificence but with the unheard-of and paradoxical luxury of fine spoken verse, floating up into the dome of a theatre intended for singers. As we write this, the same newspapers (as if our fireside thoughts had been seized upon by demons, as we slept, to publish to the world next morning!) report, as a decision by the Authorities, the very thing we would propose. In the absence of a French work so exceptional as to conquer all Europe, why not – since the programme must be national – include some works by our master-composers of the past, together with an Act from some Italian and some German opera? For it was our genius to*

218. Edouard Colonne (1838–1910), French *chef d'orchestre*. He founded the *Concert National* in 1871.

219. i.e. famous performers.

220. Ix is no doubt referring to the ridiculous scenes provoked by the performance of pieces from *Tannhäuser* and *Lohengrin* in Paris in 1860. Berlioz wrote an article about them in the *Journal des Débats,* at the time, and Baudelaire speaks of them in his 'Richard Wagner and *Tannhäuser* in Paris' (*Revue européenne,* 1 April 1861).

221. Above the great pediment of the new Opéra stands a figure of Apollo raising aloft his lyre.

teach Italy, Germany and the whole world to appreciate German, Italian and French music. Gluck, Auber and Gounod, Meyerbeer and Rossini, a concert enhanced by the magic of the site and not merely a spectacle (save for the ballet): that truly would go to make a gala evening. Who knows if, to display the full flower of our taste, the Opéra-Comique, so rich lately in revivals, could not and should not (being so much nearer to Grand Opera than to the opéra bouffe, acclaimed by Fashion) lend one of its Acts to our new Monument: either an old one, beloved of past generations, or a new one, staged more lavishly than ever before?

*We have rashly mentioned opéra bouffe, which is also known as 'operetta'. Inevitably this, distracting us from our theme, will have conjured up Judic[222] and Peschard[223] and Alphonsine,[224] if not the **Variétés** and the **Renaissance!** (That makes three actresses escaping, through their all-powerful seduction, our rule of not mentioning names, even those of plays.) But what is the good? What headman of a remote tribe of the polar seas, still in his sealskins, would need to be told what three pieces we mean, in which this divine trio compete and reign – now that even Grand Dukes of Russia know the tunes by their numbers? The theatre which gave Mme Angot a daughter,[225] and did so unaided, though boldly provoking from Litolff[226] the claim that genius is always genius, even in a 'cascade' or singing a faridondaine, is at present hesitating between two mere revivals. The **Vaudeville,**[227] without hesitation, means to reject the name that the 'French, born malicious' found for it, in order to essay a genre which, perhaps, will prove to a future age that the French can also* die *malicious. And the **Athénée,** having had no success in*

222. Anna-Marie-Louise Damiens, Mme Judic (1849–?), star of the stage and the café-concert.

223. Marie Peschard, *née* Renouleau (d. 1888), comedy actress and singer who specialised in 'breeches' parts. Her collaboration with Judic at the Bouffes was famous.

224. Jeanne-Benoist, known as 'Alphonsine' (1829–83), famous comic actress.

225. See pp. 39 and 58.

226. Henri Charles Litolff (1818–91), virtuoso pianist, music publisher and composer, of Alsatian descent.

227. The Vaudeville theatre opened in 1792. It was closed by town planners in 1869, whereupon it moved to the Chaussée d'Antin. In its heyday it staged many Labiche farces.

commissioning verse from poets, is waiting, before re-opening as a theatre for operettas, for the bonbon mottoes at its neighbour's inauguration.[228] *(This takes place on New Year's Day.)*

I weep at this state of affairs, and also laugh. Is there any real harm in such fooleries? For historical or domestic drama, and for comedy (I will, with your permission, omit any mention here of the new playbills at the **Palais-Royal,** *the* **Ambigu** *and the* **Cluny,** *reserving them for our 'Programme') there will remain three or four serious, dependable and ancient theatres. Are there more than three or four serious plays in a year? In all our contemporary drama I know, perhaps (apart from the* Diane au Bois *of Théodore de Banville) only one great comedy, the quasi-heroic and superbly buffoonish* Tragaldabas *of Auguste Vacquerie!*[229] *Abused, eulogised, celebrated and even not known, that marvel of ideal gaiety appears now as what, for any sane judge, it was from the first instant, a masterpiece; and I would regret that the Master did not give it its chance on the stage again, were it not for the satisfaction of seeing such a fine thing enjoy, in the shape of a book, a natural and serene immortality. What music, exquisite, dreamlike and brilliant, in those four Acts – if only one of you Ladies, shutting the lid on your piano, were to hear how, merely by the rhythm of the verse, the passion in the dialogue is conveyed! The discreet white leaves of a book may appeal to a poet wearied by stormy scenes; another poet may feel the need, above all, of the friendly murmur of a* salon. *But it was song we were hearing last night – song in the sonority of its syllables and the arabesques they traced round the melody of feeling – in that noble duologue* La Rencontre, *adorably spoken, before an audience of artists, by the mistress of the house and M. Fraisier of the* **Porte-Saint-Martin.**[230] *No-one in the audience but with a name with some claim to fame; and as for that of the author, whom we feted and acclaimed, remember it, to applaud it one day on the last stage to remain loyal to poetry: M. Léon Dierx.*[231]

Ix.

* * *

228. The Athenée was in rue Scribe, consequently a neighbour of the new Opéra.

229. Auguste Vacquerie (1819–95), poet, journalist and playwright.

230. The Porte-Saint-Martin, a very large theatre, was in the 1830s the home of the Romantic drama. It was burnt down in 1870 and rebuilt on the original plans.

231. Léon Dierx (1838–1912), French 'Parnassian' poet and a friend of Mallarmé's.

La Dernière Mode, 7

Sixteenth Leaf

Menu for a grand dinner

SOUP
Consommé de volailles Sévigné
Turtle soup

Oysters (Marennes, Ostend, Imperial)

HORS D'OEUVRE
Smoked goose, Prawns, Russian herrings
Prévalaye butter

ENTREES
Fillet of sole Montgolfier
Venison
Poularde du Mans Piémontaise
Caisse of Foie gras with truffles

Port wine sorbet

RELEVÉS
Woodcock sous le cendre[232]
Ham in aspic
Salade Impératrice

Ramekins of Parmesan

Victoria ice à la Bressane
Muslin brioche
Dessert chosen by the mistress of the house
Coffee, Liqueurs from the Charente and the Isles
Russian cigarettes, little canons roses au Dubèque aromatique *(Bureau Spécial)*
Cigars: Regalia-Limena-Principe-de-Galles and Partagas (Grand-Hôtel)

---

232. Roasted in a wood fire.

WINES
Iced Madeira
Château Yquem 1861
Château Léoville 1864
Château Montrose 1858 (Retour)
Château Margaux 1858
Johannisberg 1858
Veuve Clicquot

THE CHEF DE BOUCHE CHEZ BRÉBANT

* * *

Seventeenth Leaf

Panel for a new dining-room

The other day we described a ceiling-arrangement to disguise the bare plaster ceiling of rented lodgings, and people wrote to us from certain town-houses to recall us to our dignity. But how many letters, addressed from 'Fifth floor with balcony' or 'Fourth floor above the entre-sol' shall we not receive today, accusing the decoration scheme which follows of unreality, implausibility and extravagance! For it applies to an owner-occupied house, and indeed, more or less, to one that is still under construction.

Somewhere, among the miscellany of cupboards along the walls, and between the door-spaces and the window-spaces, there is always a panel in a dining-room, which, with its Indian silks or Japanese rice-paper, gives the tone (which may be exotic) to the whole room. The silk will suffer from the fumes of food and cigars, as will the wallpaper, which anyway (wherever it comes from) may be flimsy: so what wallcoverings can give us the aquatic world, which – monstrous, frail, rich, obscure and diaphanous with weeds and fishes – is so decorative? Any picture, whether painted or embroidered, casts a sort of veil, an immobility, over the mysterious life of these riverine or oceanic landscapes. How shall we possess these watery depths in their reality?

In the depths of the wall, whether a party-wall or otherwise, make an opening, as large as you please, but at least a metre above floor-level. As for a tank, cement the section of the walls, where there must be the usual conduit-and-sluice arrangement (the source of supply on the right, the overflow on the left) for the water which is to occupy this empty space, two huge sheets of tough and untarnished glass having first been set in place! One of the two rectangles of glass (the exterior one) will be pierced with a narrow channel above the water-level, for air, or whatever else one chooses to introduce; the other, which becomes a wall of the room, remains intact. What one chooses to introduce is the rarest fish and crustaceans of our shores and of distant archipelagos: goldfish, scorpion-fish, polypuses, starfish, Japanese telescope-fish, etc.; also plants.

An aquarium (lit simply by daylight or, in the evening, by gaslight): there is your panel! Magical, living, moving and extraordinary. It can have a shelf with drawers below, or merely a plain plinth; and it will attract to itself all the luxury of the room, multiplied in dark-framed mirrors.

What modern prince of taste will execute this magnificent and simple décor?

After MARLIANI
Upholsterer and Interior decorator.

* * *

GAZETTE AND PROGRAMME FOR THE FORTNIGHT

Amusements and Solemnities in 'Society'
From 6 to 20 December 1874

I. BOOKS

When the bad weather puts an end to the Tour du Lac *and all such excursions till the hour of the theatre and the ballroom, do not curse the long afternoon at the fireside, but, rather, ring your maid and ask for: at* **Michel Lévy,** Mes fils *by VICTOR HUGO (1 vol.). Verse drama:* Tragaldabas, *by AUGUSTE VACQUERIE (1 vol.); – at the* ***Bibliothèque A. Lemerre:*** *Poetry,* Le Harem, *by E. D'HERVILLY (1 vol.*); Les Élévations, *by EMMANUEL DES ESSARTS (1 vol.*); Les Princesses, *by THÉODORE DE BANVILLE (1 vol.*); Le Cahier rouge, *by FRANÇOIS COPPÉE (1 vol.). Novels:* Une Idylle normande, *by ANDRÉ LEMOYNE (1 vol.*); Une Idylle pendant le Siège, *by FRANÇOIS COPPÉE (1 vol.). Re-issue of classic authors: MOLIÈRE, vols. 7 & 8 (the last); RACINE, vols. 3 & 4 (the last); ANDRÉ CHÉNIER, two volumes (Elzevir format); – at the* ***Bibliothèque Charpentier:*** *Novels,* Fromont jeune et Risler Aîné *by ALPHONSE DAUDET (1 vol.*); Nouveaux contes à Ninon, *by ÉMILE ZOLA (1 vol.). Criticism,* Portraits contemporains, *by THÉOPHILE GAUTIER, the last volume to appear of the* Oeuvres complètes *of this great writer. – At* ***Dentu:*** *Novels,* Les Diaboliques, *by BARBEY D'AUREVILLY (1 vol.).*

These are the first of the celebrated works which, mingling with copies of La Dernière mode, *will lie, opened or unopened, on the ancient marquetry or the oriental soirées of the salon tables.*

II – THEATRES

Out of a sort of respect (!) we change nothing in our announcement of a month ago about grand Premières inaugurating the second Theatrical phase of the Season, seeming to defy Winter. Clichés? Yes, and let all our notes in this column remain a cliché. As for our most recent ones, a certain hesitation may occur until the third phase becomes definite (beginning with La Haine); *the Programme is a creature of the moment. Today, more than ever, use our predictions to form your plans, but when the moment arrives, consult your newspaper.*

Théâtre Français: Le Demi-monde, *by ALEXANDRE DUMAS* fils, *still running after so long and quite at home by now beside Molière and Beaumarchais; with **Delaunay, Got, Febvre, Thiron; Croizette, Nathalie, Tholer and Broizat** – which gives an idea of the impressiveness of these magnificent evenings. Repertory: notably* Tabarin, *a revival, then* Le Duc Job *and* Adrienne Lecouvreur.

Salle Ventadour: the ***Opéra:*** *Performances by **Faure** in* Don Giovanni*; Ottavio, the tenor **Vergnet;** Zerlina, **Mlle Lory.** When shall we see the ballet for Sangalli (the rumour is* Sylvia ou la Nymphe du Diable*) and* Le Comte Ory *(announced)? ordinarily, the repertory:* Faust *and* La Favorita *and **Rosine Bloch.***

Italiens: *Nothing but premières: To* Lucrezia Borgia, La Traviata, Il Trovatore, Il Ballo in Maschera, Il Barbiere, Martha, Violetta, Crispino e la Comare, La Somnambula, *let us add* Otello, Il Trovatore, *and* Poliuto. *So many names, and such names, brought together, do they not produce here the same dazzling effect as every evening, in the theatre, is caused by so many diamonds upon bosoms!*

Odéon: *The first performances of* La Maîtresse légitime, *an uplifting and serious work, reveal M. **Davyl** as we had guessed him to be and show **Mlle Léonide Leblanc,** once again, as perfect. As for the repertory:* Les Femmes savantes, *with M. **Dalis** as Chrysale, and Duval's* Les Héritiers, *freshened by a Mlle **Baretta.***

Opéra-Comique: Le Pardon de Ploermel ***(Zina Dalti, and Lina Bell; Bouhy, Lhérie)*** *has given up beautiful evenings to* Mireille, *performed with the portions previously cut at the Théâtre-Lyrique, and always, and most happily, with **Mme Carvalho:** and this magnificent success will give up certain days to* Beppo, *a charming one-acter by M. COMTE.*

Vaudeville: *In* Le Chemin de Damas, *in the blinding irruption of light which struck it according to the legend, there now appears* Plutus, *god of gold: an allegory which leads us to hope that further successes in simple prose or in simple verse will follow those given at the Vaudeville (literary and not musical).*

Gymnase: La Veuve, *by MEILHAC and HALÉVY, and by* FARGUEIL *and his three costumes and all his talent as varied as them;* La Princesse Georges *revived, alas! without Desclée, with* **Mlle Tallandière,** *very curious: a double evening's entertainment in which an acute and delicate spectator can compare certain analogous scenes, some charming, some tragic.*

Variétés: Les Prés Saint-Gervais, *words by Sardou (and Gilles), music by Lecocq, with Mmes* **Peschard, Paola Marie, A. Duval and B. Legrand;** *the men being* **Dupuy, Christian, Baron, Cooper,** *and* tout Paris. *Is that enough? and is it not a case where copying a theatrical poster would produce a brilliant article!*

Palais-Royal: *There are two sorts of laughter;. laughter at what we have seen a hundred times at the Palais-Royal and which draws on ancient merriment; and laughter at premières. So the revivals of this autumn are succeeded by* La Boule, *that surprise of the winter, thus exhausting both modes of Parisian joy. No need to comment on the signature, 'Meilhac and Halévy'.*

Gaîté: La Haine, *by SARDOU, which* we *shall hardly have seen by the time the programme is due; but of which, a month ago, we wrote with our eyes fixed on the future, and we write today with our eyes shut: 'Here is a triumph for La Gaîté, for* **Lafontaine,** *for Mesdames* **Marie Laurent and Lia Félix:** *for* **Rubé, Chapron, Cambom, Levastre and Desplechin,** *who have conjured up, from their magnificent dreams, the settings for five Acts, while six hundred costumes designed by M. THOMAS will evoke, bringing these costumes to life, strange and very beautiful personages as well as voices charged with emotion; for there is a drama somewhere in all this, a stirring one'.*

Porte-Saint-Martin: Le Tour du monde en 80 jours *will make the Tour of the Parisian year: from Suez to Liverpool and from October to July. What shall we say about it? One needs to see it. 'The Cave of Serpents', 'Indian Suttee', 'Explosion and Sinking of a Steamer', 'Dawnie Indians attacking a Train': they are wonderful titles but are put into the shade by the real thing, by which I mean fairy theatre!* **Dumaine, Lacressonnière, Alexandre and Vannoy; Mlles Angèle Moreau and Patri.** *There is a drama in this spectacle by D'HENNERY and JULES VERNE.*

Théâtre-Lyrique: La Jeunesse du roi Henri, *which inaugurates the new auditorium for many winters, and in which M. CASTELLANO has introduced a thousand improvements for the public, whilst remaining faithful to the scenic traditions of drama, which he has long upheld.*

Ambigu: *Why, in the middle of a success, interrupt* L'Officier de la fortune, *if not to stage* Cocagne, *by FERDINAND DUGUÉ, about which we spoke in one of our articles? But what that did not mention was the superb acting of FARGUEIL, and all those Van Dykes and Callot etchings, and the scene of 'Anne of Austria entrusting the sleeping Louis XIV to a guard of Parisians'.*

Bouffes-Parisiens: Madame l'Archhiduc: ***Théo*** *departs,* ***Judic*** *arrives: should we sigh, or rejoice? Ovations and bouquets (which in this sweet-box of a theatre* *might well be crystallised flowers); diamonds in their looks and on their shoulders: a fabulous première due to last right through the winter. Dazzled and fascinated, I shall name no-one else. Yes I shall. Beside the maestro, that other charmer, Grévin, for his costumes for the 'Trumpets of the Grand Duke'.*

Renaissance: Sometimes pink and sometimes blue, GIROFLÉ is **Mlle Garnier.** As for **Alphonsine,** who plays Aurore d'Alcarazas, this star is always Alphonsine, the unique and incomparable. It is a real opéra-bouffe, and all Paris is humming 'C'est fini le mariage', 'En tête-à-tête, faire la dinette', 'Parmi les choses délicates', and 'Matamoros, grand capitaine.' Enough! For we shall have a year to get to know it all!

Folies-Dramatiques: HELOISE ET ABELARD ***(Milher, Emmanuel; Desclauzas, Vaughel)*** *are reborn after an eternity (three years) recalled by hands all ready to applaud.*

Folies Bergère: The Gypsies! whom the gentlemen listen to and the ladies look at: for they need both to be seen and to be heard. Their music is themselves, ardent, wild and exquisite. Neither Daras Miszka nor M. **Sari** (who is a marvellous nomad himself in his tastes) will soon cease to amaze Paris. What a varied, multiple and endlessly changing spectacle, known to us from so many posters. Only lack of space forbids us to describe it.

* * *

Other places of amusement and pleasure, by day or by night, are, first, the ***Jardin d'Acclimatation*** *(animals, the reindeer and the little Ceylon Ox, also flowers, prolonged out of season, and an orchestra, prolonged likewise) a promenade which will acclimatise the winter sun.*

The ***Cirque d'Hiver*** *with a septet of prodigies, those mountain-dwellers from the Apennines drawing the voice of doves and of women out of earthenware gourds; great success of the season, like that of those extraordinary skater Goodrich and Curtis. Let us not forget the* ***Davenne*** *family (the English gymnasts), who, acclaimed every evening, are (despite what the poster says) not beginners any longer.*

The ***Théâtre Miniature,*** *itself, is not content with fairy-theatre with* Le Pied de mouton, *whose décors, costumes and general ensemble have a magnificence only limited by size; it has summoned M.* ***Vielle*** *from Hungary and makes him, every evening, conjure up Spectres or perform miracles with his fingers and little nothings! But one thing we can be sure of, we shall never, in this delightfully refurbished theatre, see the mere spectre of Mr. Punch, who enjoys every Tuesday and Sunday an indestructible and charming life.*

The ***Panorama,*** *in the Champs-Élysées, with that bad dream,* Le Siège de Paris, *magnificently brought to life by the painter PHILIPPOTEAUX, attracts us on fine afernoons in the season.*

Robert Houdin: Le Nid rose, *one of the great successes of the hour, and so many other wonderful things on the boulevard des Italiens. Whilst those of the boulevard Saint-Denis are, at the same time of day, accomplished by M.* ***Litsonn*** *at the* ***Cercle Fantastique.*** *(You must be sure to see these: flowers and sweets given away, and reduced-price tickets into the bargain, which is certainly magic.)*

For children also, every Sunday, there are exquisite matinées at ***Frascati.*** *The season for making friendships in squares and parks is over, but here is a winter Garden which allows lonely children to meet (a precious opportunity), or to make the acquaintance of the Aztecs.*

The unsigned 'Travel' section in this Issue shows Ix, or Mallarmé, at their most inventive in their devotion to *décor.* Why, they ask (we need not bother to enquire how seriously) should railway companies not advertise 'storm trains' as well as 'tide trains'?

III. – TRAVEL

Western lines

Unless London attracts you, with its November fogs, or the Atlantic, battering the coasts of ***Brittany*** *and* ***Normandy*** *with a fury unknown to bathers, the Western Line offers Paris no temptations, reserving them for the summer. All the same, these days of white or grey or black cold are the time to visit wintry places, if one wants to have seen them in their true light. It would also be good to see, in its unchained fury, the sea itself, which made a mirror for our halcyon days in July, August and September!*

An express runs in a few hours from the place du Havre[233] *(that is to say the boulevard) to the jetty at* ***Dieppe,*** *from which fine steamers sail for* ***Newhaven,*** *where one is welcomed by the South Western Railway*[234] *and soon afterwards by Victoria Station. There are 'tide trains' (I forgot to take a note of the price, but it is less than two louis*[235]*). Why are there not also 'storm trains', running to the coast, to the rocks of Penmarh and the cliffs of Etretat? At the first sign of fierce weather at sea, picked up by semaphore, a telegram would be despatched to Paris, where the walls would be covered in advertisements for this sublime and near-at-hand spectacle, unknown to Parisians.*[236]

233. The Gare Saint-Lazare.

234. An error of Mallarmé's for the London Brighton and South Coast Railway.

235. A louis was equivalent to 20 francs.

236. Mallarmé himself spent a month alone in an abandoned house on the storm-tossed Breton coast, enthralled by the savage waves and howling winds.

Not all tourists choose sunny weather to invade London, which is banal and lacks mystery at such times; but practically all holidaymakers, of whatever class, visit the sea when stripped of its grandest and wildest character.

Leaving aside its vast provincial network, the tribute to fashion of the Ligne de l'Ouest *is its suburban services, through treeless scenes, enlivened by the last races of the year at* **Le Vésinet** *et* ***Lamarche:*** *and above all, its train for parliamentary Deputies. Which means that, having borne our dreams in holiday-time, this train, for the rest of the year, carries those entrusted with fulfilling them.*

Saint-Lazare has always been a witty station and – as I said three months ago – it is the most Parisian of them all.

CORRESPONDENCE WITH SUBSCRIBERS

Let us resume our ordinary Cover, having for once changed its colour to give a special appearance to the Trimestrial issue (which contained the music written for our Readers); and on the blue (not grey) page let us recommence, not a history of the Administration's efforts, which they have already forgotten, being so eager to attempt others, but rather the regular Correspondence with Subscribers, followed by ***Good Works or Advice on Education.***

Paris, 6 December 1874.

Mme GIBS . . . , LONDON. – Certainly, madame, you may have an extra copy of our cut-out patterns with every issue, but the subscription will cost you 6 francs more for the year, which means 0 fr. 50 c. for an extra copy of the regular pattern, instead of 1 fr. 25 for one chosen arbitrarily: this is assuming, of course, that it is a model chosen by us.

Mme LA MARQUISE DE LA T . . . , L--. – Be so good, madame la Marquise, as to get in touch with Mme CHARLES, who will be glad to do all your commissions for New Year's Day; and though you may have many grandchildren, she will, I assure you, find toys for the very youngest and imaginative gifts for the older ones. It will be helpful, however, if you would let our Buyer know the ages of all that dear company, and if she would let you know in advance the objects she is choosing and their price, etc.

Mme D . . . , LILLE. – Your dress has been ordered, dear Reader; it will be sent to you to try on in a few days, but I feel sure that it will fit.

Mme B . . . , WARSAW. – We have sent you the cut-out of an overcoat, as you asked, Madame; the model is very ample, because the garment will need to be lined with fur. The new style is: straight and without plait in front and arched behind, but above all with no trimming (for this would make it exagerrated and clumsy). It reaches to within twenty centimetres of the ground and is, within three or four centimetres, as long in front as behind.

LYDIA . . . , BRUSSELS. – Yes, my dear, you will look ravishing for your first ball. White will not make you look pale; and tulle illusion, *about which you ask (prompted by our last article on festivities of the* beau monde*), will envelop you in a moving cloud. Do not be afraid; your choice was excellent; and the profit from the exchange of letters will be ours, as we shall keep your photograph. One more thing: rather than lily of the valley we picture clematis.*

Mlle LOUISE V. . . , VALENCIENNES. – At the Sphinx, *whose visiting-card we always reproduce, you will find all the Crafts for Women possible; no, only the most beautiful. They have attractive work-baskets costing 20 to 30 francs; I think one of these would look well on your grandmother's table; or, using one of their patterns, you could embroider her a foot-muff, or – perhaps – a cushion for her feet when travelling.*

TO ALL OUR SUBSCRIBERS. I have kept the following letter for the end of the CORRESPONDENCE: it touches on a serious subject, manual work, of which I have already said a word or two before. One of our forthcoming News Bulletins on Fashion will deal with this form of feminine occupation and its products, openly, frankly and simply. Anyone who has read our first six issues will realise that ours is above all a journal of high-life, a gazette of Toilettes, *of the décor amidst which they are worn, and of the brilliant personages wearing them; thus there can be no place for what ordinarily (forgive me) creates ugliness in an apartment and (forgive me again!) dishonours elegant costume or (forgive me once more!) distracts women from more noble employments: banal tapestry-work and common-place embroidery: puffs, slippers etc.! A whole world of marvels, known to certain queens of the* salon, *whose fingers have grown weary of merely handling a fan, has for some time been open to the ingenuity and good taste of all. Silence! Let us await, to speak about it, a first Essay on Pastimes for a Lady of Fashion (and the first plate illustrating it).*

ADVICE ON EDUCATION

Guided by a Professor at one of the Paris lycées, whose sure and well-informed judgements are reproduced here, we are well known for our care in informing families of such good textbooks as he draws to our attention. The teaching of foreign languages (discussed here a little while ago) is no longer regarded as one of the graceful arts (we shall say more about this soon): it has its scholastic textbooks, which, however, may be elegant as well as practical; and it is these qualities that we look for in the ordinary dry-as-dust classroom text, which publishers are revising according to today's taste. What! Grammar itself can be interesting? If you wish to convince yourselves of this, Mesdames, take a look, before you put them in the hands of your little family, at the Nouvelle grammaire française, *or even the* Petite grammaire française, *by M. Brachet*[237]*, published by Hachette, which I have no hesitation in calling masterpieces: so much order, so much clarity! The completest, or the most elementary, of these works, a pedagogical monument of today (as was, fifty years ago, the good old empirical tome by Lhomond*[238]*), is almost a work of entertainment. Exempt from all abstract aridity, and suited to the delicate and logical mind of the child, it will bring home to you that a language is not a random construction but composed like a marvellous work of embroidery or lace: the thread of ideas is never lost;* this, *though hidden, reappears a little further on connected with* that; *the threads combine in a design, complex or simple, but ideal, which is retained for ever by the memory – or I should rather say, the instinct for harmony that, old or young we have in ourselves. Impressed as we are by the method of that excellent treatise, the* Grammaire historique, *which the House of Hetzel has given us, together with the same author's* Dictionnaire étymologique de la langue française, *books that appear side by side with Littré's* Dictionnaire de la langue française *in any serious library, we hope to study two manuals of French literature in its earliest period, which complement the preceding work. Titles:* Morceaux choisis des grands écrivains du XVIe siècle, accompagnés d'une grammaire et d'un dictionnaire du XVIe siècle, *and* Recueil de morceaux choisis des écrivains français du IXe siècle à la fin du XVe, *by A. Brachet, Paris, Hachette, 1874.*

Flowers first; then, if they are flowers of rhetoric, the bouquet: the words of the language, and then its literature.

237. Auguste Brachet (1845–98).
238. Charles Francis Lhomond (1727–94).

Issue 8

HUITIÈME LIVRAISON — DIMANCHE 20 DECEMBRE 1874

LA DERNIÈRE MODE

GAZETTE DU MONDE & DE LA FAMILLE

DIRECTEUR:
MARASQUIN
9, Rue de Chateaudun, 9.

FRANCE
Un an . . . . 20 fr.
Six mois . . . 14 fr.

Paraît le 1er et le 3e Dimanche du mois, avec le Concours

DANS LA MODE ET LE GOUT PARISIEN
DES GRANDES FAISEUSES, DE TAPISSIERS-DÉCORATEURS, DE MAITRES QUEUX
DE JARDINIERS, D'AMATEURS DE BIBELOTS ET DU SPORT

EN MUSIQUE
DES PRINCIPAUX COMPOSITEURS

EN LITTÉRATURE
DE THÉODORE DE BANVILLE, LÉON CLADEL, FRANÇOIS COPPÉE, ALPHONSE DAUDET,
LÉON DIERX, EMMANUEL DES ESSARTS, ERNEST D'HERVILLY,
ALBERT MÉRAT, STÉPHANE MALLARMÉ, CATULLE MENDÈS, SULLY PRUDHOMME,
LÉON VALADE, AUGUSTE VILLIERS DE L'ISLE ADAM, ÉMILE ZOLA, ETC.

Toilette de Réception et Toilette de Visite.

In this eighth Issue (which was to prove the last), Mme de Ponty is at her most oracular and prophetic. We quoted Proust's analysis of the youthful Odette de Crécy's clothes, and their deliberate contradiction of the natural lines of the body (see pp. 25–6). This chimes well with Madame de Ponty's prognostication for the future. 'Woman will appear, as in no previous era: visible, in clear outline, herself, with the full gracefulness of her shape or the major lines of her body.'

Both Madame de Ponty and Ix have a good deal to say about Madame Rattazzi: of her good-works soirée on behalf of the St. Joseph day-nursery and the marvels of her *hôtel* in the avenue du Bois de Boulogne. (Characteristically, Ix finds ingenious reasons for reporting on the soirée before it has actually happened.) The flamboyant Madame Rattazzi was the granddaughter of Lucien Bonaparte by his second wife. Her mother, the Princess Letizia, had in 1822 married Sir Thomas Wyse, the Irish politician and diplomat, and had had two sons by him. In 1828, however, she left him, becoming the lover of a Captain Studholm John Hodgson, who had rescued her from a suicide attempt, and in 1835 a daughter was born to them, baptised as Marie Studholmina Hodgson. Marie, at the age of fifteen, married Count Frederick de Solms, and became a grand hostess in Paris, though the marriage was itself a hopeless failure. Both she and her mother were regarded as great beauties and had a genius for running extravagant households, conducting spectacular private and public quarrels and involving themselves in libel suits. Marie, who liked to claim the title of 'Princess', got into trouble with her cousin the Emperor Napoleon III, partly through her Liberal *salon* and partly by efforts to squeeze money out him, and she was expelled from France for some years, going to live in Aix-les-Bains.[239] Upon the death of her first husband, she married Urbano Rattazzi, the President of the Italian parliament (after some rumours that she might marry King Victor Emmanuel himself). Rattazzi died in 1873, whereupon she returned to Paris, an event much commented upon in the newspapers. She lived in the Hôtel Aquila, on the boulevard de l'Impératrice (now boulevard Foch), later demolished. It may have played a part in Mallarmé's interest in Madame Rattazzi that he knew one of her half-brothers, William Charles Bonaparte-Wyse, whom he got to know in Avignon, round about 1868, as a member of the Mistral circle.

239. Until 1859, Aix-les-Bains was in the Kingdom of Sardinia.

FASHION

Paris 20 December 1874

'What! From her royal dais, made of the fabrics of all ages – those worn by Queen Semiramis, and the ones created by the genius of Worth or Pingat[240] *– Fashion, parting the curtains, reveals herself to us transformed, new, and in her future glory, and you choose this moment to lay down outmoded rules for children's clothes, from three months old to eleven!' So runs the reprimand we received from the most eloquent of our Readers, apropos of our last article; whilst a thousand others, emboldened by our silence, exclaim in appealing tones: 'What about the* fanchon-frileuse *we read about in* Le Sport?' *'What about the high stick-up collar they tell us about in* La Vie parisienne? *Ought it to be, not from fashion journals, but ordinary 'society' ones (as quoted in the popular daily press), that, of a sudden, we learn pieces of news destined, in a morning, to change the face of Europe – the faces, that is to say, of the women of Europe?' So speaks their leader; and the choir intones 'For instance, the* chapeau Maréchale, *also described in* Le Sport . . . *or the long flowing veil, described in* La Vie parisienne?'

To which I answer: Thank you, dear Ladies, I appreciate all those delightful details you report to me, but let me hasten to explain: I ignored them deliberately, those accessories of this winter's dresses, being absorbed in a patient study of a current evolution in Dress. For you are right, dress is going through a metamorphosis. So that I might show you everything in its place – here, or there and strictly in proportion to its importance as part of an ensemble (foreseen and reported on by us stage by stage from our very first issue), I said nothing, wanting to say everything. Everything! I mean, to explain not only the finishing touches of a new harmony in our way of dressing, such as we have all adopted, but also where that harmony sprang from and where it will lead us: its origins, its consequences, and above all the transitions accompanying it.

In a publication studying Fashion as an art it is not enough (not by any means!) to cry: 'You must wear such-and-such'. One needs to say: 'This is why', and 'We told you so!' There is nothing brusque or immediate in Taste: I was not behindhand, I was beforehand, as you will see in a minute.

Outdone as I may be as regards certain details, I cannot resist quoting as authority, in this connection, the extracts you have made, in your impatience, from our two excellent colleagues – whom, like you, I allow to have first-hand information. 'The fanchon-frileuse,[241] *a whimsy introduced at the Élysée*[242] *by all the*

240. A fashionable dressmaker at 30, rue Louis le Grand.

241. A *frileuse* normally means a knitted woollen hood worn in winter.

242. From 1873 the Élysée Palace was the residence of the President of the Republic.

elegant women of our beau monde, *is still in the incomparable grace of its début in good society. It is made of light and wispy white tulle, draped round the face and tied under the chin: the hat proper is then set on this cloud of tulle, through which you can see the big bow which serves to secure it. The face itself is left unmasked; a long veil drops down to the chest, covering the shoulders and tied in the middle of the back.' I will continue: 'The* chapeau Maréchale, *destined to be the great success of this winter, comes in felt, velvet or tulle. It has a somewhat cunning shape, fitting closely to the head in the* Directoire *style. Over this is draped a great lace mantilla, secured at the side by a bunch of roses. Nothing could be more pretty, ideally so, than this hoodlike effect. The long lace veil need not necessarily be fastened with flowers; a beautiful bird or a long feather is sometimes used.' That's all. No, I am forgetting: 'No ruches at the neck; a tall upright collar turned back on itself, like those of the* Incroyables.[243] *It comes in the same kind of fabric as the dress, or in fur in the case of a cloak.'*

Everything perfect, exact and strictly laid down.

Now it is our turn to speak, if we dare.

What did we say in one of our issues at the beginning of autumn? That the bustle was on its way out, and that the pouff *was disappearing: we offered this as the point of departure for all probable changes during the winter. All of these have either followed, or preceded and cleared the way for, the slow process of elimination, culminating in the CLINGING DRESS, which is triumphing and will more or less make you, Ladies, into Jean Goujon's slender nymphs.*[244]

No more pouffs: *that is to say all the turned-up or tucked-up part has gone, and the tunic too; and the apron, though remaining taut and unadorned, save for a single bow at the foot, will give way to waistbands, tied very low, in the same material, two fitting closely on each hip, their function being to raise the front of the dress.*

Now, for the dress. It is trimmed, with all the ordinary decorations (ruches, pleats and flounces) rising one above the other in a charming flight towards the top of the skirt; but it also loses trimming, either in front or at the back, ending up with a bodice extending far below the waist (not to borrow technical terms from the sculptor). Finally, coronation, or a crown! For, more than ever, marabout feathers mingle their dense haze with the glitter of hair, seeming, with their playful and fluttering invasion, to want to efface the hardness and sparkle of jet. Ah, but add some fur! When this takes place – the feathers arranged in garlands and the fur spreading from the edges right across the material, in wide bands – neither will manage to outlaw its rival! Breastplates and armour etc., all the defensive and delightful gear so long combined with women's dress, will not readily give up jet,

243. The *incroyables* were the dandies of the post-Revolution epoch.

244. The nymphs carved by Jean Goujon (c.1515–68) on the Fontaine des Innocents in Paris.

with its steely scintillations, or steel itself. Though always assigning a large role to feathers – the natural ones of cock, peacock or pheasant, and dyed ones in blue or pink from the ostrich – we have hitherto believed (and here our forecasts differ from what others have said) that sequins, both glass and metal, will last through the winter.

One single proof! I only want one, but it must be definitive: and I look for it in the wonderful dress worn, only a few days ago, by the Parisienne par excellence. *For that is what she was when abroad, and as she is now in her hôtel in the Bois de Boulogne – Madame Rattazzi, Fashion's acclaimed queen. 'I have just described the décor' we are told in a delightful letter signed with well-known initials (alas! not to be able to transcribe here all that description of a magic house, but let us proceed to the magician herself!), 'and as for the Princess's costume, it was as follows. A close-fitting dress with a train, in black lace, strangely strewn with blue steel with a sword-like glitter; her hair was piled up in a diadem, with four strings of enormous diamonds intertwined in its shade and buried in its dark splendour'. What a miraculous vision, a picture to dream of rather than paint; for its beauty suggests certain impressions, deep or fleeting, of the poet.*

You will take note, Ladies (you who lectured me, and you others who echoed her), that our information does not come only from the great dressmakers, as is often said in our Journal, but also from high society. Goodbye, and thank you for having enabled us, at the beginning, to quote from two elegant and distinguished publications, it being the ambition of our Journal to lie beside them on drawing-room tables, which was not where you would have found the old Journal des modes. *The plan of this column, both before and after the kind interruptions we have been pleased to answer, was not, anyway, to speak about itself or us: it had only to present a great lady's costume, selected from several, as a quick summary of the end-result of the change taking place in Dress, of which, day by day, we have been seeing the symptoms.*

To sum up, never have rich, and even heavy, fabrics – velvet, and silver or gold brocades – reigned so proudly, but no less the light, soft and bright new cashmere, as used for evening wear; but through this envelope, whether sumptuous or plain, Woman will appear, as in no previous era: visible, in clear outline, herself, with the full gracefulness of her shape or the major lines of her body (whilst from behind, the huge grandeur of her train brings together all the folds and massive breadth of the fabric).

MARGUERITE DE PONTY

* * *

La Dernière Mode, 8

Black-and-white Engravings

First page

1. Dress for receiving: Russian grey satin; the cuirasse bodice, in the same shade of velvet, is trimmed with steel sequins.

2. Formal visiting dress: Skirt of plum-coloured faille, *with matching flounces, trimmed crosswise with velvet of the same shade. – The tunic is of quilted material, still the same shade, with large velvet* biais[245] *set lengthwise. The bottom is trimmed with strips of cock's feathers.*

Middle pages

1. Little boy, 8–9. – Jacket, waistcoat and short trousers in navy blue cloth: coat of the same material, trimmed with astrakhan.

2. Little girl, 8–9. – Blue velvet dress; plain skirt.

Miss Satin, in this issue, makes lavish propaganda for the *Lait d'Hébé* and *Crême Neige* advertised by the *Corbeille Fleurie* or *Parfumerie Pinaud-Meyer* in the boulevard des Italiens and the boulevard de Strasbourg.

THE FASHION GAZETTE

A litle bit of a chat, to expand on certain of our Cover Advertisements, they themselves being discreet and mute, as is fitting after a formal presentation.

First the visiting-card, then the visit.

Dresses, or hats? No, nor even, as on a previous occasion, fabrics.

If the harmony of her costume, whether it was ordered by herself or was a gift, is exquisite, it will distil that perfume of distinction proper to a woman: but this, though belonging entirely to the moral sphere, must not make us forget that other perfume which is derived from actual flowers, for example Parma violets. Though the soul of these flowers, destined to survive them in the cloud of a lacy handkerchief, has to undergo scientific operations before acquiring such immortality! Ask Pinaud and Meyer[246] *to explain: or rather, just sample their Extract of the aforementioned perfume, which alone will satisfy your curiosity. Snow, which chaps the skin by its temperature but gives it a lively and desirable freshness; and cream,*

245. See note 56 on p. 42.

246. See their visiting-card on p. 45.

which distends its texture but restores and feeds it: these two quite contrary whitenesses, for me, combine their virtues without their danger, in the product delightfully named Crême-Neige.[247]

Similar yet different is Le Lait d'Hébé,[248] *which someone brought me and which might well be the nectar which that goddess poured out on Olympus; for the bottle containing the marvellous liquid has within it strength as well as suppleness: that is to say all the benefits which the most delicate skins may look for when exposed to winter. A memory, not a faint one, is aroused by* l'Eau de toilette au lait d'Hébé; *and, of course! (for once that a wonder has been discovered, it must be made available in all the various forms of toilet-preparation) I am thinking of the Soap made with the same* Lait d'Hébé. To *those of you, dear Ladies, who would not be attracted by a mythological label, I propose* Opoponax *(toilet-water, cream and soap),* Exora,[249] Ylang-Ylang, *or* Nard Celtique: *strange but delicious fragrances which, when once breathed, send the mind dreaming, as does the mere pronouncing of their names.*

Very fashionable and luxurious, these perfumes have, as it were, nothing to do with the dressing-table: they fill strange-looking bottles, Dresden, Bohemian or Venetian, on the boudoir shelves. Rare glassware or porcelain emitting a precious fragrance, what a charming New Year's gift! Does a box of perfumes not hold delights very different from those of a bag of sweets? I will stop here because, on this subject, there are a thousand curious things to say.

*Who does not know the address of the Shop? But is there any need to know it? I think of them as so many ex votos hung in the chapels of beauty by grateful women – those copies of the picture which, in all the perfume shops in Paris, the provinces and abroad, intertwines the shop-sign, the streets and even the street-numbers (*A la Corbeille Fleurie, 30, *boulevard des Italiens, and 37, boulevard de Strasbourg) with its garlands, putti and clouds.*

MISS SATIN

Within Ix's conception of Fashion, as we have noticed already, the calendar plays an important part, and his advice for an old-fashioned Christmas and New Year is warmly affectionate. The enthusiasm extends to the 'Golden Notebook's' instructions for 'An ordinary Christmas tree' and is evidently Mallarmé's own. Ix's fondness for 'glacé fruits from all lands' and 'traditional sweets . . . imitating the shape of some ordinary or fantastic thing' remind one of the inventive quatrains Mallarmé would compose to accompany a New Year's gift of crystallised fruit

247. Cream-Snow.

248. The Milk of Hebe, named after the Greek goddess of youth.

249. So in the text, but the visiting card has 'Ixora'.

(some sixty-two of them have survived),[250] and the ones written in gold ink, line by line, on four red Easter eggs.

PARIS CHRONICLE

Theatres, Books, the Fine Arts;

Echoes from the salons and the seaside

The winter, the long winter, unlike the months which recall autumn or which forecast spring, does not have a daylong break, blue and clear, in the clouds: it will have to seek its days for celebration in the higher Christian heavens and the calendar. Emblem of that desire which makes us imagine delicious flavour in anything bright, oranges – in heaps at shop-doors and borne along the streets – make the first splash of splendour against the monotonous fog. Their classic appearance reminds every Parisian of a date, Christmas, and of another date, New Year. The two festivals, for their respective places of worship, hasten to choose different window-dressings, though equally designed for the pleasures of mouths and eyes: this one belongs to a former cooked-meat shop, become an international grocer; that other to a sweet-shop, preparing to candy, not just the violets of Nice, but 'fils de la Vierge'[251] *or twenty-franc coins. Happy is the toyshop man, if he really exists, in some unseen corner; or, simple fellow, unhappy, for nobody knows him, and where would he find more toys to display on his paper-lined counter?*

250. They usually turn on some inspired rhyme, as for instance 'neige' and 'n'ai-je' in the charming '*Sous un hiver qui neige, neige, / Rêvant d'Edens quand vous passez! / Pourquoi, madame Madier, n'ai-je / À donner que des fruits glacés . . . ?*' [During a winter which snows, snows, dreaming of Edens when you pass, why, Madame Madier, do I have only glacé fruits to give?]

251. Known in Britain as 'angels' hair'.

All those shops into which the children of today, skilled in manoeuvres unknown to the older European diplomacy, drag father and mother by the hand to show them, without words, that such-and-such, and no other, is the New Year's gift they are expecting – they fill me with alarm. At the counters, ladies perhaps dressed by Madame Laferrière[252] herself, eye with visible scorn the ill-bred person who would use the words 'dolls' when asking their price; whilst gentlemen, with collars turned down like visiting-cards, study the adjacent steamer, which is about to try out its engines (which run on spirits-of-wine), or discuss the chances of success of a complete electric telegraph, in a little green box, the kind one sees in offices. It would seem disrespectful even to hint the question: 'Are these jack-in-a-boxes?' Whatever happened to that age-old trade, the making of toys which were broken the very same evening, to see what was inside? Has it taken refuge in those wooden stalls with waterproof awnings which pretend to be a fair, along the astonished boulevards? By no means! Here, just as much as in the famous stores which this overgrown bazaar hopes to rival, one finds the standard Paris product, merely taxed at a more accessible rate. There you have the streets; and when my eye follows, from the doorstep of a famous shop to the door of their carriage, a lady or a gentleman preceded by a huge mysterious parcel, it is led by curiosity – yes! to know if either has by chance acquired some innocent and wonderful invention, fit to replace Mr. Punch, or the complete Noah's Ark procession, from the elephant to the fly! But almost always I am disappointed and made to think: 'What can I, a superannuated chronicler, do to restore to the faces of three- to ten-year-olds that authentic look of rapture which is always so adorable?'

Things have changed, that is all, and nothing is lost for ever, not even children's laughter . . . Cosy and intimate at home, with the Alsatian tree,[253] which we must accept without excluding the Burgundian log,[254] thus accumulating traditions; lively and noisy out of the home, in a thousand gatherings where, by a charming modern innovation, children share their joys with one another; but, change as it may, at bottom it remains the same. That is how Christmas will always be, and how the New Year will always be.

Mothers, whom this paper is usually telling what Yves or Jeanne should wear over the next fortnight, please join with me in consulting the Golden Notebook and be glad to note, beside the ideas for a New Year's Eve party, that other 'menu'

252. The third of the great Parisian dressmakers, after Worth and Pingat, at 28, rue Taitbout.

253. The Christmas tree, which originated in Germany. The force of 'Alsatian' would not have been lost on a French reader in 1874. See the 'Twentieth leaf' of the *Golden Notebook,* where the implication seems to be that the recent popularity of the Christmas tree is a gesture of solidarity with France's sometime fellow citizens in Alsace.

254. Various French provinces had a tradition of the Yule log.

whereby, piece by piece, and growing ever huger, the ceremonial fir tree is made gay and dazzling.

A quick glance at the last page (our fortnightly Gazette and Programme), where one reads the names of theatres, actors and plays, will reveal details of many Soirées, and one or two Afternoons, for children. What better or more acceptable surprise than – hidden amid the greenery, the candles and the gifts of the Christmas tree – a ticket for a box, in the name of Miss or master Baby, bearing one of those names that are magic in themselves: ***Théâtre Miniature,*** *or* ***Théâtre des Familles,*** *or* ***Robert-Houdin,*** *the* ***Bals de Frascati,*** *the* ***Cirque d'Hiver,*** *or the* ***Châtelet,*** *which has now become the* Châtelet des Pilules?[255]

In a wallet of scented notepaper (a present for the intelligent) one could still well enfold a season-ticket for the wonderful matinées at the ***Gaîté,*** *and the traditional ones at the* ***Porte-Saint-Martin,*** *or for the* ***Concerts Pasdeloup*** *or* ***Colonne;*** *for would that not be an enviable present too, the promise of noble pleasures on so many Sundays?*

Fancy devoting only the opening of this Chronicle to our rosy, fair or dark-haired darlings, sovereigns of the present moment! Their happiness is too large a subject; and I can see that, now I have nearly finished, no society gossip need distract me. Having got so far, I ought, for better or for worse, to go on in the same style. What does it matter, for instance – my absolute duty as a chronicler of Paris obliging me to tell readers abroad, or in the provinces, or even in Paris itself, that a certain delightful melody (to words printed in the present issue as 'Poem of the Day') is now a favourite on pianos weary of operetta airs and dance-tunes – whether I announce this piece of musical news under the heading 'Salons' or that of 'Festivals of the day'? For we are talking about the 'Noël' of Alphonse Daudet and Emile Pessard, a Noël simple and fresh enough to renew the sweet impression of the hymns of bygone days and yet sufficiently (how shall I put it?) full of wit and an almost Parisian dilettantism to flutter unembarrassed in the air stirred by the fans of 1875: a real success and gift from heaven, not to be neglected! How many years does Adam's lovely piece[256] have behind it, and how many does this Vierge à la crèche[257] *have before it? The same number; which is not to advise belated Readers, before acquiring the work, to wait for it to be bound up in albums; for I know no more exquisite emotion for a woman, about to open her lips and launch the first note, than the sudden thought, 'I am one of the first in the world to sing this melody'!*

---

255. See the Theatre list in this issue.

256. 'Minuit, Chrétiens', by Adolphe Adam (1803–56), composer of opéras-comiques and songs. Immensely popular in its time, it was banned in the 1930s by the French bishops as being lacking in musical taste and showing a total absence of religion.

257. Virgin at the cradle.

Still in connection with the winter's festivities, we shall describe to you in advance (the date for this festival being the 19th, the very evening we go to press) a performance to be given in the public rooms of the delightful hôtel d'Aquila, *in honour of the St. Joseph Day-Nursery – all day-nurseries and cribs recalling the one over which the star stood and the angels came down. Really and truly, is there not a charm in reporting a celebration before it happens, whereas the day after it can only be 'exquisite', implying the certainties of success? Let our Dream, clothed in satin and adorned with diamonds, climb the sumptuous staircase (reminding her of the* hôtel *built by Arsène Houssaye[258]); let her, averting her eyes from the magnificent portrait of the mistress of the house, exhibited in Vienna by Carolus Duran,[259] cross the music-room with its Herz grand piano, to view the formal drawing-room, opening on to a tropical conservatory, a fountain and cages brilliant with a thousand gem-like songbirds; then let her pause before a white marble bust, by Clesinger,[260] of the same lady as in the portrait in the hallway. But no! No doubt it will be quite different; the mansion will blaze with a thousand candles; and the invisible Person, whose appearance painting and sculpture dispute between them, will, this evening, essay new arts herself, appearing not as Madame Rattazzi but as an imaginary character in a comedy.[261] The aesthetics of Fashion or the Chronicle of a fortnight: nothing, be it theory or simple reporting, can, if it is to do its duty, escape the delightful tyranny of this Inspirer.*

But where am I getting to? Tear it all up – I mean, the first part of my causerie, not the last! – for my main task today was to have been to talk with you about new masterpieces of fiction, as I recently did about Poetry. The second edition of Zola's

258. Arsène Houssaye (1815–96), critic and art-historian and, from 1849, director of the Comédie Française.

259. Carolus-Duran (C.-E.-A. Durand) (1837–1917), the distinguished French portrait painter. The painting is now in the Museum van Schonen Kunsten at Antwerp.

260. Auguste Clesinger (1814–83), French sculptor and painter. His bust of Mme Rattazzi is also now in Antwerp.

261. The French reads, 'la figure idéale d'une saynète ou d'une comédie'. A 'saynète' is a short play or playlet.

La Conquête de Plassans, *together with his* Contes à Ninon *(and I will add* Les Héritiers de Rabourdin, *a play); also the second edition of* Fromont jeune et Risler aîné, *by Alphonse Daudet; such are the books which, alas, I give you with their pages uncut, like New Year's gifts. None, we can be sure, could be more seductive during evenings at home, when, the children in bed, the party-fever gives way, for an hour or two, to the tranquillity of the lamp.*

Thanks to these volumes, which I place as an offering on your lacquered bookshelves, to chat with you about later, I can, dear Ladies – like a friend planning a brief absence-speak to you about New Year's Day ten days in advance, so not fearing to mingle my premature greetings with those already offered by the water-carrier, the postman and the local dispenser of pain bénit.[262]

Ix.

* * *

Eighteenth Leaf

Menu for a Midnight Supper

Ostend and Marennes oysters

Consommé of plover's eggs
Black pudding à la Richelieu[263]
Fillets of sole with Montepellier butter[264]
Saddle of Nîmes Lamb with asparagus tips

Truffled bartorelles
Thrush pâté wih juniper berries
New peas à la française[265]
Buisson of crayfish with Ribeauille wine[266]

Louvres in pastry with chocolate

262. *Pain bénit* is bread that has been blessed (as distinct from consecrated) and distributed to the faithful in church to be consumed there or at home. Ix evidently supposes that the water-carrier etc. are hoping for a Christmas-box or tip.

263. Garnished with stuffed tomatoes and mushrooms, braised lettuce and roast potatoes.

264. Herbs, spinach, shallot, gherkins, capers, anchovy and garlic.

265. With lettuce, little onions and bouquet garni.

266. A Rhine wine.

Iced ceylans

Wines
Iced Château Contet. Chilled zuccho.
Roman punch
Bordeaux. Léoville. Chambertin.
Iced Saint-Marceau champagne
Dessert port

THE CHEF DE BOUCHE CHEZ BRÉBANT

* * *

Nineteenth leaf

Mulligatawny for a midnight supper.

We always have a double concern: to propagate the unique culinary genius of Paris and France through the rest of Europe and beyond; and to acclimatise products and their preparation from every part of the world. Today it is also a question of adding something foreign and modern to an old-fashioned ceremony, the midnight supper

Here is the recipe:

Brown an onion in butter with curry powder and yellow saffron from Réunion; brown a chicken, cut it in pieces and add it. Pour over it the milk obtained from the flesh of a coconut grated, pounded in a mortar and moistened in hot water.

Allow to simmer and serve with rice à la Créole.[267]

Curry, saffron from Réunion: all that and other spices can be found at 5, boulevard Haussmann, at the shop of an old friend of our Readers, the Propagateur, *to whose courtesy we are indebted for all our exotic recipes. Better still, our contributor is prepared to have this rare dish ready for the evening before the sacramental meal. Serve it between the 'saddle of Nîmes lamb' and the 'bartorelles' in Brébant's admirable menu, either as an entrée or a remove.*

The recipe was given to that shop and will be prepared there by

OLYMPE, A NEGRESS.

* * *

267. Plain boiled rice.

Twentieth leaf

The ordinary Christmas tree

Acclimatised in France from the North (especially since the war) by patriotic efforts, the Christmas tree, which until recently was reserved for rich cosmopolitan children, has now become very popular. How handsome it looks, dressed, lit and laden, in the windows of some famous confectioner! But more touching is the fir tree dressed at home, over three evenings, after the children have gone to bed.

Here is the traditional thing, in all its bare simplicity.

First, take some dozens of nuts, dampen them a little and then roll them on beaten gold foil; gilded nuts. Perform the same operation on a quantity of lady-apples, on the side opposite their rosy cheek. Add to this reminder of humble rusticity a contribution from the city, symbolised by a smaller number of mandarins and of little sponge-fingers, hung by the classic red woollen thread, or perhaps pink and blue ribbon. Then, completing the 'inevitable and essential' background, come the hundred little wax candles – coloured ones, according to the taste of some people, but white for me. The most convenient way of attaching them is by a tiny tin drip-catcher, fixed by a pin or clip and hidden under a little white paper collar (or a pink or blue one, if one is using ribbons). As reflectors, little balls of blown glass imitating steel, some bronze, others blue – like great pearls.

What next? Plant the tree itself – a fir tree a metre or two tall – without roots, in a green box decorated with gold paper, or an ordinary ceramic pot, the soil covered by moss or pretty twists of paper. The choice of a tree itself is of some importance. Choose one with long straight branches, clustering thickly and evenly.

Fantasy takes over from here; mothers, your imagination is challenged!

The infinite world of surprises at your disposal can be divided into (a) sweets: glacé *fruit from all lands, traditional sweets, especially ones made from red sugar,*[268] *and all those imitating the shape of some ordinary or fantastic thing; (b) toys: old-fashioned ones again, for instance the contents of a Noah's Ark, dispersed about the tree. There is one absolute rule: on the uppermost tip of the tree, where stands the last candle, there must be a sugar or wax doll with curly hair – the Infant Jesus.*

Everything is resplendent, glittering and dazzling; and the little musical-box, hidden among the rich gifts on the table on many lacquered trays, fills the atmosphere of joy and brilliance with its musical rain.

This is the cue for my exit: Children, you may come in!

268. i.e. light brown sugar.

Scissors, quick! setting ringing the little bell (if you have put one) on each branch, soon to be stripped bare; and may the great present-giving be repeated every evening until New Year's Day or Epiphany.

A READER FROM ALSACE

* * *

GAZETTE AND PROGRAMME FOR THE FORTNIGHT

Amusements and Solemnities in 'Society'

From 20 December 1874 to 3 January 1875

I. BOOKS
(Gifts)

Anyone who is a reader, or is merely curious, and has looked closely at the list of books we give here every fortnight will have noticed that only works of notable literary worth are mentioned: novels and poetry, always by the great writers of today and very often by our contributors. With the approach of New Year's Day, lack of space and the idea which usually governs our selection prevent us from doing otherwise than in the past. Apart from L'Inde sous les Rajahs, *a magnificently illustrated book and the leading book of the season (published by Hachette), we shall only draw to our readers' attention, as suitable gifts for their sons, brothers or husbands, the valuable book-collectors' editions published by Lemerre: noble volumes on thin and antique-looking China paper which are to books from ordinary bookshops as Bohemian glassware to heavy, cold everyday tumblers.*

We note – Poetry: Poésie et théâtre *(2 vols.) by FRANÇOIS COPPÉE;* Poésies *(2 vols.) by SULLY PRUDHOMME;* Poésies *(2 vols.) by SOULARY;* Anthologie des poètes, *and* Anthologie des prosateurs *(2 vols.): all these volumes, belonging to the well-known duodecimo collection, have been bound in cloth, with red edges, for the New Year celebration.* Oeuvres de Molière (*8 vols.*); Oeuvres de Racine *(4 vols.)*; Oeuvres de Shakespeare, *in François-Victor Hugo's translation (Vol.1): also in duodecimo, with a parchment binding.*

Albums: Les Douze travaux d'Hercule (*quarto*); *the 35 etchings, taken from Boucher, to illustrate the works of Molière.*

As for attractive childrens' books, it is a great regret to us not to have room properly to praise their illustrations, their texts and even their covers (which bear no resemblance to sweet-wrappers). Albums, and rich and serious volumes, for children are a sort of speciality of Hachette and Hetzel, who indeed invented them;

and the Bibliothèque des merveilles *of the one, or the* Bibliothèque rose *and the* Bibliothèque d'éducation et de recréation *of the other, add a new volume to their collection every year, destined to be a bestseller over the ensuing twelve months.*

You can choose from these two series with your eyes shut, or even with them wide open.

II – THEATRES
(The successes)

Théâtre français: Le Demi-monde, *by ALEXANDRE DUMAS* fils, *still running after so long and quite at home by now beside Molière and Beaumarchais; with* ***Delaunay, Got, Febvre, Thiron; Croizette, Nathalie, Tholer and Broizat*** *– which gives an idea of the impressiveness of these magnificent evenings, which are interrupted by* Une chaîne, *the revival of a revival, and* Philiberte *(or rather,* ***Mademoiselle Broizat).***

Salle Ventadour: *the* ***Opéra: Faure and Rosine Bloch*** *completely charm the public, who also take interest in the débuts of* ***Mademoiselle Daram*** *as Eudoxie in* La Juive[269] *and of* ***Madame Fursch-Madier*** *as Marguerite in* Faust. *Lovely evenings for the end of the season-ticket, and especially Sundays, with revivals from almost the beginning of the season.*

Italiens: Madame Pozzoni, *the star, is to be succeeded by that other luminary,* ***Niccolini.*** *Newcomers:* ***Mademoiselle Morio and Madame Sbolgi.*** *The complete repertory, so often set down here, will provide a wide array of magnificent evenings – to which will come rolling, with a flood of lace and satin glimpsed through their windows, all the carriages of the town, ready for the moment later when the same costumes, now fully displayed, descend the great staircase.*

Odéon: *The first performances of* La Maîtresse légitime, *an uplifting and serious work, reveal M. DAVYL as we had guessed him to be and show* ***Mlle Léonide Leblanc,*** *once again, as perfect. As for the repertory:* Les Femmes savantes, *with M.* ***Dalis*** *as Chrysale, and DUVAL's* Les Héritiers, *freshened by* ***Mlle Baretta.***

Opéra-Comique: *A revival? No, almost a première.* Le Domino noir *(**Mlle Chapuy; L'Hérie, Melchissédec**), left behind:*[270] *real luxury in costumes and singing make a new show out of this classic.*

Vaudeville: *A compliment paid to you, Ladies, if not to his niece Sarah, in M. Harmant's* Uncle Sam, *by the producing of the Gypsies after the tea-interval in the second Act; yes, the ones from the* ***Folies-Bergère,*** *whom perhaps you have not*

---

269. The opera by J.-F. Halévy, with libretto by Scribe.

270. Ix presumably means that, in this production, one would hardly recognise the original play.

seen yet, with ***Daras-Miska*** *keeping everyone hanging, in frenzy or ecstasy, on his inspired bow.*

Gymnase: *An exquisite exhibition of 1818 fashions in* Les Deux comtesses *by M. Mus; and not only that, for the excellent play, with Mesdames* ***Othon and Fromentin and Mademoiselle Legault Puzol*** *is the hit of the evening; after which* ***Lesueur,*** *a little bewildered, appears in* Les Mauriaques.

Variétés: Les Prés Saint-Gervais, *words by SARDOU (and GILLES), music by* ***Lecocq,*** *with Mmes* ***Peschard, Paola Marie, A. Duval and B. Legrand;*** *the men being* ***Dupuy, Christian, Baron, Cooper,*** *and* tout Paris. *Is that enough? No! Look at this delight again from the greasy pole, seeing the lost village from an unusual viewpoint.*

Palais-Royal: *There are two sorts of laughter; laughter at what we have seen a hundred times at the* ***Palais-Royal*** *and which draws on ancient merriment; and laughter at premières. So the revivals of this autumn are succeeded by* La Boule, *that surprise of the winter, thus exhausting both modes of Parisian joy. No need to make any comment on the signature, 'Meilhac and Halévy'.*

Gaîté: La Haine, *by SARDOU. The play can be read but must be heard, because of* ***Lafontaine*** *and of Mesdames* ***Marie Laurent and Lia Felix,*** *all of them masterly. So go and see it! For* ***Rubé*** *and* ***Chapron, Cambom, Chéret, Lavastre*** *junior and* ***Desplechin*** *have never imagined anything more extraordinary and more beautiful than their sets for the crossroads of rue Camollia, the façade of Siena Cathedral, a camp in Saint Christopher's church cloisters after the battle, Cordelia's room, the ruins of the Campo, and, finally, the interior of the cathedral by moonlight. A stage-scene of wood and canvas has perhaps never been transfigured by luxury on this scale!*

Porte-Saint-Martin: Le Tour du monde en 80 jours *will make the Tour of the Parisian year. What shall we say about it? It must be seen. 'The Cave of Serpents', 'Indian Suttee', 'Explosion and Sinking of a Steamer', 'Dawnie Indians attacking a Train': they are wonderful titles but are put into the shade by the real thing, by which I mean fairy theatre! Dumaine,* ***Lacressonnière, Alexandre and Vannoy; Mlles Angèle Moreau and Patri.*** *There is a drama somewhere in this spectacle by D'HENNERY and JULES VERNE.*

Châtelet *(also Opéra-Populaire). Re-opens with* Les Pilules du Diable, *eternally young, with a surprise for grown-up parents and babies, like the one last year. It was, you will remember, a ballet of clowns then; what will it be this time? Go and see it, Jean, Mathilde, Geneviève or Gaston, and come and tell me.*

Ambigu: Cocagne, *by FERDINAND DUGUÉ. Fargueil's superb acting, all those Van Dykes and Callot etchings, and the scene of Anne of Austria entrusting the sleeping Louis XIV to a guard of Parisians, do not quite satisfy our impatience for a (by now) well-known set: the shifting sands of Mont Saint-Michel and the moving tide.*

Bouffes-Parisiens: Madame l'Archhiduc, *or **Judic** and the lovable dragon (Madame Grivot). Ovations and bouquets (which in this sweet-box of a theatre, and on New Year's Day, might well be crystallised flowers); diamonds in their looks and on their shoulders: a fabulous première due to last right through the winter. Beside the maestro, Paris applauds that other charmer, Grévin, for his costumes for the 'Trumpets of the Grand Duke'.*

Renaissance. *Sometimes pink and sometimes blue, like the gilly-flower, **Mlle Garnier,** who plays Girofla, is the heart and soul of* Giroflé. *As for **Alphonsine,** who plays Aurore d'Alcarazas, this star is always Alphonsine, the unique and incomparable. It is a real opéra-bouffe, and all Paris is humming 'C'est fini le mariage', 'En tête-à-tête, faire la dinette', 'Parmi les choses délicates', and 'Matamoros, grand capitaine!' Enough! For we shall have a year to get to know it all!*

***Théâtre des Arts** (formerly the **Menus-Plaisirs**): Frédéric Lemaître (need we say more?) in* Le Crime de Faverne.

***Folies Bergère:** The Gypsies! whom the gentlemen listen to and the ladies look at: for they need both to be seen and to be heard. Their music is themselves, ardent, wild and exquisite. Neither Daras Miszka nor M. Sari (who is a marvellous nomad himself in his tastes) will soon cease to amaze Paris. What a varied, multiple and endlessly changing spectacle, known to us from so many posters. only lack of space forbids us to describe it.*

* * *

*Other places of amusement and pleasure, by day or by night, are, first, the **Jardin d'Acclimatation** – see its aquarium, with its Shanghai fish (fantastic fighters) and its pools of otters, playing and fishing; also flowers, prolonged out of season, and an orchestra, prolonged too. This garden can even be said to 'acclimatise' the winter sun.*

*The **Cirque d'Hiver** spares us the need to own Chantilly or rent Fontainebleau with its wonderful hunt meeting, where two stags, a doe and packs of hounds are brought together to satisfy every hunting fantasy of childhood – certainly my own! Tayaut, Halali! that is to say, Bravo!*

*The **Théâtre Miniature,** itself, is not content with its charming traditional entertainments in which décors, costumes and general ensemble have a magnificence only constrained by size. Summoned here from Hungary, M. **Vielle,** every evening, conjures up Spectres or performs miracles with his fingers and little nothings! But one thing we can be sure of, we shall never, in this delightfully refurbished theatre, see the mere spectre of Mr. Punch, who is alive and indestructible there as always.*

*The **Salle des Familles,** which the audience of the preceding theatre come back to when they are grown up and serious-minded, to applaud real premières and débuts.*

The Panorama, in the Champs-Élysées, with the nightmare of Le Siège de Paris, *magnificently brought to life by the painter PHILIPPOTEAUX, attracts us on fine afternoons in the season.*

Robert Houdin: Le Nid rose, *with its slate, on which I would write 'Miraculous'! and so many other wonderful things, on the boulevard des Italiens. Whilst the wonders of M.* **Litsonn** *and the* Cercle Fantastique *take place at the same time of day. You must be sure to see these: flowers and sweets given away, but reduced-price tickets into the bargain, which is certainly magic.*

For children, every Sunday, there are exquisite matinées at **Frascati.** *The season for making friendships in squares and parks is over, but here is a winter Garden which allows lonely children to meet (a precious opportunity), or to make the acquaintance of the Aztecs.*

* * *

For Matinées and Sunday Concerts see our Paris Chronicle and their own advertisements. Do not forget to visit the Louvre, where some of the masterpieces have been transferred from the Luxembourg; or the Cercle des Mirlitons, *which is displaying some of the recent work of Carolus Duran;*[271] *artistic walks and pastimes for the holidays.*

III – TRAVEL
(The Paris-Lyon-Mediterranée line)

The first heated express trains have long since left, transporting, in a warm fug caressing and veiling the compartment windows, a whole host of chilly, sedate and well-wrapped-up passengers, who ignore the unseen landscapes they pass through. To quit Paris and arrive where there are blue skies is their dream, and there has been no time to change this dream, after the whistle for departure, before these names burst upon them, like magic spells: MARSEILLE, TOULON. (And between these two winter resorts there are delightful and reasonable places to stay, such as La Ciotat, with its Bec d'Aigle, Saint-Cyr and the Baie des Lecques, Bandol, Ollioulesi; HYÈRES and the Îles Saint-Raphael, Antibes, Cannes, Nice, Monaco, Menton or San Remo.

Are all the travellers invalids? No, no more than all the summer excursionists were taking a seaside cure.

A custom, recently born and favourable to re-birth – one which I cannot stress too highly for the world of rich, independent lady readers among our subscribers

271. See p. 196, note 259.

– consists in leaving Paris once or twice or even three times during the winter to sample a few hours of sun and blue sky. A week of constantly depressing weather; weariness (for the ladies) of pleasures and (for their husbands) of business: it is enough to decide monsieur and madame to make use of one of those simple pieces of magic which modern life puts at the disposal of those who understand it. A change of décors for the eyes and the soul, restoring health: what is really extraordinary is that it can be had in a few hours, for a few francs! The 'Travel and Holiday Houses' columns in society journals give a glimpse of this new trend: a winter season for travel, different from the summer one and consisting of brief escapes on the very day chosen by the escapees.

As for real wanderers, they choose places for a whole season's absence which would be truly remote if the speed of the railway were not repeated by that of the steamer: ALGIERS, CAIRO and so many beneficial places in SICILY and the BALEARICS.

The island of MADEIRA, bathed by warm waters, is in 1874 a very aristocratic place of emigration.

Only the PLM line sells ticket for these paradises.

* * *

CORRESPONDENCE WITH READERS

20 December 1874

Note

In his summary of the last three months of La Dernière mode *M. Marasquin announced many surprises to come. The first is the use, for a magazine devoted to fashion and society, of the Elzevir typeface, something hitherto reserved for printing luxury editions. This, the typeface of fine editions of the past, now suddenly back in fashion, like* guipure *lace and antique jewellery, calls for a antique-style paper to go with it. It is not merely the present great vogue for the archaic that prompts us to give our paper (carefully selected for its purpose) its special yellow tinge; it is also that we want our fine black-and-white engravings to benefit from its warm, rich tone. With it, satins, velvets and all evening wear take on a sheen and a depth which a different background tint could not provide.*

Mme DE V-- . . . , ROME. My very dear Subscriber, your note proves that if you read our Fashion Column right to the last line, you also begin at the first; and Mme de Ponty confesses that her mind must have been elsewhere when an article she wrote in the first days of December was dated the day after Christmas. Instead of

26, read 6. The Programme and Letters, not to mention the Frontispiece and all the other places it occurs, confirm this correction. Thank you.

Mlle MARIE DE L. DE MONTF . . . Before I reply to your charming question, please accept our hearty and smiling congratulations. You want, you say, to owe your wedding dress to La Dernière mode; *but does not our publication owe you many of its successes among your elegant set of acquaintances? I have never had a more agreeable task than to design the outfit you want. Here it is, though too briefly described. Wedding dress in white satin, with smooth crêpe flounces with sharp pleats;* cachepoint[272] *in white jet; a tunic-scarf in white satin, trimmed with a flounce like those on the skirt. (With a bow on the train and one of the flaps held back at the waist, this tunic will be enchanting.) A train of orange-blossoms going from the waistband and finishing in the bow of the train proper. The bodice has rounded basques, very long in front and very short at the back. A* ruff *of smooth gauze edged with a garland of orange-blossom.*

When you read here certain details a little different from what our Fashion column defined as the coming style, do not think I have described anything unfashionable. Wedding dresses, as an earlier column of ours said, are the last to change; they cling to the established mode. There would be something not quite proper – particularly in your case, living so far from the capital as you do – in a bride's wishing to be in advance of fashion.

M.L. VAN . . . ECK . . . BRUSSELS. Mlle Massin's outfit in Le Chemin de Damas, *at the* Vaudeville, *has never been described in* Le Figaro, *by the 'Gentleman from the Stalls'*[273] *who usually does this sort of thing splendidly. You are right to say so; and if we have a good memory (as we do) let us recall what we ourselves saw at the première. A sky-blue taffeta dress; on both sides of the skirt, those ornaments we used to call 'quilling'*[274] *(that is, a long strip from top to bottom, widening as it reaches the bottom), then three flounces forming an apron in white lace with silver embroidery, outlined in black velvet. A low-cut cuirass bodice. A dress which, with a few alterations, one could copy and which would be as charming as the original.*

MADAME -. Goodness, you are already having a fancy-dress ball at – (You will see, dear subscriber, that your name, and that of the place which you must surely enchant, have been left blank, at your request!). Only the **Opéra-Comique,** *replacing the late grand Opéra in this respect (no pun intended), has given the signal for Carnival here, and I would not seek anything for you amid that brilliant throng. So, since the grand couturiers are not yet suppliers of fancy-dress, why hesitate, from this moment on, to copy one of the enchanting costumes from the operettas at*

---

272. An ornament, or ornamental work, concealing stitching.

273. This was the pseudonym of Arnold Mortier, author of *Les Soirées parisiennes*.

274. Small round pleats lightly sewn down the edge of the trimming.

present in vogue: from Madame l'Archiduc[275] *or* Les Prés Saint-Gervais?[276] *Judic and Paola Marie need to be seen as well as heard. See the former in her Princess dress, in pearl-grey* faille *with gold froggings; on her hair she wears a red head-scarf twisted almost into the shape of a Figaro* coiffure. *The designer is Grévin. The other actress is well suited by a Grisette costume – very short and bouffant, in soft grass-green and heart-of-tearose pink ruched silk. Her stockings are pink with gold clocks, the shoes green with high pink heels.*

YVONNE DE K . . . aun . . . , PL. -- R. Goodness, how kind you are, my dear, to avenge me for some very severe reproaches, though I think I have answered them victoriously myself in in this issue. 'Too many rules for children's clothing', so I was told by a trio of visitors; whereas you, kind elder sister that you are, write to say, 'More is needed on this subject'. So, for your sake, I shall continue; this is how, but for lack of space, I would have ended my recent article.

'Dresses for eleven-year-old girls, which ought be very plainly trimmed, should be in some kind of bure, tweed velvet: skirts down to the ankle, quite plain, and very simple tunics, ending merely with a threefold backstitching, or at the most a plait of wool or silk. I like a little jacket to match the dress, tied at the waist by a pretty faille *bow with long ends, but I forbid the dolman completely, until the age of seventeen or eighteen! A round hat, not the* chapeau Lamballe*; that charming shape is for an older friend or sister.*

'As for boys: they wear the traditional costume for first communion, apart from the collar; everyday, and taller than ever today; turned down and receding at the back, and under it a fetching bow with long drooping ends. The coat is buttoned up to the neck and does not show the shirt – that is, if one wishes not to sin against the taste of yesterday and the day before yesterday.'

I may add, for the ears of your dear mother, who, as you tell me, with a dutifulness that does you credit, gave you permission to write:

'From now on – though indeed there might be thought to be signs of it already in the fur trimmings, striped stockings and other fancies adopted by fairies and elves who are not yet young ladies and gentlemen – we hand all these young people over to Fashion. Just one remark, neither a piece of advice nor a plea: Mothers, when you take your daughter to the dressmaker or your son to the tailor, do your best to see they preserve the fleeting grace of their age and that their adolescence remains childhood for a long time.'

* * *

275. Opéra-comique by Albert Millaud, with music by Offenbach.

276. Opéra-comique by Sardou and Gille, based on Sardou's play of that title, with music by Charles Lecocq. .

ADVICE ON EDUCATION

As well as books deliberately designed as books, there are volumes composed of lines, often perfect, thrown off by inspiration in the course of a life; and, that life ended, the lines may live on, preserved by pious sympathy. Such is the Journal, Pensées et Correspondance *of JOSÉPHINE SAZERAC DE LIMAGNE, who died in 1873. This soul, who seems to me very superior even from the fragmentary thoughts she left in writing, is restored almost completely here, for anyone reading attentively, and as much in the blanks in the text as in the text itself. Grand, noble and very religious (in the strictest sense of the word), the figure of the young woman we get to know here cannot easily be blotted from memory and evokes more than one type of the old French nobility. This collection is excellent reading for the years following first communion, and many girls will be grateful to the anonymous author of the biographical note, which is interesting and, here and there, even startling.*

MME DE P.

Part III
Paris 1874: A Postface

Paris 1874

By Alex Cain

Life for fashionable French society in 1874 was an endless intricate dance movement, wherein the performers were themselves the spectators. As the seasons changed, so people moved from Paris to the country, from the *hôtel* to the *château*. In the *château*, society spent its time preparing for the Paris season by composing invitations on antique paper.

The season in Paris was about tomorrow: what will tomorrow's fashions be? The season in the *château* was about yesterday: the Third Republic harked back to the Second Empire's memories of Louis XV.

During the day, there was an appropriate costume for every hour, for every occasion; there were times to go to the Bois de Boulogne, there were days to receive and to be received: on Sunday at 5 o'clock it was chic to take a turn round the lakes in the Bois, thought Proust's Odette de Crécy, while the Eden-Théâtre was chic on Thursdays. How dull Paris was out of season! 'No theatres, no spectators. The heat has driven the bravest away . . . Our *tout Paris* has emigrated to the mountains or to the seaside ... It has moved, scattered among the casinos, the spas, the beaches of the Atlantic or the Channel. Instead of tickets for first nights, it prefers excursion tickets; travel agencies have made a fortune and theatre agencies have had to close', as Arnold Mortier comments in *Les Soirées parisiennes* (1874).

The bipolarity – rather, the complementarity – of time and place was the basic tension in the society of 1874 France, recovering from the excesses of the vulgarity of the Second Empire and interregnum brutality. Mallarmé's *La Dernière mode* occupies the period marked by a new attempt at harmonising the opposites. He makes much of this dichotomy: life in the country *(le château)* and life in Paris (*l'hôtel*), Proust tells of being able to look up a gentleman in *Le tout Paris* to find his *hôtel*, then turning to the *Annuaire des Châteaux* to find his *château*.

This complementarity was different from that existing in England, where the gentry performed a *transhumance* between the country home, the estate which was their principal home, and the house in town where they survived uncomfortably for the brief Season. There was no *éclat*, no brilliant *salon* during the London season. Life in London was but an interlude in lives spent on broad acres in Leicestershire or shooting in Scotland.

France, on the other hand, was divisible at many levels. The provinces (a better word to use than *country)* had their aristocratic pursuits which the English country house, on the whole, did not. There is nothing in England to correspond to the magic *château* of *Le Grand Meaulnes*; and the Hôtel des Guermantes in the Faubourg Saint-Germain is far removed from the closed-up town house of the Pallisers.

The peasant farmers of *la province* were peasant *proprietors*, and the distinction which they perceived between them and Paris was not so much one between an agricultural class and an urban class, as that between a solid property-owning section and an anarchist mob. The provinces feared and hated the dominance of Paris; that Paris is accustomed to govern France is a maxim that has been true for many centuries, and the provinces were determined, in 1871, that Paris should be punished for its excesses. But, though the provinces tried to do without Paris, to the extent of transferring the capital to Versailles, art and literature continued to look to Paris as their head.

Paris also represented transitoriness, as distinct from the solidity of the provinces. Paris was money, while the provinces were land. 'How many things are used up in ten years in Paris!' wrote a columnist in *La Vie parisienne* in March 1869.

Paris itself was not a unified concept either: the Buttes Montmartre, the Buttes Chaumont, the Porte d'Italie were a far cry from the Faubourgs Saint-Germain and Saint-Honoré, as the events of the Paris Commune of 1871 had so clearly demonstrated.

France in 1874 was a country in a state of uncertainty. The Second Empire itself had been a gimcrack affair, and knew it; it laboured hard to dispel the fear of the ephemeral which haunted it. Sometimes it had succeeded, as in the new layout of Paris, but more often it had merely emphasised its glittering unreality. The Second Empire had definitely come to an end on 4 September 1870, when Napoleon III had been deposed, and though there had been something like a new government proclaimed, it was by no means certain what it was called: was it, perchance, a republic? The regime acquired a President and became known as the Third Republic, with laws of governance but no constitution, until its demise in 1940, but its whole existence was always ghostly. Similarly, in 1874 France had no capital; the government sat in Versailles, but Paris, punished for its Communard activities, had no special place. Like the Thermidor revolution, this was the revenge of the provinces on Paris.

France was uncertain as to what kind of government she wanted. Not an empire, in the sense of Napoleon III's Empire, and yet there was a new colonialist spirit abroad, directed towards Cochin China and Annam, bringing with it a revival of interest in *chinoiserie* in art and oriental products into the market. Not a return to the Bourbon monarchy, although the comte de Chambord was waiting in the wings, ready to ascend the throne as Henri V with the white flag of the *ancien régime*. And yet, what was certainly not wanted was a Paris-based, revolutionary state. It turned out that there would be a remarkable continuity between the Second

Empire and the new republic, and this is most obvious in the nostalgia that was felt by the post-war generation for the quality of life it believed it had lost with the war. In 1874, Jennie Jerome recorded with surprise that the French thought plumed hats and Louis XV heels were suitable for country wear, just as the Empire itself had harked back to an existence *à la* Watteau for its country pleasures and costumes. There were other echoes of eighteenth-century dress in the 1870s, such as the black velvet choker – Madame de Ponty's *collier-bagatelle* – that could be dramatically set off with diamonds or pendant pearls. Commentators of the time refer to the *revival* of Second Empire gaiety with the production of *La Fille de Madame Angot* in 1873 as a desirable event, though *gaiety* had been almost a term of reproach when referring to life under Napoleon III. The reception of this play was all the more surprising, considering the strong revolutionary overtones of Madame Angot herself, an archetype of the Parisian *femme du people* whose most recent reincarnation in urban mythology had been the *pétroleuse* of the 1871 Commune. *La Fille* was conveniently set in the period of the Directoire, but the couplet 'Ce n'était pas la peine assurément / De changer le gouvernement' ('It certainly wasn't worthwhile changing the government') was daring in its contemporary implications for the recent revolutionary changes with a prospect of reaction ahead.

The one bright light on the politico-economic scene in France was the astonishing ability of the French economy to revive and produce enough hard cash to pay off the enormous reparations Bismark had demanded in the Treaty of Frankfurt (he had made the practical methods of payment as difficult as possible), on top of the humiliation of the surrender of the industrialized territories of Alsace and Lorraine. This was done largely by raising patriotic loans, the French people demonstrating their confidence in their country, and also by a protectionist excise, not favourable to the import of foreign produce like tobacco or food, thus compelling France to be, for a while, self-sufficient.

The disasters of the Franco-Prussian War and the subsequent troubles in Paris had brought to a temporary halt the French dressmaking industry. Under the influence of the Empress Eugénie, crinolines had been at their most extravagant. And this was one of the excesses that moralists had decried. From one extreme to another, the dark days of the Siege of Paris saw women actually wearing trousers: this was, admittedly, a very brief fashion, nor was it generally popular, but it was a sign of a retreat from frivolity, that was more usually demonstrated by a conservative style for women. Women in men's clothes, indeed, were denounced as typical of the rot in the fabric of French society which had caused the downfall of the country. There was a new seriousness abroad. The post-war generation needed to be uplifted morally and spiritually, and 1874 saw the unveiling of a statue of Joan of Arc in the place des Pyramides (even though she *was* burned at the stake for cross-dressing), and the previous year had seen the laying of the foundation stone of the Sacré-Coeur in Montmartre. But in spite of high-mindedness, frivolity kept breaking in; and it was not forgotten that the fashion industry in Paris was an important contributor to the French economy. In similar circumstances, Christian Dior would have the same message in 1947. It was the very shifting vagaries of fashion that promoted the economic upswing: Paris was the past mistress in the art of making fashion changes, and the workers in the fashion industry excelled in selling, and in selling at great price: a writer remarks that fabric worth 200 francs would fetch 1200 francs when turned into a 'creation'.

Mallarmé's two fashion correspondents exemplify the two strands of Fashion. On the one hand, Madame de Ponty – a married lady, with a *particule* suggesting nobility, dispensing advice and comfort – on the other, Miss Satin, the independent-minded English 'Mees', a forerunner of 'Miss Sacripant' and 'Miss Tanguy'; these two, in fact, represent two different traditions in magazines themselves, from both of which Mallarmé inherits. As well as the fashion magazine properly speaking there was another kind of publication, aiming at helping the bourgeoisie overcome the pitfalls which might await them in their social ascent, the *savoir-vivre* books. There was an essential tension between these two – though both are equally prescriptive – the latter looked back to an ideal past, the former looked forward to an ideal future. So it was in the social and political life of France in 1874.

Fashion and *Style* are two very different things, and Miss Satin was right in introducing the English word *Fashion* into her causeries. The world of fashion is a fertile world for nonce words – Madame de Ponty's words for colour, for example, are often hard to identify – for a fashion comes but once; a fashion 'revival' is not the same thing repeated, one cannot step into the same fashion twice. *Style* can be explained rationally, it has a certain classicism, a sense of balance; *Fashion* is like a neurosis, fleeting, baroque.

Fashion has two maxims: 'Carpe diem' and 'Memento mori'. A society which is obsessed with fashion is obsessed with death; it is so obsessed with death that it sees it everywhere. The Parisian of our period, argued Maxime Du Camp in his monumental work *Paris* (1869–75), 'does not wish to grow old, but above all to stay unchanged'.

There is, however, a positive side to the mutability of fashion, for it is indicative of a perpetual quest. To quote Du Camp again: 'Fashion is the search for an ideal superior beauty – always in vain, sometimes ridiculous, occasionally dangerous.'

Ridiculous the creations of M. Worth could be, with some heavy decorative fantasies, the vital *haute couture* stamp of uniqueness ranging from the bizarre to the pointless, that element of 'conspicuous outrage' which has been seen as one of the pursuits of Veblen's leisured classes. A particular example of conspicuous outrage in the 1870s was the hat, so designed to display the hair and face, whereas the earlier bonnet was intended to cover the head and face with a blinkered effect. Modest women understood that a hat would not do in church, only a bonnet was respectable. Of Veblen's other conspicuousities, conspicuous consumption, though not so obvious as in the court of the Empress Eugénie, ran riot in the many layers of clothes which were required in 1874, not all with the purpose of keeping warm. The illustrations in *La Dernière mode* usually show skirts looped up in front to display an elaborate underskirt, then tailed away into a train, which would eventually be gathered up into a bustle. Jewels are the most obvious example of *conspicuous wealth*. But it should be remembered that it was the wife's *duty* to reflect her husband's wealth; one of the bridegroom's first duties was to provide the *corbeille de mariage* (and Madame de Ponty has much to say about this), and it is the wife's duty to wear the jewels therein. Madame's children have to suffer from the needs of *vicarious consumption*, as the illustrations indicate, as do her suggestions for one's daughters' jewellery.

All social life in Paris is *spectacle*. 'Every time that there are uniforms to see somewhere, dresses to look at, the Parisian rushes there,' says Du Camp. The great entertainment consists in *looking* and in *being looked at*. This is true of going to the café, such as the celebrated Tortoni's where one sat at little tables on the pavement to watch the world go by; of going on holiday, when *le tout Paris* moved to the seaside in order to meet up with each other; of going to the theatre itself, where the audience spent more time watching other members of the audience than they did in watching the stage; Mary Cassatt's painting *At the Opera* shows a woman looking through her opera glass, not at the stage, but at another box.

Mallarmé rightly devoted a large part of *La Derniére mode* to theatre, as being an essential part of fashion. The theatre was part of the lifeblood of the Parisian, and a gauge of the spirit of the time. It had all but stopped during the terrible days of the Siege and the Commune, with many theatres destroyed in fighting; but by 1873 it had come to life again, and most theatres had been rebuilt. Even Napoleon III's grand design for an opera house was revived, and Garnier's monumental building would be opened in 1875.

Paris theatres had been strictly controlled since the days of Napoleon I in a strict table of precedence. Mallarmé's listings of the week's theatrical events follow this table, beginning with the state-subsidised houses, the Opéra, the Opéra-Comique and the Comédie-Française. At this latter, only the recognised classics could be performed, and only here. The classics had to be treated with respect. There were at this time 41 regular theatres in Paris (that is, with regular nightly shows) and 17 others playing once or twice a week. Napoleon I's law of 8 June 1806 specified which particular drama form each house must specialise in. On top of this, there was also the state censor to contend with, who looked after citizens' moral and spiritual well-being. These regulatory powers had continued into the Third Republic.

The Parisian theatre audience, however, was scarcely affected by these restrictions. Serious pieces played little part in their theatre-going, as Zola and Flaubert found to their cost in 1874, when their plays, appearing at a little-frequented theatre on the Left Bank, flopped disastrously. On the stages of the 41 regular theatres and 70 others there appeared a succession of plays, virtually identical one with the other, which disappeared again without leaving any marks on the memory. A special kind of show had been invented to satisfy the theatre-goers' fancy, popularly known as '*pièces à femmes*'. A very slender plot spread over several acts interposed with ballet, pretty girls in stunning costumes, or with a lack thereof, showing as much leg, arm or shoulder as the police might allow; Bengal lights, gas lights, electric lights; frantic music. 'It's not theatre, it's only spectacle,' said Du Camp, who was totally cynical about the moral or artistic or intellectual worth of the French theatre. 'This kind of play ought to be put on backwards, you must turn your back on the stage and watch the auditorium. The audience are just as curious to watch as the painted women who strike up poses in the middle of cardboard architecture.' Spectators become spectated; everything is *spectacle.*

The theatrical piece which would dominate the Parisian stage during the period of *La Dernière mode* was Sardou's *La Haine*. Dramatically, it was a historical melodrama of little literary worth; Ix will have much to say about its visual impact, which appears to resemble that of a Cecil B. de Mille film. It is praised, probably with tongue in cheek, for its cast of hundreds, its costumes, its scenery, its lighting, in fact for everything except the script. Again, it was *spectacle*. One thing that struck all critics was the cost: 360,000 francs. 'All that so that a hundred actors rigged out in expensive mediaeval armour can strut on the stage to no purpose, and so that the little dramatic interest in the play would be drowned in a wave of velvet and brocade,' was one comment.

A very interesting example of changing taste at the end of the Second Empire and the beginning of the Third Republic is the case of Offenbach. Under the glitter of the Empire, he had been the most popular composer for the musical stage, but with the coming of a new post-war seriousness, his great satirical works (they were thought of as 'cynical') fell from favour; in his last work, *The Tales of Hoffmann,* he symbolised the earlier culture in Olympia, the heartless doll. The new patriotic spirit, the defence of the national heritage, revolted against parodies which trivialised the classics (curiously, the classical gods and goddesses of *La Belle Hélène* were sacrosanct in the eyes of a Church-dominated educational system), or mocked court life (even though the Grand Duchess of Gerolstein was manifestly German). Consequently he turned to the production of *féerie*, a curious dramatic form based on spectacular effects and rich settings. It had been popular before the war, and the Théâtre de la Porte Saint-Martin had been a very successful home to luxurious productions. *Féeries*, in the period immediately following 1871, distracted the public from eternal preoccupations with political questions, and at the same time they avoided the frenzy, the *ivresse* of the Empire. Offenbach rewrote *Orpheus in the Underworld* as a *féerie;* the satire and the parody were removed to be replaced by innumerable balletic pieces at every interval, and even the music was made subsidiary to 'special effects'. The original production had had a limited cast; the new version had 120 in the chorus and 68 dancers. 'Tableaux' were even more striking than ballets, with a particularly striking one of sunrise over Olympus. 'An exhibition of legs and stage sets,' said one scornful critic. His *Madame l'Archiduc*, produced in October 1874 and mentioned in *La Dernière mode,* misses completely the satiric wit of *La Grande Duchesse*, and its characters have lost all touch with reality, like fairytale characters, like dolls. In fact there is a doll-like quality about the whole of *La Dernière mode*; dresses are created for dolls, actresses are dream-like figures (Patti has become *la marquise*, a mythological figure), even Madame de Ponty's correspondents inhabit castles in Spain.

The ruling quality of the *féerie*, said Daudet in his essay *Féeries et dêcors*, is naivety, and naivety is not simplicity. It is 'a spectacle for the eyes'. The stage adaptation of Jules Verne's *Round the World in Eighty Days*, which was immensely popular in 1874, was full of characters and incidents, but in Daudet's eyes, it remained a *féerie*, 'the most sumptuous, the most original of all.'

Offenbach himself was not concerned with the permanence of the pieces he wrote: 'The piece that is born makes you forget the piece that has died, you don't make comparisons or look for analogies; it's a series of fleeting pictures as in a magic lantern, and once they have vanished, the most terrific success weighs no more in the spectator's mind than the most shattering flop' (quoted by Siegfried Kracauer in *Orpheus in Paris*, 1938).

It is a sign of the new seriousness that Zola despised operetta, 'a public enemy that should be strangled behind the prompter's box like a savage beast'. He took the somewhat Platonic view that it hid folly behind an attractive screen, encouraged vice and led the public away from serious things. There was, however, a tendency at the time for literary men to abhor all forms of music. Daudet quotes Gautier as thinking it 'the most disagreeable of all noises' and comments, 'whenever the piano is opened, Goncourt frowns.'

The sense of *spectacle* extended beyond the theatre house. There had developed in the 1860s a new Parisian institution, the department store. In real life, Le Bon Marché, La Samaritaine and others, and in fiction Au Bonheur des Dames, provided a new fascination for women. Zola's novel, *Au Bonheur des Dames,* provides a key text for the importance of shopping as an end in itself. Zola describes, first of all, the small family-run shop, dark and unwelcoming, with a limited supply and specialised stock, where ladies needed to know in advance what they wanted, and contrasts it with the new-style department store which revels in its fantastic display of treasures, tempting its visitors (and sometimes tempting them to disastrous ends), with ever-increasing ranges of goods. Madame de Ponty immediately opens an Aladdin's cave, with its glitter and its splendour and its riches. It is the display of the exotic and sensuous, like the oriental display of carpets and costly goods that greeted the astounded customers of *Au Bonheur des Dames*; and goods that were also trumpery, things which made but a brave display, like the cheap fans in the department store and Madame's costume jewellery. To visit the store was an end in itself, like going to the Louvre (there is a department store called *Au Louvre* and to this day there reigns a certain confusion about one's destination). Women could meet their friends in the reading rooms and, as in the theatre, be seen as well as see. It is important to remember that these stores develop from small shops essentially devoted to women's needs – haberdashery, fabrics for dresses, ribbons, and the like – *nouveautés*. Although there was a growing market for ready-made clothes, most women's clothes were made at home, as *La Dernière mode* makes abundantly clear. The rich might patronise the great couture houses like Worth, but most middle-class women made their clothes at home, buying lengths of material and creating something with the aid of a paper pattern – one of which would be included in each copy of *La Dernière mode* – and the sewing machine; Madame de Ponty has great praise for this most revolutionary machine, which brought quite complicated dressmaking within the purview of quite ordinary women – though she does suggest that it might be a good idea for one's servant to have lessons in its use.

This brings us to wonder who exactly were the audience Mallarmé had in mind for his paper. The price indicates a fairly modest income level (50 centimes would be the equivalent of UK 65p, US $1 in 2002); the illustrations of women's activity on the cover send a very mixed message. The domestic scenes contrast strongly with activities of the 'new woman' participating in sports. Again, Madame de Ponty dispenses fashion advice without considering the cost, without warning his lady readers that somehow at the end of the month accounts ('*la douloureuse*') will have to be presented to husbands, for it must be remembered that at this period French married women had few rights to income; but there was a new independent class of office and shop workers who were enthusiastic, on a limited income, about new fashions. And we remember that Emma Bovary, in the depths of Normandy, subscribed to *La Corbeille* and *Le Sylphe des Salons*, and 'she devoured, without missing anything, all the reviews of first nights, racing events and evening parties, and interested herself in the debut of a singer, the opening of a shop. She knew the new fashions, the addresses of good tailors, the days for the Bois or the Opera'.

However, the existence of the department store provided a free entertainment, that is, so long as the window shoppers were not carried away by what was then considered a new neurosis whereby otherwise respectable women were led to shoplifting. Zola stresses the sensuous thrill some women felt, plunging their hands into offerings of fine lace which they did not need but which they could not resist.

Even behind closed doors, the life-as-*spectacle* continued. The most dramatic event of life in the *hôtel* was the salon, that essentially French form of socio-cultural life. To be seen in a *salon* no matter what its social or cultural level, was to go into society, *aller dans le monde*, the young Daudet thought, and later in life he would mock middle-class attempts at creating an 'artistic' *salon,* with music and recitation, and a modicum of food and drink. *Ridiculous salons,* he calls them: When the bourgeois get up to being *fantaisistes (* fanciful), you never know where they will stop. He fails to realise that the whole of the *salon* scene is *fantaisiste*, and that his description of a pathetic lower middle-class attempt at a *salon*, with the piano pushed up against the kitchen door, glasses of *sirop* on top of volumes of music and the maid listening to a singer with her elbows on the piano is no more ridiculous than Madame Verdurin's affected cries on hearing Vinteuil's music. Mallarmé takes Madame Rattazzi as an archetypical *salon* hostess and envisages her as the 'figure idéale d'une saynète ou d'une comédie', after having led us in our imagination through the halls of her *hôtel*, up the sumptuous staircase, past the works of art, through the music room, and finishing up in the reception room with its conservatory and fountain: a grand entrance to a theatre culminating in a perfect setting for a 'well-made play'. Mallarmé was right to refer to the *salon* in a women's magazine, for this was the one area where women ruled supreme; the literary salon was essentially presided over by 'a prepossessingly mature Muse'.

Ladies did not eat in restaurants in 1874, so Mallarmé creates a special restaurant atmosphere in the home for them by offering recipes from *Chez Brébant*, a restaurant which played a leading part in the social life of literary circles, and had been particularly memorable during the Siege of Paris.

Mallarmé goes further in his treatment of the domestic interior as a stage setting. This was a time when articles of the home were frequently concealed under the guise of something else; this would later be one of the main features of Art Deco, and had previously figured in the Baroque – all ages of uncertainty and flux. Mallarme's DIY household tips consist of disguise: turning an oil lamp into a gas lamp; creating false beams; giving an appearance of a leather-clad room. One dressed a room as one dressed a body, and Madame de Girardin, according to Goncourt in his journal for 26 April, 1872, used the word 'habiller' to describe her decoration of her bedroom 'with embroidered satin from Worth, at the cost of 60,000 francs'. Creating a dress, or a room, is like creating a self.

We have seen that the immediate post-war period in France in the 1870s was a period of great instability and uncertainty; to foretell the political or economic future of the country was difficult. This state of flux is well translated by Madame de Ponty into the field of fashion. Art, too, seemed to be in a state of flux; the new school of impressionism tried to catch the evanescence of light itself, though Mallarmé does not refer to the seminal exhibition of 1874.

An increase in the possibility of moving around the country is indicated by the amount of advertising in *La Dernière mode* for train travel. French people had not originally taken to the railway train in the way the English had; the first public railway line from Paris to Versailles was dismissed as a passing novelty. However, it soon became apparent that there was a life beyond the change between *hôtel* and *château,* that one could visit the thermal stations in the mountains or the seaside resorts, where elegant hotels (in the English sense of the word) were beginning to spring up. Country visiting had existed as a pastime, but it was in the sense of *villégiature*, which essentially meant going to stay with family or friends – 'the *châteaux,* the pride of hospitable France,' said Barbey d'Aurevilly in *L'Ensorcelée* (1889). It was only shop assistants who went picnicking by the side of the Seine, and no-one indulged in sport, with the exception of hunting. Ladies could go riding *en Amazone.* The Parisian's interest in sport was largely an extension of the fashion parade, 'the procession of horsemen, of amazons and elegant carriages that go round the two lakes in the Bois de Boulogne in the afternoon'. Mallarmé's conceit of the sport of lark-catching is a charming fancy. But the railway travel feature in *La Dernière mode* has a considerable seriousness about it, with details about special excursions and fares, which imply that this would be of more than a passing interest to his readership and, as he suggests, some people might even go as far as Madeira. One suspects that these seaside or mountain resorts were to a great extent merely extensions of Paris society, that there was a reconstruction of one's habitual circle in different surroundings. Madame Verdurin brought her 'petit clan' with her when she rented a house in Normandy; and people went to Deauville or Trouville to be seen, and to see, exactly as if they were going to the Bois de Boulogne. This new freedom of movement, therefore, is no liberation from the old pattern, but merely the establishing of the same pattern in a different place.

For shorter outings, Mallarmé recommends the parks of Paris, which are many. Some of them might even have flowers, although there has always been a feeling among French gardeners that parks are mainly for walking in. This stems from Lenôtre, whose designs for the gardens of Versailles consisted largely of gravel paths. Only nursemaids, he considered, required flower beds to look at; society made conversation while promenading.

It is particularly fortunate that the brief run of *La Dernière mode* covers 1–2 November, the Feasts of All Saints and All Souls, both major occasions for Parisians to visit cemeteries. In fact, there seems to have arisen a veritable cult of cemeteries at this time. On this very 2 December, 1874, Goncourt records in his diary: 'In the middle of modern materialism and utilitarianism, one lonely immaterial and disinterested feeling remains in France: the cult of the dead'. In the week of 1–7 December 1875, for example, 68,035 people visited the cemeteries of Paris, whereas on 1–2 November alone there was an astounding total of 870,000 – and the weather was bad. Cemeteries, which for centuries had been wretched, cramped places, breeding death and pestilence, had, in the nineteenth century, become spaces, green places where people could take pleasure in walking. The prime example in Paris is the Père Lachaise cemetery, originally laid out in 1804. Ix refers to the cemetery 'Cayenne', so-called from its remoteness, actually in the suburb of Saint-Ouen, which was opened in September 1872. The scene as described by

Maxime Du Camp is not so gloomy and desolate as Ix pictures it, and in fact presents a two-faced image which Ix would have enjoyed. The road to the cemetery, starting from the Porte de Clignancourt in the north of Paris is 'lined on both sides with constructions of wood, clay or zinc derived from demolition work, the embryo of a budding village: taverns, dance halls, arbours, bowls, quoits, skittles, swings; all a madding gaiety, the people are really alive and are scarcely put out by passing funerals'. There was an even more remote cemetery planned at Méry-sur-Oise, in the valley of Montmorency, but it was still being discussed in August 1874, and involved the use of railway access. Note that, despite Ix's comment on the urn as an alternative to the tomb, cremation was illegal in France at this point.

It is not easy to determine to what extent religious sentiment entered into this cult of the cemetery, and how much was ancestor worship. The most striking funeral processions tended to be civil. The Ix persona does not come over as a deeply religious person. Paris was noted for its non-religious attitudes, although the social divide between working class and bourgeois would be replicated in religious practices. Certainly our period saw the increasing cult of Joan of Arc, and contemporary illustrations of her new statue in the place des Pyramides, 1874, show a predominantly female, bourgeois audience, and the laying of the foundation stone of the basilica of the Sacré Coeur in 1873, planned as an expiation for the anti-clerical activities of the working-class of Paris in the Commune, equally reflects a new devotion to the Sacred Heart of Jesus. Catholic practice was already beginning to find its chief home in the bosoms of the right-wing political parties, a sad event which was to culminate in the Dreyfus Affair. Religious *passion*, in spite of such flourishing cults, in spite of Bernadette and Lourdes, in spite of authors like J.K. Huysmans or Léon Bloy, was now directed to the cult of the *grand magasin*, the new temple where women paid their devotions.

It is by no means a sign of religious devotion that Madame de Ponty recommends to one of her correspondents that she send her daughter to one of the schools run by sisters of the Sacred Heart. In the days before state secondary education for girls was introduced in the 1880s, only religious orders would undertake the task, and these sisters of the Sacred Heart had a great reputation for high standards in teaching literature and other humane studies. It is to be noticed that the grandmother of Proust's narrator was educated by them.